Understanding the European Union

A Concise Introduction

Fifth Edition

John McCormick

palgrave
macmillan

First published 1999
Second edition 2002
Third edition 2005
Fourth edition 2008

This edition published 2011 by
PALGRAVE MACMILLAN

Palgrave Macmillan in the UK is an imprint of Macmillan Publishers Limited, registered in England, company number 785998, of Houndmills, Basingstoke, Hampshire RG21 6XS.

Palgrave Macmillan in the US is a division of St Martin's Press LLC, 175 Fifth Avenue, New York, NY 10010.

Palgrave Macmillan is the global academic imprint of the above companies and has companies and representatives throughout the world.

Palgrave® and Macmillan® are registered trademarks in the United States, the United Kingdom, Europe and other countries

ISBN-13: 978-0-230-29882-8   hardback
ISBN-13: 978-0-230-29883-5   paperback

This book is printed on paper suitable for recycling and made from fully managed and sustained forest sources. Logging, pulping and manufacturing processes are expected to conform to the environmental regulations of the country of origin.

A catalogue record for this book is available from the British Library.

A catalog record for this book is available from the Library of Congress.

10 9 8 7 6 5 4 3 2 1
20 19 18 17 16 15 14 13 12 11

Printed and bound in Great Britain by
MPG Books Group, Bodmin and King's Lynn

THE EUROPEAN UNION SERIES

General Editors: Neill Nugent, William E. Paterson

The European Union series provides an authoritative library on the European Union, ranging from general introductory texts to definitive assessments of key institutions and actors, issues, policies and policy processes, and the role of member states.

Books in the series are written by leading scholars in their fields and reflect the most up-to-date research and debate. Particular attention is paid to accessibility and clear presentation for a wide audience of students, practitioners and interested general readers.

The series editors are **Neill Nugent**, Professor of Politics and Jean Monnet Professor of European Integration, Manchester Metropolitan University, and **William E. Paterson**, Honorary Professor in German and European Studies, University of Aston. Their co-editor until his death in July 1999, **Vincent Wright**, was a Fellow of Nuffield College, Oxford University.

Feedback on the series and book proposals are always welcome and should be sent to Steven Kennedy, Palgrave Macmillan, Houndmills, Basingstoke, Hampshire RG21 6XS, UK, or by e-mail to s.kennedy@palgrave.com

---

General textbooks

Published

Desmond Dinan **Encyclopedia of the European Union** [Rights: Europe only]

Desmond Dinan **Europe Recast: A History of European Union** [Rights: Europe only]

Desmond Dinan **Ever Closer Union: An Introduction to European Integration** (4th edn) [Rights: Europe only]

Mette Eilstrup Sangiovanni (ed.) **Debates on European Integration: A Reader**

Simon Hix and Bjørn Høyland **The Political System of the European Union** (3rd edn)

Paul Magnette **What Is the European Union? Nature and Prospects**

John McCormick **Understanding the European Union: A Concise Introduction** (5th edn)

Brent F. Nelsen and Alexander Stubb **The European Union: Readings on the Theory and Practice of European Integration** (3rd edn) [Rights: Europe only]

Neill Nugent (ed.) **European Union Enlargement**

Neill Nugent **The Government and Politics of the European Union** (7th edn)

John Peterson and Elizabeth Bomberg **Decision-Making In the European Union**

Ben Rosamond **Theories of European Integration**

Esther Versluis, Mendeltje van Keulen and Paul Stephenson **Analyzing the European Union Policy Process**

Forthcoming

Laurie Buonanno and Neill Nugent **Policies and Policy Processes of the European Union**

Magnus Ryner and Alan Cafruny **A Critical Introduction to the European Union**

Dirk Leuffen, Berthold Rittberger and Frank Schimmelfennig **Differentiated Integration**

Sabine Saurugger **Theoretical Approaches to European Integration**

Also planned

The Political Economy of European Integration

Series Standing Order (outside North America only)
ISBN 0–333–71695–7 hardback
ISBN 0–333–69352–3 paperback
Full details from www.palgrave.com

Visit Palgrave Macmillan's
EU Resource area at
www.palgrave.com/politics/eu/

The major institutions and actors

Published

Renaud Dehousse **The European Court of Justice**
Justin Greenwood **Interest Representation in the European Union** (3rd edn)
Fiona Hayes-Renshaw and Helen Wallace **The Council of Ministers** (2nd edn)
Simon Hix and Christopher Lord **Political Parties in the European Union**
David Judge and David Earnshaw **The European Parliament** (2nd edn)
Neill Nugent **The European Commission**
Anne Stevens with Handley Stevens **Brussels Bureaucrats? The Administration of the European Union**

Forthcoming

Wolfgang Wessels **The European Council**

The main areas of policy

Published

Michelle Chang **Monetary Integration In the European Union**
Michelle Cini and Lee McGowan **Competition Policy In the European Union** (2nd edn)
Wyn Grant **The Common Agricultural Policy**
Sieglinde Gstöhl and Dirk de Bièvre **The Trade Policy of the European Union**
Martin Holland **The European Union and the Third World**
Jolyon Howorth **Security and Defence Policy in the European Union**
Johanna Kantola **Gender and the European Union**
Stephan Keukeleire and Jennifer MacNaughtan **The Foreign Policy of the European Union**
Brigid Laffan **The Finances of the European Union**
Malcolm Levitt and Christopher Lord **The Political Economy of Monetary Union**
Janne Haaland Matláry **Energy Policy in the European Union**
John McCormick **Environmental Policy In the European Union**
John Peterson and Margaret Sharp **Technology Policy In the European Union**
Handley Stevens **Transport Policy in the European Union**

Forthcoming

Karen Anderson **Social Policy In the European Union**

Hans Bruyninckx and Tom Delreux **Environmental Policy and Politics in the European Union**
Jörg Monar **Justice and Home Affairs In the European Union**

Also planned

Political Union
The External Policies of the European Union

The member states and the Union

Published

Carlos Closa and Paul Heywood **Spain and the European Union**
Alain Guyomarch, Howard Machin and Ella Ritchie **France in the European Union**
Brigid Laffan and Jane O'Mahoney **Ireland and the European Union**

Forthcoming

Simon Bulmer and William E. Paterson **Germany and the European Union**
Brigid Laffan **The European Union and Its Member States**
Baldur Thórhallsson **Small States in the European Union**

Also planned

Britain and the European Union

Issues

Published

Derek Beach **The Dynamics of European Integration: Why and When EU Institutions Matter**
Christina Boswell and Andrew Geddes **Migration and Mobility in the European Union**
Thomas Christiansen and Christine Reh **Constitutionalizing the European Union**
Robert Ladrech **Europeanization and National Politics**
Cécile Leconte **Understanding Euroscepticism**
Steven McGuire and Michael Smith **The European Union and the United States**
Wyn Rees **The EU/US Security Relationship: The Tensions between a European and a Global Agenda**

Contents

List of Boxes, Tables, Figures and Maps   viii
List of Abbreviations and Acronyms   x
Introduction   xii

1 **What is the European Union?**   1
    The EU in the international system   2
    Understanding regional integration   5
    Explaining the EU today   13
        Federalism   16
        Confederalism   19
    Conclusions   22

2 **The Idea of Europe**   24
    Europe's changing identity   25
    Where is Europe?   32
    Europeanism   39
    Conclusions   46

3 **The Evolution of the EU**   48
    Postwar Europe   49
    First steps towards integration (1948–55)   52
    The European Economic Community (1955–86)   54
    Economic and social integration (1979–92)   59
    From Community to Union (1992–2003)   61
    The euro, Lisbon, and beyond   67
    Conclusions   72

4 **The European Institutions**   74
    A constitution for Europe   75
    The European Council   78
    The European Commission   80
    The Council of Ministers   84
    The European Parliament   88
    The European Court of Justice   92
    Specialized institutions   95
    Conclusions   97

5 **The EU and its Citizens**   98
    Public opinion and Europe   99

The democratic deficit   104
The people's Europe   107
Participation and representation   111
    European elections   111
    Referendums   115
    Interest groups   116
    Other channels   120
Conclusions   121

6 The EU Policy Process   **123**
The changing balance of authority   124
The policy environment   127
The policy cycle   132
    Problem identification and agenda-setting   132
    Formulation and adoption   134
    Implementation   135
    Evaluation   136
Features of the policy process   138
    Compromise and bargaining   138
    Political games   139
    Multi-speed integration   139
    Incrementalism   140
    Spillover   141
The EU budget   142
Conclusions   146

7 Economic Policy   **148**
Completing the single market   149
Effects of the single market   151
    Freedom of movement   151
    Trans-European networks   152
    Liberalization of air travel 155
    Mergers and acquisitions   156
    Competition policy   159
Inside the eurozone   162
Conclusions   170

8 Managing Resources   **172**
Levelling the playing field   173
Agricultural policy   176
Cohesion policy   182
Environmental policy   190
Conclusions   194

9	**The EU and the World**	**196**
	Towards a European foreign policy	197
	Towards a European defence policy	201
	Europe's global economic presence	206
	Relations with the United States	209
	Relations with the neighbourhood	212
	Development cooperation	214
	Conclusions	217

Appendix 1: Europe in Numbers — 220
Appendix 2: A Chronology of European Integration — 222
Sources of Further Information — 226
    Books — 226
    Periodicals and EU publications — 228
    Websites — 229
Bibliography — 230
Index — 243

List of Boxes, Tables, Figures, and Maps

Boxes

1.1	Pros and cons of regional integration	6
1.2	Mitrany's working peace system	8
1.3	Regional integration around the world	12
2.1	Early thoughts on European cooperation	29
2.2	The Turkish question	37
2.3	Promoting European culture	44
3.1	The Marshall Plan	51
3.2	Early steps on the road of integration	56
3.3	Social issues move up the agenda	62
4.1	Intergovernmental conferences	77
4.2	European Union law	85
5.1	Euroscepticism	102
5.2	The knowledge deficit	103
5.3	Political groups in the European Parliament	112
6.1	Principles of the EU policy process	126
6.2	Europeanization	141
6.3	Battles over the budget	144
7.1	Justice and home affairs	153
7.2	Europe and the aerospace industry	157
7.3	The European Central Bank	165
8.1	Living the European Dream	177
8.2	The Common Fisheries Policy	181
8.3	The (bad) luck of the Irish	185
9.1	The European External Action Service	202
9.2	A European or an Atlantic defence?	204
9.3	The overlooked superpower	210

Tables

2.1	Official languages of the EU	33
2.2	Key features of Europeanism	45
3.1	Prospective members of the EU	69
3.2	Key elements of the Treaty of Lisbon	71
4.1	The major treaties	76
4.2	Presidents of the European Commission	83

4.3   Rotation of presidencies of the Council of Ministers   87
4.4   Votes in the Council of Ministers   88
4.5   Seats in the European Parliament   90
4.6   Specialized EU institutions (selected)   96
5.1   National referendums on EU issues (selected)   117
6.1   The division of policy authority   128
9.1   The ACP states   216

Figures

1.1   Levels of political organization   4
1.2   Federalism and confederalism compared   20
2.1   Changing European identities   39
4.1   The institutional structure of the EU   89
5.1   Public opinion on EU membership   100
5.2   How much do Europeans know about the EU?   104
5.3   Turnout at European Parliament elections, 2009   114
6.1   The policy cycle   133
6.2   Infringements of EU law, 1952–2008   137
6.3   The European Union budget   146
7.1   The world's biggest corporations, by region   159
8.1   Per capita GDP in the European Union   174
8.2   Unemployment in the European Union   188
9.1   The EU in the global economy   208

Maps

0.1   The European Union   xiv
2.1   Europe Today   35
3.1   Growth of the EU, 1952–86   58
3.2   Growth of the EU, 1990–95   65
3.3   Growth of the EU, 2004–07   68
7.1   The eurozone   166
9.1   The EU and its neighbourhood   212

List of Abbreviations and Acronyms

ACP	African, Caribbean, Pacific
CAP	Common Agricultural Policy
CFSP	Common Foreign and Security Policy
Coreper	Committee of Permanent Representatives
DG	directorate-general
EADS	European Aeronautic Defence and Space company
EC	European Community
ECB	European Central Bank
ECSC	European Coal and Steel Community
ecu	European currency unit
EDC	European Defence Community
EEA	European Economic Area/European Environment Agency
EEAS	European External Action Service
EEC	European Economic Community
EFTA	European Free Trade Association
EMS	European Monetary System
EMU	economic and monetary union
EP	European Parliament
EPC	European Political Cooperation
ERDF	European Regional Development Fund
ERM	Exchange Rate Mechanism
ESDP	European Security and Defence Policy
ESF	European Social Fund
EU	European Union
EU-15	The 15 member states of the EU prior to the 2004 enlargement
EU-27	The 27 member states of the EU following the 2004–07 enlargement
Euratom	European Atomic Energy Community
GATT	General Agreement on Tariffs and Trade
GDP	gross domestic product
GNP	gross national product
IGC	intergovernmental conference
IGO	intergovernmental organization
IO	international organization
IR	international relations
MEP	Member of the European Parliament

NAFTA	North American Free Trade Agreement
NATO	North Atlantic Treaty Organization
NGO	non-governmental organization
OECD	Organization for Economic Cooperation and Development
OEEC	Organization for European Economic Cooperation
PR	proportional representation
QMV	qualified majority voting
SAP	Social Action Programme
SEA	Single European Act
TEN	trans-European network
UN	United Nations
VAT	value-added tax
WEU	Western European Union
WTO	World Trade Organization

The member states:

AT	Austria		IT	Italy
BE	Belgium		LT	Lithuania
BG	Bulgaria		LU	Luxembourg
CY	Cyprus		LV	Latvia
CZ	Czech Republic		MT	Malta
DE	Germany		NL	Netherlands
DK	Denmark		PL	Poland
EE	Estonia		PT	Portugal
EL	Greece		RO	Romania
ES	Spain		SE	Sweden
FI	Finland		SI	Slovenia
FR	France		SK	Slovakia
HU	Hungary		UK	United Kingdom
IE	Ireland			

Introduction

This is a book about the European Union (EU), whose impact on the lives of Europeans and non-Europeans has deepened dramatically in recent years, but which still has a remarkable capacity to confuse, bemuse, and confound. The problem starts with trying to pin down its character and personality; in other words, just what is the European Union? It is much more than a standard intergovernmental organization, because its powers, roles, and responsibilities go far beyond those of any other intergovernmental organization that has ever existed. But it has not yet become a European superstate, or a United States of Europe, and there are many in Europe who are keen to make sure that this never happens. Just where this leaves it on the continuum between an intergovernmental organization and a superstate remains contested.

Beside the basic challenge of defining the EU, we are faced with a host of additional problems and questions. What role does it play in the daily life of politics, economics, and society in its 27 member states? Is it a bona fide political system, and if so, how do we explain and characterize its relationship with its 27 member states? Are the member states independent actors, or should we think of them as part of a club, whose rules, norms, and expectations they must follow? What does the EU mean for policy making in Europe? And what has been the impact of the EU on the identity and meaning of Europe? Is it any longer realistic or useful to make a distinction between Europe and the EU?

What of Europe's place in the world? What difference has the EU made to how Europe deals with the rest of the world, and to how the rest of the world deals with Europe? Are the statistics as impressive as they seem: the wealthiest marketplace in the world, controller of one of the world's two leading international currencies, the biggest trading power in the world, the biggest market for mergers and acquisitions in the world, and the biggest source of foreign direct investment and official development assistance in the world. Or are there still too many problems and divisions among Europeans to allow Europe to flex its international political and economic muscle?

And what of the future? Is the hold of the EU strengthening over time, or is opposition to the directions being taken by integration finally beginning to have an impact? Will the accumulation of doubts and crises prove too much, or will European leaders continue to adapt and make the EU both more stable and more widely accepted? Perhaps no publication has made quite such a habit of predicting the end of the

EU as *The Economist*, whose cover in March 1982 showed a tomb-stone bearing the words 'EEC: Born March 25 1957, Moribund March 25 1982, capax imperii nisi imperasset' (thought capable of ruling until it actually tried). Since then, *The Economist* has declared the Community, the EU, and the euro to be on the verge of collapse more times than can be counted, and yet somehow it survives. But how long can this continue?

The number of responses to these questions has grown with time, but agreement on the best is as remote as ever. We cannot even agree on whether the EU is a good idea, and a project worth pursuing, or whether it has involved the surrender of too much state sovereignty and identity, and has aspirations above its station. Opinion polls find that only about half of Europeans approve of the EU, while the other half either disapproves or is not sure what to think. Polls also find that most Europeans do not know how it works, begging the obvious question of how far we can rely on their opinions on the EU. Critics point accusing fingers at interfering Eurocrats, and disapprove of the authority given to European institutions that are portrayed as secretive, elitist, and unaccountable. They also question the extent to which integration can be credited with the peace, economic growth, and prosperity that has come to Europe since 1945. But supporters take the opposite view, see many political and economic advantages in integration, and are ready to credit much of Europe's renewal and revival to the opportunities provided by integration, and to think of themselves more as Europeans than as citizens of particular states.

Even with all the doubts, it is hard to see the structure of European integration being undone. The member states of the EU have spun a web of links that would be all but impossible to unravel. None of the laws that once limited free movement and trade among European states are likely to return. The physical and psychological barriers that for so long reminded Europeans of their differences have come down, and while national and regional identities are still alive and well, Europeans are no longer willing to fight each other to assert those identities. Twenty years ago, the EU was only a marginal factor in the lives of most Europeans, but today – with the completion of the single market, policy cooperation on a wide range of issues, the development of a system of European law, the adoption of the euro, eastern enlargement, moves towards a common foreign policy, and important global challenges that demand responses from its leaders – Europe has become impossible to ignore.

This is an introductory book about the European Union, written for anyone who wants to understand how it works and what it means for the half a billion people who live under its jurisdiction. It sets out to introduce the EU from first principles: to look at the debates over what

Map 0.1   *The European Union*

it is and how it has evolved, to describe and assess the way it works and reaches decisions, to examine its impact on the individual states of Europe and their citizens, to review the effects of European integration on a range of critical policy issues, and to discuss its changing global role. The analysis in the chapters that follow has been coloured by two core influences.

First, the emphasis is on brevity. This book has never been intended to be a detailed analysis of the EU, but nor has it ever been designed as a mere whistle-stop description of the EU, reciting key facts, names, and dates. Instead, it sets out to review and synthesize the major points in the analytical debate about the EU, the key steps in its history, the work of its major institutions, the ways in which ordinary Europeans relate to its work, and its key policy outputs, all the while engaging and challenging its readers, and tying up the basic facts with reflection and context. While some textbooks on the EU now top a remarkable 600 pages, *Understanding the European Union* has never been more than half that length, and this new edition brings the story up to date while also being nearly five per cent shorter than the last edition. Anyone looking for a more in-depth treatment might want to consider my other textbook, *European Union Politics*, also published by Palgrave Macmillan, of which *Understanding the European Union* is – in essence – a brief but somewhat wider-ranging version.

Second, much of the academic writing on the EU – particularly at the introductory level – has done us a disservice by shrouding the EU in a fog of theoretical debates, treaty articles, arcane jargon, and convoluted philosophical theses that have helped make one of the most fascinating developments in European history sound dull and bureaucratic, and has too often divorced European integration from the real, daily life of Europeans. Events at the European level are just as full of drama, of success and failure, of bold initiatives and weakness, and of visionary leadership and mercenary intrigue as events at the national level, and it is important in books such as this to show clearly why the EU changes all of our lives in real and substantial ways.

It was in 1997 that Steven Kennedy at Palgrave Macmillan first asked me to write a book that would provide a brief and broad-ranging survey of the EU. The first edition of *Understanding the European Union* was published in 1999, and happily struck a note; new editions followed in 2002, 2005, and 2008, and this fifth edition follows in short order. There is something of a perception in the academic world that new editions of books rarely involve many changes, but while that may be so in some fields of study, it is impossible for those of us dealing with the EU: it keeps evolving, its rules are regularly amended, its personality keeps changing, and new layers of analysis and interpretation are regularly added to the debate over integration. Not least among the changes since the fourth edition have been the final adoption of the Treaty of Lisbon and the fallout from the global economic downturn of 2007–10 and the eurozone crises of 2010–11.

While the fifth edition preserves the overall goals and structure of its predecessors, it has been substantially updated to take account of recent developments, shortened wherever possible, the arguments tightened and adjusted as needed, and new boxes, figures, and tables inserted to present information more visually. As a result it looks quite different in several places.

Chapter 1 on theory remains relatively unchanged, the thorough reorganization and revisions made to the fourth edition holding firm: explanations of how the EU evolved (which come mainly out of international relations theory) are distinguished more clearly from explanations of what the EU has become (which come mainly out of comparative politics and public policy).

Chapter 2 on the meaning of Europe has been overhauled, with cuts made in the opening section on the identity of Europe in order to make room for an expanded section on the meaning of Europeanism, discussing the political, economic, and social norms and values that distinguish the region and its inhabitants.

Chapter 3 on the history of the EU has been revised to cut back on some of the early developments in order to make room for more analysis of the international environment in which integration took place, and to take the story up to the Treaty of Lisbon and the recent trials and tribulations on the economic front.

Chapter 4 on institutions has been revised and reorganized in light of Lisbon and with a view to clarifying the often confusing decision-making processes of the EU.

Chapter 5 on the EU and its citizens was formerly Chapter 6, and has had new material injected on public opinion, euroscepticism, and the democratic deficit, and has seen the sections on representation and participation reorganized and fine-tuned to bring in new information on elections, referendums, and interest groups.

Chapter 6 was formerly Chapter 5, and began life in earlier editions as a study of the relationship between the EU and the member states, and has since been converted into a full-blown study of the policy process.

Chapter 7 on economic policy has seen much of the historical background taken out, more details added on the effects of the single market (and particularly on competition policy), and more details and discussion incorporated on the story of the euro.

Chapter 8 has also seen a substantial reduction in historical background, making way for an assessment of changes in agricultural, fisheries, and cohesion policy, and an almost complete rewrite of the section on environmental policy.

Chapter 9 includes developments arising out of Lisbon and more on EU relations with its neighbourhood, as well as offering more in the way of discussion about the changing global role of the European Union.

My thanks as ever to Steven Kennedy for the constant energy, reassurance, and excellent judgement that he provides, and to Juanita Bullough, Helen Caunce and the staff at Palgrave Macmillan for their work on the production. And my love and thanks as always to Leanne, Ian and Stuart.

JOHN MCCORMICK

Chapter 1

What is the European Union?

When we study international relations, and try to understand our place in the international system, the standard point of reference is the state. World maps show continents divided by state frontiers, marking out territories under the administration of sovereign governments and subject to independent systems of law. When we travel from one state to another, we must usually show passports or other documents, and are reminded that we are in transit until we return to our 'home' state: the one to which we legally 'belong' and with which we feel a sense of identity.

States dominate our thinking because they have been the primary actors in the global system for 300 years or more, and because the study of international relations has long involved the study of alliances, changing patterns of cooperation and conflict, and fluctuations in the balance of power between and among states. But there are many who argue that states are in decline, their credibility undermined by their long-time association with self-interest and conflict, and their independence reduced by the effects of globalization. Borders no longer matter as much as they once did, runs the logic, and in order to truly understand the modern world we need to expand our analytical horizons.

In few places has the prestige and hold of the state been more aggressively challenged than in Europe, where centuries of conflict and tension reached a climax with the horrors of two world wars, driving home the dangers of nationalism and emphasizing the urgency of inter-state cooperation. Political divisions were further emphasized by the cold war, which made many realize that states seemed unable to guarantee the safety of their citizens except through a balance of violence with other states, and found Europe caught in the middle of a political and ideological competition between the superpowers, the west obliged to follow the lead of the United States, and the east trapped in the Soviet bloc.

Alarm at the internal and external threats to European security led to a new debate about how best to build a lasting peace in the region, the most important result of which was the creation of what is now the European Union. But although the EU is today a fixed part of the international political landscape, there is little agreement on how it evolved, or on what it is, or what it might one day become. Did it

1

grow out of the deliberate actions of governments, or was there a more complex set of internal and external pressures at work? Were states the core elements in the story, or was cross-state functional cooperation the key driving force? And what exactly is the EU? It is more than a typical intergovernmental organization, but it is not a European super-state. So how do we explain it?

Most analyses of European integration have come out of the study of international relations, because the EU (and the European Community before it) was long approached by most scholars of integration – and by European political leaders – as an international organization. But since the 1990s there has been growing support for understanding the EU as a political system in its own right, and for looking at explanations coming out of the fields of comparative politics and public policy. There is still no grand theory of European integration, and no agreement about how best to understand and describe the EU today, but the parameters of the debate are changing, as this chapter will show.

The EU in the international system

Look at a map of the world and you will find it divided into nearly 200 states. As a unit of administration, the state has dominated the way we think about political relations among humans for generations – some say since the Renaissance, some since the 1648 Peace of Westphalia (see Chapter 2), and others since the beginning of the nineteenth century. A state is a legal entity which has four key qualities:

- It operates within a fixed *territory* marked by borders, and controls the movement of people, money, goods, and services across those borders.
- It has *sovereignty* over that territory and over the people and resources within its borders, and has the sole right to impose domestic laws and taxes.
- It is legally and politically *independent,* and both creates and operates the system of government under which its residents live.
- It has *legitimacy,* meaning that it is recognized both by its people and by other states as having jurisdiction and authority within its territory.

None of these qualities is absolute: there may be political disputes that create uncertainties about the borders of a territory; there may be legal, economic or political difficulties that limit the sovereignty of a state; the independence of states is qualified by external economic and political pressures; and levels of legitimacy vary according to the extent to which the citizens of a state (and the governments of other states) respect the powers and authority of that state (see Vincent, 1987; Gill, 2003). Furthermore, the viability of the state system has come under increased scrutiny of late, and there are many who argue that the state is in retreat (see Strange, 1996; van Creveld, 1999), the result mainly of three critical developments.

First, public loyalty to the state – and the strength of state identity – has long been compromised by economic, social and political divisions. In Europe, most states are home to multiple different nations, or groups of people linked by history, language and culture. Occasionally, a nation will coincide with a state (for example, most of the residents of Portugal are Portuguese), but most European states are home to multiple different nationalities. Thus Spain is a state, but its population is divided among Andalusians, Aragonese, Basques, Cantabrians, Castilians, Catalans, Galicians, Navarese, Valencians and others. In many parts of the world, the focus of people's allegiance has changed as national minorities have become more assertive and demanded greater self-determination, and even independence in some cases, as with the Scots in Britain, the Kurds in Turkey/Iraq/Iran, and the Québécois in Canada.

Second, international borders have been weakened by the building of political and economic ties among states, driven mainly by the need to trade, to expand markets, to develop security alliances, and to borrow money. Perhaps nothing today poses as much of a threat to the state as globalization: increased economic interdependence, changes in technology and communications, the rising power of multinational corporations, the growth of international markets, the spread of a global culture, and the harmonization of public policies in the face of shared or common problems such as terrorism, transboundary pollution, illegal immigration, and the spread of disease. At the same time, people have become more mobile: complex new patterns of emigration have been driven by a combination of economic need and personal choice, and mass tourism has broken down many of the psychological borders among states.

Third, states have not always been able to meet the demands of their residents for security, justice, prosperity, and human rights. States have frequently gone to war with each other, their democratic records have been mixed, many have failed to manage their economies and national resources to the benefit of all their residents, and even the wealthiest and most progressive of states still often struggle with poverty and social division. Many states have also failed to meet the needs of their consumers for goods and services, a problem that has combined with the rise of multinational corporations in search of new markets and profits to change the nature of production, and to make state boundaries more porous.

The decline of the state has run in tandem with growing interstate cooperation on matters of mutual interest, ranging from the narrowly focused to the broadly idealistic. Cooperation has been most clearly

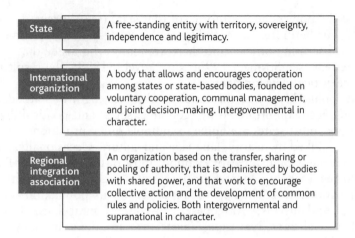

Figure 1.1 *Levels of political organization*

obvious in the work of international organizations (IOs), bodies that promote voluntary cooperation and coordination between or among their members, but have neither autonomous powers nor the authority to impose their rulings on members. Some IOs have national governments as members; they include intergovernmental organizations (IGOs) such as the United Nations (UN), the World Trade Organization (WTO) and the North Atlantic Treaty Organization (NATO). Others are non-governmental organizations (NGOs), including multinational corporations (such as Wal-Mart, Royal Dutch Shell, Toyota or ING), or private organizations with specific interests (such as Amnesty International, Doctors Without Borders, Friends of the Earth or Oxfam).

In the case of IGOs, decision making is described as intergovernmental: IGOs are forums within which government representatives can meet, share views, negotiate and work to reach agreement. Membership is voluntary, management is communal, decisions are the result of the joint will of their members, and IGOs depend for revenue on contributions from their members. They do not have independent powers, they do not normally have the means or authority to enforce their decisions, and they normally cannot impose fines on recalcitrant members, or impose sanctions other than those agreed by the membership as a whole. In most cases, IGOs are limited to imposing moral pressure (playing by the rules) or either suspending or terminating members.

Taken to another level, IGOs can evolve into regional integration associations (RIAs). This happens when a group of states agree to take collective action and develop common rules and policies on shared interests. Regional integration involves the transfer, sharing or pooling of sovereignty, and the creation of regional institutions with a high degree of authority to oversee the making of new rules and regulations in areas where their members have agreed to cooperate. However, the final say on the adoption of those rules and regulations is left to the member states, and the regional institutions are denied direct powers of execution, which are left to the governments of the member states.

The EU is the benchmark case of an RIA. In many respects it is a standard IGO in which decisions are taken as a result of negotiations among the leaders of the states, and its institutions mainly carry out the wishes of the member states. But in other respects it has moved into the realms of supranationalism: a form of cooperation which results in the creation of a new level of authority that is autonomous, above the state, and has powers of coercion that are independent of those of participating member states. In policy areas where the member states have ceded or transferred authority to the EU institutions, those institutions have the power to make laws and policies that are binding on the member states. In some areas, such as trade, the EU has been given the authority to negotiate on behalf of the member states collectively, and other countries work with the EU institutions rather than with the governments of the member states. In several other policy areas, such as agriculture, the environment, and competition, decisions are taken at the level of the EU rather than of the member states.

Matters are complicated, though, by the different personalities of EU institutions. Some (notably the European Council and the Council of Ministers) are more clearly intergovernmental, because they are meeting places for the representatives of the governments of the EU member states, and decisions are reached as a result of compromises based on competing state interests. Other institutions (notably the European Commission and the European Court of Justice) are more clearly supranational, because they focus on the general interests of the European Union, and their decision makers are not national representatives. But the debate about the logic and personality of the EU has provided few hard answers, in part because of competing opinions about how the EU has evolved, but also because of questions about whether it is even a good idea (see Box 1.1). Opinion polls have found that only about half of all Europeans support European integration, but they have also found most Europeans to have only a passing understanding of how it works and what it means (see Chapter 5). Under the circumstances, pinning down the character of the EU is fraught with difficulty.

Understanding regional integration

States have a long history of cooperation or coalescence, the pressures to come together stemming from a variety of sources:

Box 1.1   Pros and cons of regional integration

Few Europeans would question the merits of peace, cooperation and trade, but opinions about the benefits of regional integration as a means to achieving these ends are mixed. Some feel that they can be achieved without the compromises that are demanded by integration, while others argue that the record of centuries of conflict and war proves that only integration can keep Europeans peaceful and prosperous. In the resulting debate, it has so far been easier to assess the costs than to outline the benefits. Those costs include the following:

1. Loss of sovereignty and national independence.
2. Loss of national identity as laws, regulations and standards are harmonized.
3. Reduced powers for member state governments.
4. The creation of a new level of distant and impersonal European 'government'.
5. Too little reference to public opinion regarding key decisions on integration.
6. Increased competition and job losses brought by the removal of market protection.
7. Handicaps on progressive states as standards are reduced to help integrate states with lower standards.
8. Increased cross-border crime and illegal immigration arising from the removal of internal border controls.
9. Problems related to controversial initiatives such as recent bailouts of economically troubled eurozone states.

For pro-Europeans, the benefits of integration include the following:

1. Cooperation makes war and conflict less likely.
2. Member states working together enjoy new global power and influence.
3. The single market offers European businesses a larger pool of consumers, and offers consumers more choice and lower prices arising out of competition.
4. Mergers and takeovers create world-class European corporations, helping the EU better compete in the global marketplace.
5. Greater freedom of cross-border movement within the EU eases travel.
6. It pools the economic and social resources of multiple member states.
7. Less advanced member states 'rise' to standards maintained by more progressive states.
8. Funds and investments create new opportunities in the poorer parts of the EU.
9. Democracy and capitalism are promoted in less advanced member states.

- States may be brought together by force, as they were in Europe by Napoleon and Hitler.
- They may come together out of the need for security in the face of a common external threat, as did the members of NATO during the cold war.
- They may share common values and goals, and agree to cooperate or share resources in selected areas, as have the Nordic states on transport, education, and passports.
- They may decide that they can promote peace and improve their quality of life more successfully by working together rather than separately, as have the members of the United Nations.

Interstate relations in Europe were long influenced and driven by the first pair of motives, but since 1945 there has been a shift to the second pair. In other words, compulsion has been replaced by encouragement. But just why and how the process has evolved the way it has remains a matter of debate. At first, there was an idealistic notion that out of the ruins of postwar Europe, and before state governments could reassert themselves, there was an opportunity to break with the past and create a new European federation. Federalism was based on the argument that states had lost their political rights because they could not guarantee the safety of their citizens (Spinelli, 1972), and that if the prewar system was rebuilt there would be a return to nationalism and further conflict. Federalists hoped that political integration would be followed by economic, social and cultural integration. With this optimistic idea in mind, the European Union of Federalists was created in 1946, but by the time it met at its first Congress in 1948, national political systems were on the mend and federalist ideas fell by the wayside. The Congress was able to agree only on the creation of the Council of Europe, with its more modest goal of intra-European cooperation.

Postwar thinking about international relations instead came to be dominated by the more pessimistic notion of realism, which argues that states are the most important actors on the world stage (because there is no higher sovereign power), and that states strive to protect their interests relative to each other. Realists speak of the importance of survival in a hostile global environment, and argue that states use both conflict and cooperation to ensure their security through a balance of power with other states (see Waltz, 2008). Under this analysis, the EU today would be best understood as a gathering of sovereign states, which retain authority over their own affairs, transfer authority to new cooperative bodies only when it suits them, and reserve the right to take back that authority at any time. In short, realists argue that the EU exists only because the governments of the member states have decided that it is in their best interests. Realism was a response to the tensions that arose out of the nuclear age, but it

Box 1.2   Mitrany's working peace system

At the core of thinking about the mechanics of regional integration are the ideas of the Romanian-born British social scientist David Mitrany (1888–1975). His treatise *A Working Peace System* (first published in 1943) became the basis of functionalism, defined as an attempt to link 'authority to a specific activity, [and] to break away from the traditional link between authority and a definite territory' (Mitrany, 1966:27). He argued that transnational bodies would not only be more efficient providers of welfare than national governments, but that they would help transfer popular loyalty away from the state, and so reduce the chances of international conflict (Rosamond, 2000:33). He argued for the creation of separate bodies with authority over functionally specific fields, such as security, transport, and communication. They should be executive bodies with autonomous tasks and powers, he argued, and do some of the same jobs as national governments, but at a different level. This focus on particular functions would encourage international cooperation more quickly and effectively than grand gestures, and the dimensions and structures of these international organizations would not have to be predetermined, but would instead be self-determined (Mitrany, 1966:27–31, 72).

Once these functional organizations were created, Mitrany argued, they would have to work with each other. For example, rail, road, and air agencies would need to collaborate on technical matters, such as the coordination of timetables, and agreement on how to deal with different volumes of passenger and freight traffic. As different groups of functional agencies worked together, there would be coordinated international planning. This would result not so much in the creation of a new system as in the rationalization of existing systems through a process of natural selection and evolution. States could join or leave, drop out of some functions and stay in others, or try their own political and social experiments. This would eventually lead to 'a rounded political system ... the functional arrangements might indeed be regarded as organic elements of federalism by instalments' (Mitrany, 1966:3–84).

Mitrany was not much interested in regional unification, which he felt would simply expand the problems of the state system and replace inter-state tensions with interregional tensions, and nor did he support the idea of world government, which he felt would threaten human freedom. Nonetheless, his ideas were at the heart of the thinking of the two men most often described as the founders of the European Union, French bureaucrat Jean Monnet and French foreign minister Robert Schuman (see Chapter 3). They believed that the integration of a specific area (the coal and steel industry) would encourage integration in other areas. As Schuman put it, 'Europe will not be made all at once or according to a single plan. It will be built through concrete achievements which first create a *de facto* solidarity' (Schuman Declaration, reproduced in Weigall and Stirk, 1992:58–9).

did not explain the rising tide of cooperation that followed the Second World War, left many unanswered questions about the motives behind international relations, and has recently lost some support.

An alternative view was offered by functionalism, based on the idea of incrementally bridging the gaps between states by building functionally specific organizations (see Box 1.2). So instead of trying to coordinate big issues such as economic or defence policy, for example, functionalists believed they could 'sneak up on peace' (Lindberg and Scheingold, 1971:6) by integrating relatively non-controversial areas such as the postal service, or a particular sector of industry, or by harmonizing technical issues such as weights and measures. While realists spoke of competition, conflict, and self-interest, functionalists focused more on cooperation. While realists were concerned with relations among governments, functionalists focused on cooperation promoted by technical experts. Looking at the internal dynamic of cooperation, they argued that if states worked together in limited areas and created new bodies to oversee that cooperation, they would come to work together in additional areas through an 'invisible hand' of integration. In short, functionalists argued that European integration had a logic that participating states would find hard to resist.

The first in-depth study of European integration, by Ernst Haas in 1958, led to the expansion of these ideas as neofunctionalism. This argued that preconditions were needed before integration could occur, including a switch in public attitudes away from nationalism and towards cooperation, a desire by elites to promote integration for pragmatic rather than altruistic reasons, and the delegation of real power to a new supranational authority (see Haas, 1958, and Rosamond, 2000, Chapter 3). Once these changes took place there would be an expansion of integration caused by spillover, described by Lindberg (1963:10) as a process by which 'a given action, related to a specific goal, creates a situation in which the original goal can be assured only by taking further actions, which in turn create a further condition and a need for more action'. For example, the integration of agriculture would only really work if related sectors – say, transport and agricultural support services – were integrated as well. Equally, the integration of an international rail system would inevitably increase the pressure to integrate road systems and air routes as well.

Spillover is a valuable analytical concept, but it is broad and ambiguous, and is better understood when it is broken down into more specific varieties, of which there are at least three:

- *Functional spillover* implies that economies are so interconnected that if states integrate one sector of their economies (for example), it will lead to the integration of other sectors (Bache and George, 2006:10). So many functional IGOs would have to be created to oversee this process, and so many links built among states, that the power of national government institutions would decline, leading eventually to economic and political union.

- *Technical spillover* implies that disparities in standards will cause states to rise (or sink) to the level of the state with the tightest (or loosest) regulations. For example, Greece and Portugal – which had few if any environmental controls before they joined the EU – were encouraged to adopt such controls because of the requirements of EU law, which had in turn been driven by economic pressures from states with tight environmental controls, such as Germany and the Netherlands.

- *Political spillover* assumes that once different functional sectors are integrated, interest groups (such as corporate lobbies and labour unions) will switch from trying to influence national governments to trying to influence regional institutions (which will encourage them in an attempt to win new powers for themselves). The groups would appreciate the benefits of integration and would act as a barrier to a retreat from integration, and politics would increasingly be played out at the regional rather than the national level (Bache and George, 2006:10).

The forerunner of today's European Union was the European Coal and Steel Community (ECSC) (see Chapter 3). Founded in 1952, it was created partly for short-term goals such as the encouragement of Franco-German cooperation, but Monnet and Schuman also saw it as the first step in a process that would eventually lead to political integration. Few people supported the ECSC at the start, but once it had been working for a few years, trade unions and political parties became more supportive because they began to better understand it, and the logic of integration in other sectors became clearer. But there was only so far it could go, argues Urwin (1995:76), because it 'was still trying to integrate only one part of complex industrial economies, and could not possibly pursue its aims in isolation from other economic segments'. This was part of the reason why – six years after the creation of the ECSC – agreement was reached among its members to achieve broader economic integration within the European Economic Community.

Neofunctionalist ideas dominated studies of European integration in the 1950s and 1960s, but briefly fell out of favour in the 1970s, in part because the process of integrating Europe seemed to have ground to a halt, and in part because the theory of spillover needed further elaboration. The most common criticism of neofunctionalism was that it was too linear, and needed to be expanded or modified to take account of different pressures for integration, such as changes in public and political attitudes, the impact of nationalism on integration, the influence of external events such as changes in economic and military threats from outside, and social and political changes taking place separately from the process of integration (Haas, 1958:xiv–xv).

Variations on the theme of spillover were described by Philippe Schmitter (1971), including the following:

- *Spillaround*: an increase in the scope of the functions carried out by an IGO (breadth) without a corresponding increase in authority or power (depth). For example, governments of the EU member states have allowed the European Commission to become involved in new policy areas, but have worked to prevent it winning too many new powers over the policy process.
- *Buildup*: an increase in the authority or power of an IGO (depth) without a corresponding increase in the number of areas in which it is involved (breadth). Nye (1971a:67) has written about 'rising transactions' (or a growing workload) which 'need not lead to a significant widening of the scope (range of tasks) of integration, but to intensifying of the central institutional capacity to handle a particular task'. This, for example, would explain why the workload of the European Court of Justice led to the creation in 1989 of a subsidiary Court of First Instance (now the General Court) to deal with less important cases (see Chapter 4).
- *Retrenchment*: an increase in the level of joint arbitration between or among member states at the expense of the power and authority of the IGO. This has happened at times of crisis in the EU, such as when member states pulled out of attempts to build exchange rate stability in the 1980s and early 1990s as a prelude to establishing the single currency, or wrestled with the challenges of the eurozone crisis in 2010–11.
- *Spillback*: a reduction in both the breadth and depth of the authority of an IGO. This has yet to happen in the case of the EU, although the powers of the Commission over policy initiation have declined in relative terms as those of the European Parliament and the European Council have grown.

Neofunctionalism was given a boost by Nye (1971b:208–14) when he suggested taking it out of the European context and looking at non-western experiences. He concluded that experiments in regional integration involve an integrative potential that depends on several different conditions, including the economic equality or compatibility of the states involved, the extent to which the elite groups that control economic policy in the member states think alike and hold the same values, the breadth of interest group activity, and the capacity of the member states to adapt and respond to public demands, which in turn depends on the level of domestic stability and the capacity – or desire – of decision makers to respond.

Box 1.3   Regional integration around the world

The European Union is the example of regional integration that has attracted the most international attention and that has had the most evident effects both on its member states and on states doing business with the EU. But regional integration is very much a global affair, and there are similar experiments underway on every continent. Levels of progress have been mixed, regional groupings do not always have the same levels of ambition, and their integrative potential varies. Extrapolating from the arguments made by Nye, the chances of success are greatest where the states involved have the most in common and where there are obvious advantages to integration. So, for example, while the five-member East African Community and the 10-member Association of Southeast Asian Nations (ASEAN) bring together countries with often common historical experiences and comparable political and economic conditions, the 53-member African Union faces enormous challenges in bringing its members together.

Since its creation in 1994, the North American Free Trade Agreement (NAFTA) has tried to open up trade among the United States, Canada, and Mexico. But it has been handicapped by economic differences, minimal political support, public indifference, and concerns about international terrorism and the enormous challenge of controlling illegal immigration into the United States. The US is much wealthier than Mexico, elite groups in Mexico are more in favour of state intervention in the marketplace than those in the United States and Canada, trade unions in the United States have been critical of NAFTA, public opinion in Mexico is more tightly controlled and manipulated than in the United States and Canada, and both Mexico and Canada are wary of the political, economic and cultural power of their giant neighbour.

Elsewhere, the four-member Mercosur grouping in Latin America, the eight-member Central American Integration System, the 15-member Caribbean Community (Caricom), and the 21-member Asia-Pacific Economic Cooperation (APEC) have all had teething troubles, but have made progress toward encouraging their member states to work together on issues of mutual interest, notably internal trade. With its common history, language, religion and culture, the Arab world would seem to offer strong prospects for integration, but the Arab League, the Council of Arab Economic Unity, the Gulf Cooperation Council, and the Arab Maghreb Union have all been handicapped by the political and religious divisions of the region.

On all these counts the EU has always had a relatively high integrative potential: the member states are economically compatible (in the sense that their goals and values are generally the same, even if Eastern European members are still shaking off the effects of central planning), elite groups may disagree on the details but they tend to have broadly similar goals and values, interest groups have taken advantage of the rise of a new level of European decision making (see Chapter 5), and the democratic processes and structures of EU member states are responsive to public demands, even if there is sometimes a mismatch between what majority public opinion says and what political leaders do. By contrast, similar exercises in integration in other parts of the world generally have more handicaps to overcome (see Box 1.3).

A response to criticisms of neofunctionalism came in the form of intergovernmentalism, a theory which draws on realism and takes neofunctionalism to task for concentrating too much on the internal dynamics of integration without paying enough attention to the global context, and for overplaying the role of interest groups. Intergovernmentalism argues that while organized interests play an important role in integration, as do government officials and political parties, the pace and nature of integration are ultimately determined by national governments pursuing national interests; they alone have legal sovereignty, and they alone have the political legitimacy that comes from being democratically elected. Put another way, governments have more autonomy than the neofunctional view allows (Hoffman, 1964). A variation on this theme is liberal intergovernmentalism, a theory which emerged in the 1980s and 1990s, and combined the neofunctionalist view of the importance of domestic politics with the role of the governments of the EU member states in making major political choices. Proponents argue that European integration has moved forward as a result of a combination of factors such as the commercial interests of economic producers, and the relative bargaining power of important governments (see Moravcsik, 1998).

Whatever the debates about how and why the EU evolved, there is no question that its institutions as a group today constitute an additional level of political authority in Europe, being involved in making decisions that impact both the governments and the residents of the member states. So while the debates over how the EU reached its present state are interesting, of more immediate interest now are attempts to understand what the EU has become, and to tie down its contemporary personality and character. Here again, there are many competing explanations and not much agreement.

Explaining the EU today

The EU today sits somewhere along the continuum between an international organization and a state, moving away from the former as it moves closer to the latter. But just where it sits on that continuum is a matter for debate. As noted earlier, it has many of the typical features of an intergovernmental organization, in that membership of the EU is voluntary, the balance of sovereignty lies with the member states, decision making is consultative, and the procedures used to direct the work of the EU are based on consent rather than compulsion. At the same time, it also has some of the qualities of a state: it has internationally recognized external borders, there is a European system of law to which all member states are subject, it has administrative institutions with authority that impacts the lives of Europeans, the balance of responsibility and power in many policy areas has shifted to the European level, and in some areas – such as trade – the EU functions as a unit.

That so much emphasis has been placed on analyzing the EU as an international organization can be explained in part by the dominance in the academic debate of principles coming out of theories of international relations (IR). IR has made important contributions, but it is concerned with interactions between or among states, and pays little attention to the internal characteristics and qualities of the states themselves. As long as the EU was mainly an association of states, this presented few problems, but once the EU began to develop a life and personality of its own, and its institutions accumulated stronger roles, so IR analyses became less useful. As a result, there has been growing support since the early 1990s for approaching the EU as a political system in its own right (Sbragia, 1992; Hix, 2005), and for making greater use of the analytical methods of comparative politics and public policy.

With its focus on institutions and processes, comparative politics can help us better understand how political power is exercised at the European level, how Europeans relate to EU institutions, and how EU-wide administration is influenced by political parties, elections, and interest groups. In other words, instead of studying the process of integration, we can try to better understand the structure of the EU using the comparative method, defined as the process by which different cases or samples are systematically studied in order to establish empirical relationships among two or more variables while the others are held constant (Lijphart, 1971). In other words, we can focus less on assessing the EU as an international organization, and more on comparing its institutions and procedures with those found in states, and in other regional groupings of states. Meanwhile, the methods and theories of public policy can help us better understand the European decision making process: the forces and limitations that come to bear on decision making, the relative balance of influence of the EU and the member states, and the steps involved in setting the European agenda, developing plans of action, implementing decisions, and evaluating the results. There are many different models and theories of the policy process that are applicable to the EU case, including the process model, rational choice, incrementalism, group theory, elite theory, and game theory – see Chapter 6 for more details.

The greatest problem with trying to encourage the use of comparative and public policy analyses is how quickly most European leaders and scholars of the EU shy away from the idea that there is a European government. The term *government* typically refers to the institutions and officials that make up the formal administrative structure of a state, and the context in which it is normally used implies that they have discreet powers to make laws and set the political agenda. But while the EU clearly has a network of 'governing' institutions and full-time officials, that network is rarely described in the language used to describe national systems of government. Instead, it is more usual to see the system of authority within the EU described as *governance*, a term which plays down the role of institutions and focuses instead on processes: governance is the exercise of authority through interactions involving a variety of actors, which in the case of the EU includes member state governments, EU institutions, interest groups, and other sources of influence.

At the heart of any such discussion is the question of sovereignty, defined as the right to hold and exercise authority. A state is sovereign over its territory in that it has the power to decide what happens within that territory, and to make laws that govern the lives of the people who live there. More specifically, sovereignty is usually said to lie in the hands of the institutions that exercise control over the territory, which in democratic systems means the national executive, legislature and judiciary. Theoretically, there are no legal constraints on a sovereign power, only moral and practical ones – sovereign institutions are not answerable to any higher authority, but can only exert their powers to the extent that those under their authority will allow, and to the extent that they can practically implement their decisions.

The complaint made most often by critics of European integration is that it has involved the surrender of sovereignty. But whether or not this is true depends upon how we understand the EU and the changing role of its member states, the point being that sovereignty has not been lost so much as redistributed. Where sovereign power was once monopolized by the governments of the member states, it is now shared by those governments and by the institutions of the European Union. But just how is it shared, and how do national governments interact with EU institutions?

One analytical concept that has gained popularity in recent years has been multi-level governance (MLG), which describes a system in which power is shared among the supranational, national, sub-national, and local levels, with considerable interaction among them all (see Puchala, 1975; Marks, 1993; Bache and Flinders, 2004). The debate within academic circles about the value of MLG has been vigorous, but once again inconclusive. And what almost everyone has failed to acknowledge is that MLG is a conceptual cousin of two other, older concepts which also play a role in the debate. The most important of these is federalism, which has generated often heated debates among European political leaders and publics, more often being used as a red flag marking what the EU should be avoiding than as an objective measure of what it has become, or might become. Less important, but only because it has rarely been discussed in the context of the EU, is confederalism, a looser form of administration which historically has been a stepping stone to federalism.

Federalism

Although there is no fixed template for federalism (see Burgess, 2006, Chapter 1; Watts, 2008), it can be defined as an administrative system in which at least two levels of government – national and local – coexist with separate or shared powers, each having independent functions, but neither having supreme authority over the other. A federation usually consists of an elected general government with sole power over monetary, foreign and security policy, and separately elected local governments with powers over such issues as education and policing. There is a single state currency and a common defence force, a written constitution that spells out the relative powers of the different levels of government, a court that can arbitrate disputes between them, and at least two major sets of law, government, bureaucracy, and taxation. The cumulative interests of the local units help define the interests of the general government, which deals mainly with those matters better addressed at the state rather than the local level.

There are about two dozen federations in the world, including Australia, Canada, Germany, India, Mexico and Nigeria, but the best known and most thoroughly studied is the United States. It has been a federal republic since 1788, when the Articles of Confederation were replaced with a federal union by which states voluntarily gave up power over such areas as security, retaining their own sets of laws and a large measure of control over local government. American states today can raise their own taxes, and have independent powers over such policy areas as education, land use, the police, and roads. But they are not allowed to make treaties with other states or foreign nations, or to have their own currencies, to levy taxes on imports and exports, or to maintain their own armies. Meanwhile, the federal government in Washington DC cannot unilaterally redraw the borders of a state, impose different levels of tax by state, give states different levels

of representation in the US Senate (where each state has two representatives), or amend the US constitution without the support of two-
thirds of the states. Meanwhile – an important point – the US
constitution (in the Tenth Amendment) reserves to the states or the
people all the powers not delegated to the national government by the
constitution or prohibited by it to the states.

EU member states can still do almost everything that the states in
the US model *cannot* do: they can make treaties, still have a near
monopoly over tax policy, maintain independent militaries, and have
had no obligation to adopt the euro. The EU institutions, meanwhile,
have few of the powers of the federal government in the US model:
they cannot levy taxes, they can make few independent decisions on
law and policy, they do not yet enjoy the undivided loyalty of most
Europeans, and they do not have sole power to negotiate all agreements on behalf of the member states with the rest of the world.
Despite this, the EU does have some of the features of a federal
system:

- It has a complex system of treaties and laws that are the functional
  equivalent of a constitution, are uniformly applicable throughout the
  EU, apply to all the member states and their citizens, and are interpreted and protected by the European Court of Justice.
- It has several levels of administration, ranging from the European to
  the local, that each have some autonomy in different areas of policy.
- In those policy areas where the member states have agreed to
  transfer authority to the EU – including intra-European trade, the
  environment, agriculture, and social policy – EU law supersedes
  national law.
- It has a directly elected representative legislature in the form of the
  European Parliament, which has growing powers over the process
  by which European laws are made. As those powers grow, so the
  powers of national legislatures are declining.
- Although still small by comparison to most national budgets (just
  under €143 billion in 2011), the EU budget gives the EU institutions
  an element of financial independence.
- The European Commission has the authority to oversee negotiations
  with third parties on behalf of all the member states, in those areas
  where it has been given authority by the member states.
- Seventeen of the EU member states have their own currency, the
  euro, meaning that they have transferred monetary policy from their
  own national central banks to the European Central Bank in
  Frankfurt.

One way of looking at the practice of European federalism is to
picture the EU as a network in which individual member states are

increasingly defined not by themselves but in relation to their EU partners, and in which they prefer to interact with one another rather than
third parties because those interactions create incentives for self-inter-
ested cooperation (Keohane and Hoffmann, 1991:13–14). It has been
argued that the EU has become 'cooptive', meaning that its participants have more to gain by working within the system than by going it
alone (Heisler and Kvavik, 1973). Once they are involved, governments of the member states must take some of the responsibility for
actions taken by the EU as a whole, and find it increasingly difficult to
blame the European institutions.

Federalism is not an absolute or a static concept, and it has taken on
different forms in different situations and at different times according
to the relative strength and nature of local political, economic, social,
historical, and cultural pressures. For example, the US model of federalism was in place long before that country began its westward expansion, explicitly includes a system in which the powers of the major
national government institutions are separated, checked, and balanced,
and was adopted more to avoid the dangers of chaos and tyranny than
to account for social divisions. Furthermore, it has changed over time
as a result of an ongoing debate over the relative powers of national
and local government. In India, by contrast, federalism was seen as a
solution to the difficulty of governing a state that was already in place,
and that had deep ethnic and cultural divisions; the national government has a fused executive and legislature on the British model, and
while India is a federal republic like the United States, political reality
has ensured that powers have often been much more centralized in the
hands of the national government.

The most committed European integrationists would like to see a
federal United States of Europe in which today's national governments
would become local governments, with the same kinds of powers as
the *Lander* governments have in Germany or state governments in the
United States. Before this could happen, there would need to be – at
the very least – a directly elected European government, a constitution,
a common tax system, a single currency, and a common military, and
EU institutions would have to be able to act on behalf of all the
member states in foreign relations. But the political resistance to a shift
of powers on this scale would be substantial, and just how far the
process of integration would have to go before there was a federal
Europe is debatable. There are several quasi-federations in existence –
including Argentina, Britain, Spain, and South Africa – which have
some of the features of a federal system without having formally
declared themselves as federations. In many ways the EU could be
added to this list, and there is no reason why European federalism
(should it ever come) would have to look like the US, Indian or even
German models.

Confederalism

A confederation is a loose system of administration in which two or more organizational units keep their separate identities but give limited and specified powers to a central authority for reasons of convenience, mutual security, or efficiency. Lister (1996, especially pp. 22–3) argues that if a federation is a union of peoples living within a single state, then a confederation is a union of states. The balance of power in a confederation is tilted towards the member states, central authorities are kept subordinate, the shifting of authority to those authorities must be approved by the states, ultimate authority remains firmly fixed with the national governments of the member states (which exercise it jointly in the various confederal decision making bodies), and the loyalty of individuals remains focused on their home states. 'In a confederal setting,' Lister argues, 'the central institutions are both the agents of the member states and the instruments that enable those states to attain the degree of political union that is provided for in their treaty-constitutions' (Lister, 1996:83).

Put another way, the member states in a confederation are sovereign and independent, and the central authority is relatively weak, existing at the discretion of the members, and doing only what they allow it to do. If states were to form a confederation, then the citizens of those states would continue to relate directly to their own governments, and only indirectly to the higher authority (see Figure 1.2). Unlike a federal system, where government exercises power over both its constituent units and its citizens, and there is a direct relationship between citizens and each level of government, the higher authority in a confederation does not exercise power directly over individuals.

One example of confederalism in practice was the United States in 1781–88. Following the end of the War of Independence, the original 13 states cooperated under a loose agreement known as the Articles of Confederation, or a 'league of friendship'. Central government could declare war, coin money, and conclude treaties, but could not levy taxes or regulate commerce, and founded its system of 'national' defence on a network of state militias. The Articles could not be amended without the approval of all 13 states, and treaties needed the consent of at least nine states. There was no national executive or judiciary, and the powers of the confederation lay in the hands of an elected Congress in which each state had one vote. Congress rarely met though, and had no permanent home, so its powers were exercised by committees with variable membership. The assumption was that the states might cooperate enough eventually to form a common system of government, but they did not. It was only in 1787 that work began on developing the federal system of government that we find in the United States today.

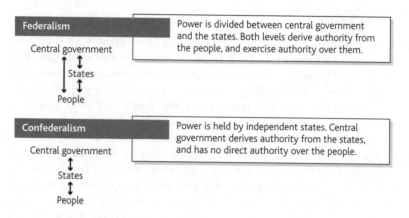

Figure 1.2   *Federalism and confederalism compared*

Confederalism was also used in Germany in 1815–71, when a 39-member confederation was created under the domination of Austria and Prussia following the Congress of Vienna in 1815. Based on the old Holy Roman Empire, it was more an empire than a new state. Few restrictions were placed on the powers of the member kingdoms, duchies, and cities, whose representatives met sporadically (just 16 times in the history of the confederation) in a diet in Frankfurt. Amendments to the constitution needed near-unanimity, and most other measures required a two-thirds majority. Regular business was conducted by an inner committee in which the 11 largest states had one vote each, and the smallest had six between them. There were no common trade or communications policies, and the development of a common army was frustrated by the refusal of smaller states to cooperate (Carr, 1987:4–5).

Switzerland, too, was confederal until 1798, and although it now calls itself a federation, it has given up fewer powers to the national government than has been the case with other federations, such as Germany, the United States, or Russia. Its 1874 constitution allocates specific powers to the federal government, the rest being reserved to the 20 cantons and six half-cantons. The Swiss encourage direct democracy by holding national referendums, have a Federal Assembly elected by proportional representation, and are governed by a seven-member Federal Council elected by the Assembly. Comparable arrangements can be found today in Bosnia and Hercegovina. Even though it is formally described as a federation, and the federal government has accumulated more powers with time, the two partner states – the Bosnian Muslim-Croat Federation of Bosnia and Hercegovina and the Bosnian Republika Srpska – still have considerable independence. Each has its own system of government, with a president, a legislature, a court, a police force and other institutions, but they come together under a joint Bosnian government with a presidency that rotates every eight months between a Serb, a Bosnian Muslim, and a Croat.

The European Union has several of the features of a confederal system:

- The citizens of the member states do not relate directly to any of the EU institutions except Parliament (which they elect), instead relating to them mainly through their national governments. Despite their powers of making and implementing policy, the key institutions of the EU – the European Commission, the Council of Ministers, the European Council, and the European Court of Justice – derive their authority not from the citizens of the member states, but from the leaders and governments of the member states. They are run either directly by national government leaders (the Council of Ministers and the European Council), or are appointed by those leaders (the Commission and the Court of Justice).
- The member states still have their own separate identities, have their own systems of law, can sign bilateral treaties with other states, can act unilaterally in most areas of foreign policy, and can argue that the EU institutions exist at their discretion. There is no European government in the sense that the EU has obvious leaders – such as a president, a foreign minister, or a cabinet – with substantial power to make policy for the EU member states. The most important political leaders in the EU are still the heads of government of the individual member states.
- There is no generalized European tax system. The EU raises funds in part through levies and customs duties, which are a form of tax, but the vast majority of taxes – income, corporate, property, sales, estate, capital gains, and so on – are raised by national or local units of government, which also make tax policy.
- There is no European military or defence system. The armies, navies, and air forces of the member states still answer to the governments of the member states, although contingents have come together as the seeds of a European security force (see Chapter 9). In this sense they are the functional equivalent of the militias that existed in the American confederal system.
- The EU may have its own flag and anthem, but most of the citizens of the member states still have a greater sense of allegiance to their own national flags, anthems, and other symbols, and there has been only limited progress towards building a sense of a European identity (see Chapter 2).

Interestingly, the concept of confederalism is rarely mentioned in conjunction with the EU (see Majone, 2006 and Moravcsik, 2007 for exceptions), in spite of how much it clearly offers the debate. There are several possible reasons for this: federalism is more often found in practice and has been more thoroughly studied, federalism has been at the heart of the criticisms directed by eurosceptics at the EU, confederalism falls short of what the most enthusiastic European federalists would like for Europe, and in those few cases where confederalism has been tried in practice it has always evolved ultimately into a federal system. In his 1981 study of confederation and the European Economic Community (EEC), Forsyth argued that studies of federalism seemed to have little connection with the realities of European integration, and that if we were to look more closely at historical examples of confederations, we would find that the EEC was clearly an economic confederation in both content and form (Forsyth, 1981:x, 183). Lister agrees, describing the EU as a 'jumbo confederation' whose member states and governments continue to dominate the EU's institutions (Lister, 1996:ch. 2).

Conclusions

What, then, is the European Union? The answer depends upon who you ask, and what preferences they bring to their analysis. It is clearly far more than a conventional international organization, but it has not yet been comfortably slotted in to discussions about the state. It often appears in the company of states, as in peacekeeping operations in world trouble spots, where EU soldiers might be operating alongside those from individual states, or as in so many of those statistical tables produced by the UN that list all the countries of the world and will often have a separate listing for the EU. But it is generally understood that it is in a class apart.

   In spite of all the energy that has been devoted since the 1950s to first understanding the process of European integration, and then to understanding the personality of the EU, about all that anyone can agree is that there is nothing in the political lexicon that captures the essence of the EU, and that it is *sui generis* (unique). To describe it as such is really to avoid the question, and to avoid taking a position. And yet to take a position, and to describe the EU as federal, confederal, quasi-federal, an exercise in multi-level governance, or any of the other labels that have appeared in the debate, is to invite additional debate which rarely results in a conclusion. To take the plunge and to argue that it is an arrangement on the road to a United States of Europe is to risk either the ire or the confusion of others in the debate. This is one of the great frustrations of studying the EU. No one can quite agree on what it is, it constantly changes form, it is on the path to an end-state whose features are unknown, everyone has different opinions about when the end-state will be reached, and it is unlikely that we will even know we have reached that end-state until many years after the event. For former Commission president Jacques Delors, it was an 'unidentified political object'. For political scientist Michael Burgess, the most we can say is that 'the EU works in practice but not in theory' (Burgess, 2006:245).

What cannot be denied is that the EU is an entity with which we are all becoming more familiar. This is especially true in Europe, because the laws and decisions that govern the lives of Europeans are being made less at the local or national level, and increasingly as a result of negotiations and compromises among the EU member states. Developments at the EU level are becoming as important for Europeans to understand as those in their national capitals. Not long ago an 'informed citizen' was someone who knew how their national system of government worked, how their national economy functioned and how their national society was structured. To be 'informed' now demands a broader horizon, and familiarity with a new set of institutions, processes, and political, economic, and social forces.

Opinions on the value of regional integration – and its long-term prospects – will remain divided as long as they are confused and obscured by questions and doubts about the conditions that encourage integration, the logic of the steps taken towards integration, and the end product. Comparing the European Union with a conventional state can give us more insight, but we are still some way from agreement on what drives the process, and from understanding what we have created. Most confusingly, the goals of regional integration are only vaguely defined. The next three chapters will attempt to address some of the confusion by looking at the personality, evolution, and structure of the European Union.

Chapter 2

The Idea of Europe

We live in a European world. It is a multicultural world, to be sure, but most of it has been colonized at some point by one European power or another, and most people today live in societies that are either based on the European political and cultural tradition or influenced by the norms and values of that tradition. The 'world culture' described by the American political scientist Lucien Pye (1966) is ultimately European in origin, even if it has been most actively promoted and exported by the United States (which is itself mainly a product of European culture). For 'western', we could as easily think 'European'.

It is all the more ironic, then, that the idea of Europe remains hard to pin down. Its political and cultural qualities are hard to define (beyond being an accumulation of national identities), its geographical boundaries are debatable, and there is little agreement on what 'Europe' represents. Europeans have had much to unite them over the centuries, but they have had much more to divide them. Their common historical experiences have been rare, they speak many different languages, they have struggled with religious and social divisions, their views of their place in the world have changed, wars have broken out among them with depressing frequency, and the map of Europe has frequently had to be redrawn in response to changes in political affiliation.

But all is now changing. Although Europeans after the Second World War were too focused on rebuilding their economies and political systems to think outside their own states, they could not ignore their perilous situation astride the divisions of the cold war. First the western part of the continent built ties through the European Community (and then the European Union), and then with the end of the cold war the east entered the equation. Through a complex process of trial and error, Europeans have discovered their common interests, goals, and values, collectively labelled Europeanism. Outsiders have also had to review their perception of Europe, which is now less a collection of sovereign states and more a regional collective. North American and Asian business and government leaders see the EU as a new source of competition for economic and political influence, while most Eastern Europeans and Russians see it as an assertive new force for democratic and free-market change.

And yet the idea of European unity is nothing new. Since the Early Middle Ages, monarchs, popes, generals, and philosophers have dreamed about European cooperation, and have written and spoken of unity as a means of defending Europe against itself and outsiders since at least the fourteenth century. But for them it was to prove no more than an ideal; modern Europeans have seen the practical application of those ideas, and even though European integration has been made up on the fly, with no clear final destination, its effects are impossible to ignore, and the implications for the idea of Europe have been profound. As a result, we need to better understand the meaning of Europe. What are its political, economic, social, and cultural dimensions, and how can these help us better understand the significance and impact of European integration? Has integration simply been an intergovernmental project pursued by elites and bureaucrats, or does it build upon – and help strengthen – a European political, economic, and social model? Is there a distinctively European way of interpreting domestic and international problems, and of addressing those problems? In short, what is the idea of Europe?

Europe's changing identity

Defining *Europe* and *European* has never been simple, thanks to disagreements about the outer limits of the region and the inner character of its inhabitants. The rise of the EU has added a new dimension to the challenge, obliging us to think of the inhabitants of the region not just as Spaniards or Belgians or Poles or Latvians, but also as Europeans. And to add yet more spice to the debate, macro-integration has been accompanied by a micro-level loosening of ties as national minorities in several countries – such as the Scots in Britain, the Catalans in Spain, the Flemings and Walloons in Belgium, and multiple nationalities in the Balkans – express themselves more vocally, and remind us that European identity is being re-formed not only from above but also from below.

Europe has never been united, and its long history has been one of repeated fragmentation, conflict, and the reordering of political boundaries. Parts of Europe have been brought together at different times for different reasons – beginning with the Romans and moving through the Franks to the Habsburgs, Napoleon, and Hitler – but while many have dreamed of unification, it has only been since the Second World War that the idea of setting aside insular nationalism in the interests of regional cooperation has been put into practice. For the first time in its history, almost all of Europe has been engaged in a joint integrative exercise that has encouraged its inhabitants to think collectively rather than as members of smaller cultural or national groups that happen to inhabit the same landmass. But there is one key problem that crops up repeatedly throughout European history: Europeans have often been better at defining themselves in relation to outsiders than in relation to each other.

The word *Europe* is thought to come from Greek mythology: Europa was a Phoenician princess who was seduced by Zeus disguised as a white bull, and was taken from her homeland in what is now Lebanon to Crete, where she later married the King of Crete. It is unclear when the term *European* was first applied to a specific territory or its inhabitants, but it may have been when the expansion of the Persian Empire led to war in the fifth century BC. Greek authors such as Aristotle began to make a distinction between the languages, customs, and values of Greeks, the inhabitants of Asia (as represented by the Persians), and the 'barbarians' of Europe, an area vaguely defined as being to the north. Maps drawn up by classical scholars subsequently showed the world divided into Asia, Europe, and Africa, with the boundary between Europe and Asia marked by the River Don and the Sea of Azov (Delanty, 1995:18–19; den Boer, 1995).

The Roman Empire – at its peak from approximately 200 BC to 400 AD – brought much of Europe for the first time under what has been described as a 'single cultural complex' (Cornell and Matthews, 1982). The Roman hegemony came with a common language (Latin), a common legal and administrative system, and – following the adoption of Christianity in AD 391 – a common religion. However, the Roman Empire was centred on the Mediterranean and included North Africa and parts of the Middle East as well, and so was not exclusively European. Because the Romans presided over an empire, there was no prevailing sense that everyone living under Roman rule was part of a region with a common identity. The situation was further confused with the end of Roman hegemony in the last part of the fourth century AD, when Rome was invaded by the northern 'barbarians' and Europe broke up into feuding kingdoms. The invasions separated Europe culturally from its classical past, and the Dark Ages that followed witnessed redefining movements of people as different tribes – notably the Huns, the Vikings, and the Magyars – invaded other parts of Europe.

The birth of Europe is often dated to the Early Middle Ages (500–1050), which saw the emergence of a common civilization with Christianity as its religion, Rome as its spiritual capital, and Latin as the language of education. The new sense of a European identity was strengthened by the development of a rift between the western and eastern branches of Christianity, the expansion of Frankish power from the area of what are now Belgium and the Netherlands, and the development of a stronger territorial identity in the face of external threats, notably from the Middle East. The retreat of Europeans in the face of Asian expansionism reached its peak in the seventh and eighth centuries with the advance of Arab forces across North Africa and into Spain and southern France. They were turned back only in 732 with their epic defeat by Charles Martel near Poitiers, in west-central France.

The term *European* was used by contemporary chroniclers to describe the forces under the command of Martel (Hay, 1957:25), but it would not become more widely used until after 800, when his grandson Charlemagne was crowned Emperor of the Romans by Pope Leo III and hailed in poems as the king and father of Europe. His Frankish Empire covered most of what are now France, Switzerland, Austria, southern Germany, and the Benelux countries (an area that supporters of European unity in the 1950s liked to point out coincided with the territory of the six founding member states of the European Economic Community.) Although the Frankish Empire helped promote the spread of Christianity, and passed on to his son after Charlemagne's death in 814, it was later subdivided and ultimately evolved into the Holy Roman Empire.

Medieval Europe was peripheral to the development of civilization. Central authority declined and intra-European trade ended in the wake of further invasions from Scandinavia and central Europe, and feudalism strengthened as large landowners exercised new authority. It was not until the beginning of the High Middle Ages in the mid-eleventh century that commerce revived, agricultural production and population grew, towns became centres of intellectual and commercial life, a new class of merchants emerged, and monarchs and the aristocracy imposed greater control over their territories. The threat of invasion from outside Europe largely disappeared, and Europe became the aggressor. As Christian armies gathered from all over the region to take part in the Crusades (1095–1291), aimed at recapturing Jerusalem and the Holy Land from the Muslims, Europe became more tightly defined.

By the fifteenth century it had become more usual for scholars to use the term *Europe*, which to outsiders was synonymous with *Christendom*. This was ironic, given the turbulence that followed in the wake of famines, the Black Death, and the Hundred Years' War (1337–1453), which saw the rising power of monarchs, and challenges to the authority of the papacy that led to the Reformation and the emergence of the modern state system. Religious divisions strengthened as Protestant churches expressed their independence from the Roman Catholic Church, and for much of the sixteenth and early seventeenth century Europe was destabilized by religious warfare. But this did not stop Europeans from embarking on voyages of discovery to Africa, the Americas, and Asia, there was an expansion of education based on the classical works of Greek and Latin authors, and a revolution in science was sparked by the findings of Copernicus, Sir Isaac Newton, and others. These developments combined to give Europeans a new confidence and a new sense of their place in the world.

Delanty (1995:42) argues that cultural diversity within Europe ensured that the idea of European unity was limited to matters of foreign conquest. The earliest proponents of unity were moved in part by their belief that a united Christian Europe was essential for the revival of the Holy Roman Empire and by concern about Europe's insecurity in the face of gains by the Turks in Asia Minor; most of the proposals for unity were based on the argument that the supremacy of the papacy should be revived (Heater, 1992:6). But then the Renaissance (roughly 1350–1550) saw loyalty shift away from the Church, with growing support for individualism and republicanism, and the Church had become so divided by the end of the sixteenth century that the idea of a united Christian Europe was abandoned, and those who still championed the idea of regional unity (see Box 2.1 for examples) saw it as based less on a common religion than on addressing the religious causes of conflict and the growing threat of Habsburg power. But the borders of European states were achieving new permanence, weakening the notion of a wider European identity. With the Peace of Westphalia in 1648, and two treaties bringing an end to the Thirty Years War and the Eight Years War and leaving many territorial adjustments in its wake, the grip of the state strengthened.

The tumult of the French Revolution and the Napoleonic wars encouraged several prominent thinkers and philosophers to explore the notion of European peace through unity. Jean-Jacques Rousseau wrote in favour of a European federation; Jeremy Bentham, in *A Plan for an Universal and Perpetual Peace* (1789), wrote of his ideas for a European assembly and a common army; Immanual Kant's *Thoughts on Perpetual Peace* (1795) included suggestions for the achievement of world peace; and the Comte de Saint-Simon published a pamphlet in 1814 titled *The Reorganization of the European Community,* in which he argued in support of a federal Europe with common institutions, but within which national independence would be maintained and respected.

Others had come to the conclusion that conquest was the best response, but they found themselves foiled by the sheer size of the task and by resistance from key actors to changes in the balance of power. The attempts by Charlemagne, Philip II of Spain, and the Habsburgs to establish a European hegemony all failed, argues Urwin (1995:2), because of the 'complex fragmented mosaic of the continent ... [and] the inadequate technical resources of the would-be conquerors to establish and maintain effective control by force over large areas of territory against the wishes of the local populations'. The first attempt to achieve unity by force in modern times was made by Napoleon, who brought what are now France, Belgium, the Netherlands, Luxembourg, and parts of Germany and Italy under his direct rule. He saw himself

Box 2.1 Early thoughts on European cooperation

The challenge of how best to encourage Europeans to set aside their differences has exercised the minds of many thinkers over the centuries, some of their suggestions looking remarkably like parts of today's European Union:

- Pierre Dubois (1255–1312), a French advocate, suggested that the princes and cities of Europe form a confederal 'Christian Republic', overseen by a permanent assembly of princes working to ensure peace through the application of Christian principles. In the event of a dispute, a panel of nine judges could be brought together to arbitrate, with the Pope acting as a final court of appeal (Heater, 1992:10; Urwin, 1995:2).
- King George of Bohemia (1420–71) and his diplomatist Antoine Marini proposed a European confederation in response to the threat posed by the Turks in the mid-fifteenth century. Their plan involved an assembly meeting regularly and moving its seat every five years, a college of permanent members using a system of majoritarian decision making, a council of kings and princes, and a court to adjudicate disputes (de Rougemont, 1966:71).
- The Duc de Sully (1560–1641), in his Grand Design, proposed a redrawing of administrative lines throughout Europe so as to achieve equilibrium of power, and the creation of a European Senate with 66 members serving three-year terms (Heater, 1992:30–5).
- William Penn (1644–1718) published in 1693 his *Essay Towards the Present Peace of Europe*, proposing a European diet or parliament that could be used for dispute resolution, and suggesting that quarrels might be settled by a three-quarters majority vote, weighted according to the economic power of the participating states: Germany would have 12 votes, France ten, England six, and so on (Heater, 1992:53–6; Salmon and Nicoll, 1997:3–6).
- The Abbé de Saint-Pierre (1658–1743) published in 1717 his *Project for Settling an Everlasting Peace in Europe,* arguing for free trade and a European Senate. His ideas inspired the German poet Friedrich von Schiller to write his 'Ode to Joy' in 1785, which – sung to the main theme of Beethoven's Ninth Symphony – is today the European anthem: 'Thy magic reunites those whom stem custom has parted, All men will become brothers under thy gentle wing'.

as the 'intermediary' between the old order and the new, and hoped for a European association with a common body of law, a common court of appeal, a single currency, and a uniform system of weights and measures.

Despite rapid economic, social, and technological change, nineteenth-century Europe was driven by nationalism, boosted by the effects of the 1815 Congress of Vienna on great-power rivalry, and tracing its evolution through to the unification of Italy in the 1860s, of Germany in 1871, and beyond. It also prompted rivalry among European states, both within Europe and further afield in the competition to build colonial empires. Dreams of a United States of Europe nonetheless continued to inspire nineteenth-century intellectuals such as the French poet and novelist Victor Hugo, who in 1848 declared that the nations of Europe, 'without losing [their] distinctive qualities or ... glorious individuality, will merge closely into a higher unity and will form the fraternity of Europe ... . Two huge groups will be seen, the United States of America and the United States of Europe, holding out their hands to one another across the ocean.' But nationalism prevailed, feeding into militarization and the outbreak in 1914 of the Great War, when all the competing tensions within Europe finally boiled over in what was effectively a European civil war. One of the consequences was chaos in much of central Europe, and the peace arranged under the 1919 Treaty of Versailles did little more than fan the fires of nationalism, particularly in Germany.

The horrors of the Great War helped create a more receptive audience to notions of European integration and unity, the new debates involving not just intellectuals but politicians as well. The strongest support came from the leaders of smaller states that were tired of being caught up in big-power rivalry, and several made practical moves towards economic cooperation. Thus Belgium and Luxembourg created a limited economic union in 1922, including fixing the exchange rates of their currencies relative to each other, and in 1930 joined several Scandinavian states in an agreement to limit tariffs.

One of the most convinced champions of European unity was Count Richard Coudenhove-Kalergi (1894–1972), the son of an Austrian diplomat and his Japanese wife, and co-founder in 1922 of the Pan-European Union. In his 1923 manifesto *Paneuropa*, Coudenhove-Kalergi argued in favour of large-scale cooperation within a network of five 'global power fields': the Americas (excluding Canada), the Soviet Union, Eastern Asia (China and Japan), Paneuropa (including continental Europe's colonies in Africa and southeast Asia), and Britain and its empire. He proposed a four-stage process for the achievement of European union: a conference of representatives from the 26 European states, the agreement of treaties for the settlement of European disputes, the development of a customs union, and the drafting of a federal European constitution. He also suggested that English should become the common second language for Europe, since it was becoming the dominant global language. His ideas failed to generate a mass following, but they impressed several leading figures in the arts, as well as several contemporary or future political leaders, including Georges Pompidou, Thomas Masaryk, Konrad Adenauer,

Winston Churchill, and two French prime ministers, Edouard Herriot and Aristide Briand.

The prevailing view in France was that European cooperation was an impossible dream, and that the best hope for peace lay in French strength and German weakness (Bugge, 1995:102). Herriot disagreed, and in 1924 he called for the creation of a United States of Europe, to grow out of the postwar cooperation promoted by the League of Nations. For his part, Briand called for a European confederation working within the League of Nations, and in May 1930 distributed a memorandum to governments outlining his ideas (Salmon and Nicoll, 1997:9–14). In it he wrote of the need for 'a permanent regime of solidarity based on international agreements for the rational organization of Europe'. He used such terms as 'common market' and 'European Union', and even listed specific policy needs, such as the development of trans-European transport networks, and anticipated what would later become the regional and social policies of the EU. But all thought of European cooperation was now swept aside in the gathering storm of tensions sparked by the rise of Nazism.

Adolf Hitler was obsessed with correcting the 'wrongs' of Versailles and creating a German 'living space'. He spoke of a 'European house', but only in terms of the importance of German rule over the continent in the face of the perceived threat from communists and 'inferior elements' within and outside Europe. The nationalist tensions that had not been resolved by the Great War now boiled over once again into pan-European conflict. Almost every European state was dragged in, and Hitler was able to expand his Reich to include Austria, Bohemia, Alsace-Lorraine, and most of Poland, and to occupy much of the rest of continental Europe.

With the end of the Second World War in 1945, the need to deal with the pre-existing economic and social divisions of Europe was joined in European calculations by the question of how to deal with the ideological rift between a capitalist west and a socialist east. The circumstances would have seemed unfavourable to supporters of unity and regional integration, and yet it was to be the very depth of the threats posed to Europe by the cold war that was to allow the dreamers to begin taking the substantive actions needed to move beyond theory and philosophy into the realms of practical political, economic, and social change. Europe was still potentially a threat to itself, but it now faced the far greater threat of global rivalry between two superpowers armed with nuclear weapons. At no time in its history had it been so divided, or had its future been so patently out of its control. The dismay at the depths to which it had been reduced by centuries of conflict now combined with cold war division to spark a new interest in European cooperation and independence; the first modest step was taken in 1952 with the creation of the European Coal and Steel Community, and the second in 1958 by the creation of the European Economic Community (see Chapter 3).

Western Europeans continued to build ties among themselves during the 1960s and 1970s, so that by the time the cold war came to an end in 1990–91, the foundations for the economic integration of the entire continent were firmly in place. There are still many divisions: Eastern Europe (or Central Europe, as some prefer to call it) has not yet entirely rid itself of the heritage of state socialism, Germans still distinguish between those from the east and those from the west, Italy is culturally and economically divided into north and south, and Britain is an amalgam of English, Scottish, Welsh, and Northern Irish influences. Cultural and economic differences also continue to complicate European identity: the Mediterranean states to the south are distinctive from the maritime states to the west or the Scandinavian states to the north. And the rivalries, suspicions, and stereotypes that have their roots in centuries of conflict still surface periodically.

But compared with just a generation ago, what unites Europeans has become more distinct and important than what divides them. Europeans are more individually mobile, the communications revolution has made Europe a smaller place, there has been a growth in intra-European trade, and there is a new awareness of what Europeans have in common and of how their values and priorities differ from those of the United States, China, and Russia. Many still have their doubts about the wisdom of regional integration, and Europeans still have their political and cultural differences, but at no time in its history has the idea of Europe had so much clarity as it does today.

Where is Europe?

In spite of the new definition given to the meaning of the terms *Europe* and *European*, many differences remain. First, few European states are culturally homogeneous, and there is no such thing as a European people or race. The repeated reordering of territorial lines over the centuries has bequeathed to almost every European state a multinational society, and has left several national groups – such as the Germans, the Poles, the Basques, and the Irish – divided by national frontiers. Many states have also seen large influxes of immigrants since the 1950s, including Algerians to France, Turks to Germany, and South Asians to Britain. Not only is there no dominant culture, but most Europeans rightly shudder at the thought of their separate identities being subordinated to some kind of homogenized Euroculture; at least part of the resistance to integration is generated by concerns about threats to national cultural identity.

Table 2.1   *Official languages of the EU*

Bulgarian	German	Polish
Czech	Greek	Portuguese
Danish	Hungarian	Romanian
Dutch	Irish	Slovak
English	Italian	Slovene
Estonian	Latvian	Spanish
Finnish	Lithuanian	Swedish
French	Maltese	

Second, the linguistic divisions of Europe are substantial: its natives speak more than 40 languages, which are defended as symbols of national identity. Multilingualism in Europe also means that all official EU documents are translated into the 23 official languages of the member states (see Table 2.1), although the work of EU institutions is increasingly carried out in English and French. Supported by its rapid spread as the language of global commerce and diplomacy, the dominance of English grows, and it is slowly becoming the language of Europe. This worries the French in particular and other Europeans to some extent, but it is too late, and it at least gives Europeans a way of talking to each other, and helps reduce the cultural differences that divide them.

Third, while the histories of European states overlapped for centuries as they colonized, went to war, or formed alliances with each other, those overlaps often emphasized their differences rather than giving them the sense of a shared past. When it came, European integration grew in part out of the reactive idea of ending the conflicts that arose from those differences. Historical divisions were further emphasized by the external colonial interests of European powers, which encouraged them to develop competing sets of external priorities at the expense of cultivating closer ties with their immediate neighbours. Even now, Britain, France, Spain, and Portugal have close ties with their former colonies, while Eastern European states have still not entirely cut their ties with Russia.

Finally, it is not clear exactly where Europe physically begins and ends. It is often described as a 'continent', but continents are defined by geographers as large, unbroken, and discrete landmasses that are almost entirely surrounded by water. Strictly speaking, Europe is no more than part of the Asian continent, but no one would seriously describe Europeans as Asians. The western, northern, and southern boundaries of Europe offer no difficulties, because they are conveniently demarcated by the Atlantic, the Arctic, and the Mediterranean. Unfortunately, there is no handy geographical feature to mark Europe's eastern boundary. It is usually defined as running down the

Ural Mountains, across the Caspian Sea, along the southern edge of the Caucasus Mountains, across the Black Sea, and through the Bosporus Strait. But these are no more than convenient physical features that have been adopted despite political and social realities.

The Urals are considered a boundary of Europe only because they were nominated as such by an eighteenth-century Russian cartographer, Vasily Tatishchev, so that Russia could claim to be an Asian as well as a European power. If we accept them as a boundary, then six former Soviet republics – Belarus, Moldova, Ukraine, and the three Baltic states (Estonia, Latvia, and Lithuania) – are part of Europe. The Baltic states offer no problems, because they have historically been bound to Europe, and are now members of the European Union and NATO. But Belarus, Moldova, and Ukraine are all still caught in a residual struggle for influence between Russia and Europe. Belarus is a political outlier, having resisted the wave of democracy that has swept over most of its neighbours. Ukraine underwent its famous Orange Revolution in 2004 and has made clear its aspirations for membership of the EU, but there are many political and economic hurdles to cross before that becomes a reality. In Moldova, meanwhile, political leaders have hinted at an interest in EU membership, but the country is poor and has strong historical and cultural links with Russia.

The major problem with the Urals is that they are deep in the heart of Russia. Russians are sometimes defined as European, and Russia west of the Urals was long known as Eurasia because of the distinctions imposed on the region by Europeans, but opinion on Russia's identity remains mixed: some Russians see their country as part of Europe and the West, others distrust the West and see Russia as distinctive from both Europe and Asia, and yet others see it as a bridge between the two (Smith, 1999:50). The most obvious problem with defining Russia as European is that three-quarters of its land area is east of the Urals in Siberia, and most Siberians – including Buryats, Yakuts, and Siberian Tatars – are unquestionably non-European. Further south, meanwhile, the Caucasus Mountains present similar problems as a boundary; should the republics of Armenia, Azerbaijan, and Georgia be considered European? They are all members of the Council of Europe, after all, and there have been hints here, too, as in Ukraine, of EU and NATO membership down the line. But are they too politically and economically tied to Russia?

In central Europe, changes in the balance of power long meant that the Poles, the Czechs, and the Slovaks were caught in the crossfire of great-power competition, which is why this region was known as the 'lands between'. The west looked on the area as a buffer against Russia, a perception that was helped by the failure of its people to form lasting states identified with dominant national groups. During the cold war the distinctiveness of Eastern Europe was further empha-

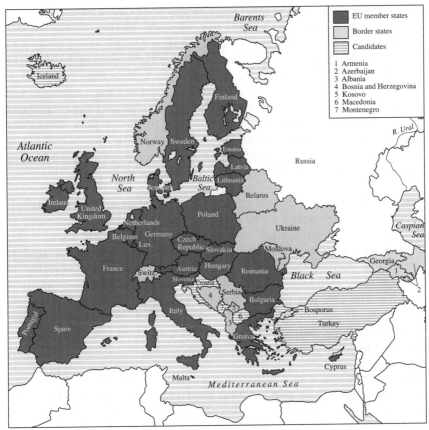

Map 2.1 *Europe Today*

sized by the ideological divisions between east and west, despite the historical ties that meant Poland was actually closer to Western Europe than to Russia. But the end of the cold war meant a rapid reorientation of central Europe towards the west, and all states in the region are now members of the EU and NATO.

For their part, the Balkans occupy an ambiguous position between Europe and Asia, being a geographical part of the former but historically drawn towards the latter. They were long regarded as an extension of Asia Minor, and until relatively recently were still described by Europeans as the Near East (Hobsbawm, 1991:17). Frequent changes of authority – whether it was the Macedonians, the Romans, the eastern Roman empire, Slavic tribes, Christianity, the Kingdom of Hungary, the Venetians, or the Ottoman Turks – has helped create what Delanty (1995:51–2) describes as 'frontier societies in the intermediary lands' between great powers. The Slavs in particular were split between those who accepted Catholicism, Greek Orthodoxy, or Islam, which resulted in cultural heterogeneity in spite of the greater linguistic homogeneity that existed among Slavs than among the peoples of Western Europe (Delanty, 1995:54). Slavs continue to have affiliations with Russia, which is part of the reason why NATO was wary of becoming too deeply involved in the conflicts in Bosnia and Kosovo in the 1990s. Since the break-up of Yugoslavia there has been a trend for Balkan national groups to look to the EU; the Slovenians were the first to become members in 2004, Croatia, Macedonia, and Montenegro have been accepted as candidate countries, and other Balkan republics have broached the prospect of eventual EU membership.

By far the most troubling question in the debate about the boundaries of Europe relates to Turkey. The Bosporus is usually regarded as the border between Europe and Asia, which means that about 4 per cent of the land area of Turkey lies inside Europe. Turkey indicated its interest in joining the European Economic Community as early as 1963, and is currently considered a candidate country, meaning that its application for membership has been accepted and negotiations on the terms of membership are under way. But numerous problems stand in the way, including its relative poverty, doubts about its democratic record, its large size, and the fact that it is a Muslim state (see Box 2.2.)

So where, then, is Europe? If its borders with Turkey, the Caucasus, and Russia are taken as its eastern limits, then it consists today of 40 countries: the 27 members of the EU, three other Western European states (Iceland, Norway, and Switzerland), and ten Eastern European states. If a broader definition of Europe's boundaries is accepted, then it includes four more countries: Armenia, Azerbaijan, Georgia, and Turkey. Stretching the limits of credibility, some (such as former Italian prime minister Silvio Berlusconi) have even suggested that Israel should be considered European, and might qualify for EU membership, but this view has little support.

Whatever Europe's external boundaries, its inner personality has been driven by two critical developments. First, the cold war division of Europe has faded into the mists of history as Western and Eastern Europeans have buried their political, economic, and ideological differences, and as the bonds among them have tightened and strengthened. Political and economic investments have flowed from west to east, and workers in search of new opportunities have moved from east to west. Second, enlargement of the European Union has helped reduce the distinctions between 'Europe' and the 'European Union'. As recently as 2004, less than half the states of Europe were members of the EU, which was home to only two-thirds of Europeans. Today, the EU covers three-quarters of the land area of Europe, includes two-thirds of

Box 2.2   The Turkish question

When it comes to defining the borders of Europe, and deciding the limits of EU enlargement, the Turkish question has a special place in the debate. The European Community agreed as long ago as 1963 that Turkish membership was possible, and it became an associate member of the Community that same year. It applied for full membership in 1987, a customs union between the EU and Turkey came into force in December 1995, Turkey was formally recognized as an applicant country in 1999, and negotiations on EU membership opened in 2006. But a string of difficult questions has muddied the waters, not least being the matter of whether or not Turkey is a European country. If EU member Cyprus is European, then presumably so is Turkey, in geographical terms at least.

But the problems with Turkey are less geographical than they are political, economic, and religious. The EU has agreed three criteria for aspiring members, known as the Copenhagen conditions: an applicant must be democratic, capitalist, and willing to adopt the existing body of EU laws. Turkey is clearly capitalist, and has made great efforts to meet the third of these requirements, most notably abolishing the death penalty in 2004. But while it is capitalist it is also poor, with a per capita GDP one-tenth that of the EU average, and current EU members fear not only that billions of euros in subsidies and investments will be diverted to Turkey if it joins the EU, but that large numbers of Turks will move to wealthier parts of the EU in search of jobs. As to Turkish democracy, its record on human rights has been poor, with concerns – for example – about the role of the military in politics, about the treatment of the Kurdish minority, and about women's rights.

But the most telling – if usually unspoken – concern about prospective Turkish membership of the EU is religious. Turkey is a Muslim state, and even though its brand of Islam is secular and western-oriented, the potential difficulties of integrating 76 million Turkish Muslims into a club that often emphasizes its Christian credentials, and that has been struggling with accommodating its own existing Muslim minorities, are substantial. If Turkey was small, poor, and Muslim (like Albania) it might be less of a problem, but its size means that it would become the second largest member state of the EU by population after Germany. The resulting doubts have divided European public and political opinion, which tends to focus on the challenges rather than the opportunities offered by Turkish membership. Among the latter: a large new market and labour pool, and the importance of Turkey in helping Europe strengthen its geopolitical relationship with the Middle East and the Muslim world. (For further discussion, see Morris, 2005.)

the states of Europe, accounts for 93 per cent of the economic wealth of Europe, and is home to four out of every five Europeans. We may still quibble about the eastern borders of Europe, but the differences between the EU and Europe are rapidly disappearing.

All these changes have reordered the way in which Europeans regard one another, and approach their understanding of the division of policy interests. Europeans are slowly transferring their loyalty from individual states to a more broadly defined European identity, and are thinking of themselves less as Germans or Belgians or Slovaks and more as Europeans. It has been a slow process, to be sure, but recent Eurobarometer polls have found that slightly more than half of Europeans think of themselves as European in addition to their own nationality (see Figure 2.1), and that about 60 per cent feel proud to be European. Fligstein (2008:250) divides Europeans into three camps: one (making up about 10–15 per cent of the population) has deep economic and social ties to Europe, from which it benefits materially and culturally; a second (40–50 per cent) is aware of what is going on across borders but is still wedded to national language, culture, and politics; the third (40–50 per cent), made up mainly of older, poorer, and less educated Europeans, is more wedded to home, does not travel or consume culture from other societies, and is more fearful of European integration.

Critics of integration have long argued that one of the greatest dangers posed by integration is the homogenization that comes as member states lose their individuality in the move towards Europe-wide standards and regulations. They argue that authority is shifting from national governments mandated by the people towards a European superstate that lacks such a mandate. But this depends upon how the EU is understood; if it is a European federation, then many problems remain. But if it is a confederation, in which citizens have the closest ties to their home states, and national governments set the pace of regional integration, then there is little to worry about. And rather than lead to a homogenized Europe, integration has actually helped promote a reassertion of cultural differences as Europeans have grown to better understand and appreciate the variety of the regions in which they live.

Indeed it is often argued that a Europe of the regions may come to rival or even replace a Europe of the states. In the interests of correcting economic imbalances, and prompted by growing demands for greater decentralization, European states began to regionalize their administrative systems in the 1960s, and as a result regions have emerged as important actors in politics and policy (Keating and Hooghe, 1996). They have come to see the EU as an important source of investment and of support for minority cultures, and in some cases this has given more confidence to nationalist movements (such as those

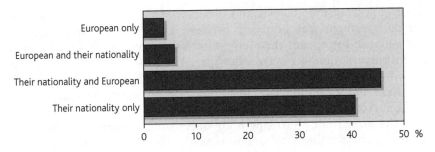

Figure 2.1   *Changing European identities*
Data from European Commission, *Eurobarometer* 61, Spring 2004.

in Scotland and Catalonia), as they feel less dependent on the support of the state governments. It has also reduced the overall importance of interstate relations within the EU, and drawn new attention to interregional relations. The logical conclusion is that forces of this kind will lead to Europe centralizing and decentralizing at the same time, with the member states as we know them today squeezed in the middle.

Europeanism

There is an old and well-worn joke that heaven is where the police are British, the cooks are French, the mechanics are German, the lovers are Italian, and everything is organized by the Swiss. Meanwhile, hell is where the police are German, the cooks are British, the mechanics are French, the lovers are Swiss, and everything is organized by the Italians. National stereotypes such as these abound in Europe (as they do everywhere), some based on a modicum of truth, some with no redeeming qualities, and most nonetheless perpetuated by the media and popular culture. But even if such stereotypes are typically wrong (or wrong-headed), what they tell us is that Europe is a region of diversity, with every European state claiming to have a distinctive personality arising out of a combination of history, culture, norms, and values.

Out of this melange of competing identities, is it possible to pin down a distinctive European personality? Surely the histories, cultures, and social structures of European states are too deeply ingrained to make such an exercise credible? And those who doubt the wisdom and effects of European integration are more than ready to point to the many instances where EU member states still squabble and disagree. The open disagreement over the US-led invasion of Iraq in 2003 is a prime example, often touted as evidence of the underlying weaknesses of the European experiment, notably in the area of foreign policy. But what almost all the analysts and observers failed to mention was that the disagreement was primarily between European governments, and not between Europeans themselves. Indeed, opinion polls found a near uniformity of opinion across Europe, with 70–90 per cent of those polled expressing opposition to the war, even in countries whose governments supported the war, including Britain, Spain, Italy, Denmark, and the Netherlands.

At the same time, a growing body of research indicates that there are many common values and opinions across the EU on a broad array of issues, ranging from welfarism to capital punishment, immigration, international relations, environmental protection, and the relationship between Church and State. Much remains to be done to better understand and clarify the commonalities, and to move the analysis beyond the fascination with what divides rather than unites Europe, but the outlines have achieved a new clarity in recent years, particularly since the end of the cold war finally allowed Europeans from east and west to begin expressing and exerting themselves without being limited by the constraints of rivalry between the Americans and the Soviets. (For more details on the arguments that follow, see McCormick, 2010. See also Fligstein, 2008.)

Europeanism is usually understood to mean support for the process of European integration. Hence Scruton (1996:180) defines it as the 'attitude which sees the well-being, destiny and institutions of the major European states as so closely linked by geographical and historical circumstances that no cogent political action can be successfully pursued in one state without some reference to, and attempt to achieve integration with, the others'. But it is also used to signify the collective values and principles associated with Europe and Europeans. An initial attempt was made to pin down those values in 2003, when – inspired by the massive demonstrations against the impending invasion of Iraq that were held in every major European city on 15 February – the German and French philosophers Jürgen Habermas and Jacques Derrida hailed the birth of a 'European public sphere', noted that there had been a reaction to nationalism that had helped give contemporary Europe 'its own face', and argued that a 'core Europe' (excluding Britain and Eastern Europe) should be built as a counterweight to US influence in the world. They listed several features of what they described as a common European 'political mentality', including secularization, support for the welfare state, a low threshold of tolerance for the use of force, and support for multilateralism (Habermas and Derrida, 2003 [2005]).

During the cold war, the outlines of a distinctive European identity had been hard to find, divided as the sub-continent was by the lines of the conflict, and subject as most European states were to the political lead of the United States (in the west) or of the Soviet Union (in the east). Since then, though, and encouraged by the twin effects of European integration and the removal of cold war ideological and social divisions, there has been an emerging sense that Europeans have much in common, and a set of values that give them a distinctive identity. The key elements of Europeanism can be found in four major areas: political values, economic values, social values, and attitudes towards international relations.

On the political front, Europeans are clearly champions of democracy, human rights, and the rule of law, but they also have a particularly European view of the nature and purposes of democracy. Institutionally, the structure and distribution of power is driven by the principles of parliamentary government, which – while not peculiar to Europe – were born in Europe and today form the basis of all national European political systems, albeit with local variations. One effect of the system is that political parties play a more central role in European politics than they do in much of the rest of the world (in spite of the many suggestions that European party systems are on the decline), the distribution of seats in national legislatures determining the make-up of governments, and the variety and ideological spread of parties reflecting and driving the diversity of voter opinion (Mair, 2001).

In terms of how they identify themselves politically, Europeans live in the part of the world where the modern state system first emerged and where many now argue that it is most rapidly declining. As state borders have become more porous and Europeans travel in greater numbers to neighbouring states, so identification with states has declined and a sense of patriotism – if it is understood as love of country – has also declined, to be replaced by a belief in democratic ideas, otherwise known as constitutional patriotism (see Müller, 2007). Europeans have become more aware of their national and European identities, and this has encouraged them to adopt views of the world, and of their place in it, that are driven more by two other perspectives: cosmopolitanism and multiculturalism. The first is the idea that humans can associate themselves more with universal ideas and that they belong to a single moral community that exists above the level of states and nations (for background, see Rumford, 2007, and Beck and Grande, 2007). The second suggests that Europeans have become more used to contacts and integration with other cultures and no longer see the world exclusively from their own national or cultural perspective. But this is only a factor in relation to other Europeans; when it comes to racial or religious tolerance the European record is not so strong.

In terms of how they conceive political rights, Europeans stand in particular distinction to Americans; while the latter emphasize individual rights and place an emphasis on self-reliance, Europeans are more communitarian in their approach: they support more of a balance between individual and community interests, and are more tolerant of the argument that in some cases society may be a better judge of what is best for individuals than vice versa (for more detail on the qualities of communitarianism, see Etzioni, 1998). At the heart of this concept are positive rights, meaning those which permit or oblige action, perhaps making way for the offering of services by the state, and which stand in contrast to negative rights, which prevent actions by others (in areas such as freedom of speech and religion, for example). Hutton (2003:54–8) argues that while the American liberal definition of rights does not extend beyond the political to the economic and social, the European conception of rights is broader, including free health care, free education, the right to employment insurance, and so on.

On the economic front, Europeans are committed capitalists and supporters of the free market, but they place a premium on the redistribution of wealth and opportunity, and on the responsibility of government to maintain a level playing field. As Prestowitz puts it, a key difference between the American and European economic models is that 'Americans emphasize equality of opportunity, [while] Europeans focus more on equality of results' (Prestowitz, 2003:236–7). Europeans have a higher level of tolerance than Americans for the collective society: the idea that key services (such as education and health care) should be managed and offered by the government, and paid for out of taxes. One American observer – Jeremy Rifkin – has gone so far as to talk of a new European dream that is threatening to eclipse the much-vaunted American dream. He contrasts the American emphasis on economic growth, personal wealth, and individual self-interest with the European emphasis on quality of life and community, and concludes that the EU is developing a new social and political model better suited to the needs of the globalizing world of the new century (Rifkin, 2004).

Europeans have not yet been able to address the problems of persistent poverty and unemployment (just as no one has), but their welfarist approach stands in contrast to those of the United States, which places an emphasis on self-reliance and on the private delivery of key services. There has been recent debate about just how much European governments agree on the economic responsibilities of the state, and an interest in the distinctions between the 'Anglo-Saxon' and 'continental' or Rhenish European economic models (see Albert, 1993). The former features lower levels of tax and regulation, a greater reliance on the private sector to provide key services, and a greater level of market freedom, while the latter argues that the state must intervene more actively to redistribute wealth and address poverty. Whatever the differences, though, Europeans are more ready than Americans to believe that the state has a responsibility to encourage as level a playing field as possible, to criticize capitalism as a source of economic and social ills, and to support the core goals of sustainable development.

On the social front, there may not yet be a distinctive European society, and regional integration has not been able to overcome the considerable barriers posed by language differences, by the absence of pan-European media, and by cultural differences (see Box 2.3), and yet there are many trends which suggest substantial agreement among Europeans on a variety of issues. For example, Europeans are willing to concede that government may have a role in making moral decisions or defining the social choices of individuals; this can be seen in relation to issues such as abortion, capital punishment, gun control, censorship, doctor-assisted suicide, and same-sex civil unions and marriage.

In few social areas is there a more distinctive European identity than in religion; the evidence suggests that Europe is the only part of the world where belonging to a religion is on the decline, and much of the explanation for this can be found in history. Despite the central role that the Church has played in European public and political life over the centuries, it has never been a uniting force (Dunkerley *et al.*, 2002:115). First there was the division between the Latin and Orthodox Churches, then the division between the Catholic and Protestant Churches, and more recently there has been the rise of religious diversity as new immigrants have brought Islam, Hinduism, Buddhism, Sikhism and other religions into the equation. During the discussions over the European constitutional treaty, it was suggested that the preamble should include reference to the Christian heritage of Europe, but this was turned down on the grounds that it would not reflect the religious diversity of the new Europe, and would send a particularly worrying message to Muslims and Jews (see discussion in Schlesinger and Foret, 2006).

European society is also distinguished by important demographic changes that are routinely quoted as sources of concern and as indicating weaknesses in the future success of Europe, and yet are at the core of European identity. Prime among these is declining birth rate, which has helped bring about a fundamental redefinition of the family: fewer Europeans are marrying (or are delaying marriage), divorce rates are growing, fewer Europeans are having children, and single-parent or no-child households have become the norm. At the same time, Europeans are working fewer hours and are taking more time off (a 40-hour week and five weeks of paid vacation are now the norm), which is changing their attitudes towards both work and leisure. But how far they can continue to sustain an ageing population while working fewer hours is currently the topic of much debate.

In international relations, Europeans have a preference for multilateralism, the use of smart power (a balance between soft power – encouragement and opportunity – and hard power – coercion and force; see Chapter 9), and for using civilian means for dealing with conflict. They take a liberal view of the international system, arguing

Box 2.3   Promoting European culture

The stability of a state is usually predicated upon a high degree of legitimacy (public acceptance), which is in turn predicated upon a strong sense of national identity, in which a sense of a common culture is a critical element. Conversely, the instability of states often arises out of social and cultural divisions, which weaken the sense of a common national identity. France is an example of a state with a high level of cultural unity, while British national identity is weakened by divisions among the English, the Scots, the Welsh, and the Northern Irish, and Belgium is weakened by divisions between its Flemish and Wallonian communities.

Historically and culturally speaking, Europeans are insular and inward-looking, often knowing little about the history or culture of even their closest neighbours. The EU has tried to address this problem by promoting the idea of a common European culture (even though such promotion may be anathema to some – how can culture be legislated or 'promoted' as a policy goal?). Despite the results of Eurobarometer polls showing a majority in favour of cultural policy being left to the member states, Maastricht introduced a commitment that the EU would 'contribute to the flowering of the culture of the Member States' with a view to improving knowledge about the culture and history of Europe, conserving European cultural heritage, and supporting and supplementing non-commercial cultural exchanges and 'artistic and literary creation'.

What this has so far meant in practice has been spending funds on restoring historic buildings, supporting training schemes in conservation and restoration, preserving regional and minority languages, subsidising the translation of works by European authors (particularly into less widely spoken languages), and supporting cultural events. For example, the EU has funded a Youth Orchestra and a Baroque Orchestra to bring young musicians together, declared since 1985 European 'Capitals of Culture' (including Graz in Austria, Genoa in Italy, and Cork in Ireland), and established a European Cultural Month in cities in non-member states (such as Basel, Cracow, and St Petersburg).

While the sentiments behind these projects are laudable, it is difficult to see how cultural exchanges and the development of a European cultural identity can work unless they are driven by Europeans themselves. It is easy to argue that Shakespeare, Michelangelo, Voltaire, Goethe, Picasso, and Mozart are all part of the heritage of Europe, but the notion of promoting a modern pan-European popular culture is a beast of an entirely different stripe. Even the most mobile of art forms – film and rock music – come up against the barrier of national preferences, and little that is not produced in English has had commercial success outside its home market.

Table 2.2   *Key features of Europeanism*

Democracy	Welfarism
Parliamentary government	Sustainable development
Constitutional patriotism	Secularism
Cosmopolitanism	Redefinition of the family
Multiculturalism	Multilateralism
Communitarianism	Smart power
Capitalism	Civilian power
Collective society	

that states can and must cooperate and work together on matters of shared interest, and placing an emphasis on the importance of international organizations and international law. The European view once again stands in particular contrast to that of the United States, which has a reputation for the promotion of national interests, an emphasis on military solutions to problems, and a distrust of international organizations. While Europeans have become used to working together, the United States has long been wary of alliances and jealously guards its independence. Where many Europeans long ago acknowledged that they were citizens of an international system, and are prepared to act multilaterally, there are still many Americans for whom there are only two realistic options: American leadership, or isolationism.

The best–known recent analysis of the contrasting worldviews of the EU and the US was offered in 2003 by Robert Kagan, an American political commentator (Kagan, 2003). He argued that the two sides no longer share a common view of the world, and that 'Americans are from Mars and Europeans are from Venus.' What he meant was that while Europe has moved into a world of laws, rules, and international cooperation, the United States believes that security and defence depend on the possession and use of military power. While the United States sees the world as divided between good and evil, and between friends and enemies, Europeans see a more complex global system, and prefer to negotiate and persuade rather than to coerce. Kagan argues that the differences are a reflection of the relative positions of the two actors in the world; when Europe was powerful it was willing to use violence to achieve its goals, while Americans had no choice but to use soft power. But now that they have traded places, they have also traded perspectives. Critics have taken issue with this analysis, arguing that Europeans do not use soft power because they have no choice, but precisely because they have a choice. Europe is not a continent of pacifists, but one where the 'just' causes of war are actively debated and where there are different opinions about the role of military force (Menon *et al.*, 2004).

These four sets of features can help us pin down the nature of Europeanism, but – just as with Europe's eastern borders – it is not easy to draw firm lines around those features, many of which are shared with other parts of the world. In geographical, political, economic, and social terms it has never been easy to pin down Europe, particularly given its enormous internal diversity. But one of the effects of integration has been to encourage more efforts to understand what Europeans have in common. There is still much resistance among political leaders, academics, and Europeans themselves to the idea that generalizations can be drawn across national borders, but the common themes in both the meaning of Europe and in the values and norms that are represented by Europe are easier to identify today than ever before.

Conclusions

The idea of European unity is nothing new. The conflicts that brought instability, death, and changes to the balance of power in Europe over the centuries prompted many to propose unification – or at least the development of a common system of government – as a means to the achievement of peace. The rise of the state system undermined these proposals, but interstate conflict ultimately reached a level at which it became clear that only cooperation could offer a path to peace. The two world wars of the twentieth century – which in many ways began as European civil wars – emphatically underlined the dangers of nationalism and of the continued promotion of state interests at the expense of regional interests.

New thinking has dramatically altered the idea of Europe over the past two generations, and the nature of the internal relationship among the states that make up Europe has changed out of all recognition. Not everyone is a supporter of European integration, and the criticisms of the directions it has been taking have grown, but there has been a generational shift since 1945, as memories of the horrors of the Second World War fade into history, and the idea of Europe is one associated with peace and progress. Where intellectuals and philosophers once argued in isolation that the surest path to peace in Europe was cooperation, or even integration, the costs of nationalism are now more broadly appreciated, ensuring a wider and deeper consideration of the idea of regional unity.

Europeans still have much that divides them, and those differences are obvious to anyone who travels across the region. There are different languages, cultural traditions, legal, education and health-care systems, social priorities, cuisines, modes of entertainment, patterns of etiquette, styles of dress, ways of planning and building cities, ways of spending leisure time, attitudes towards the countryside, and even sides of the road on which to drive (the British, Irish, Cypriots, and Maltese drive on the left, everyone else on the right). Europeans also have differences in the way they govern themselves, and in what they have been able to achieve with their economies and social welfare systems.

Increasingly, however, Europeans have more in common. The economic and social integration that has taken place under the auspices of the European Union and its precursors since the early 1950s has brought the needs and priorities of Europeans closer into alignment. It has also encouraged the rest of the world to see Europeans less as citizens of separate states and more as citizens of the same economic bloc, if not yet the same political bloc. Not only has there been integration from the Mediterranean to the Arctic Circle, but the 'lands between' – which spent the cold war as part of the Soviet bloc and part of the buffer created by the Soviet Union to protect its western frontier – are now becoming part of greater Europe for the first time in their history. The result has been a fundamental redefinition of the idea of Europe. In the next chapter we will look at the key steps in the evolution of the European Union, the underlying motives of integration, and the debates involved in the process.

Chapter 3

The Evolution of the EU

The idea of 'Europe' has been evolving for centuries, but serious efforts to encourage regional integration date back only to the end of the Second World War, when three critical needs came to the fore: economic reconstruction, security in the face of cold war tensions, and efforts to prevent European nationalism spilling over once again into conflict. At the core of European calculations was concern about the traditional hostility between France and Germany, and the belief that if these two states could cooperate it might provide the foundations for broader European integration.

A modest early step was taken in 1949 with the creation of the Council of Europe, but this did not go far enough for committed integrationists, who looked instead to the creation of new institutions with supranational powers. On 9 May 1950, French foreign minister Robert Schuman announced a plan under which Europe's national coal and steel industries would be brought together under a joint authority. The European Coal and Steel Community began life in 1952 with just six member states (France, West Germany, Italy and the three Benelux countries), but with its creation began a complex and often controversial process of experimentation, opportunism, intrigue, crisis and serendipity that eventually led to the European Union as we know it today.

The next step was the creation in 1958 of the European Economic Community, with the same six member states but a more ambitious set of goals, including the development of a single market within which there would be free movement of people, money, and services, and common policies on agriculture, competition, trade and transport. As it became clear that the Community was working, other countries applied for full or associate membership. The first enlargement came in 1973 with the accession of Britain, Denmark, and Ireland, followed in the 1980s by Greece, Portugal, and Spain, and in 1995 by Austria, Finland and Sweden.

The single market was given a boost in 1986 with agreement of the Single European Act, setting a five-year deadline for removal of remaining barriers. There was progress, too, on monetary union, with the launch in 1999 of the euro, which finally replaced 12 national currencies in 2002. The focus of enlargement shifted eastwards; after lengthy preparations, 12 new mainly Eastern European countries joined the EU in 2004-07, bringing membership to 27 and the population of the EU to nearly 500 million. Other countries now wait in line for membership, including Croatia, Iceland, Macedonia, Montenegro, and Turkey.

Along the way, progress has been made on developing common policies on a wide range of issues, although those who hoped that Europe would play a more assertive and united role in foreign and security policy have been disappointed. There was also disappointment for supporters of a new European constitution, which was drafted in 2005 but collapsed after negative public votes in France and the Netherlands. Agreement was instead reached on a new Treaty of Lisbon that preserved most of the content of the constitutional treaty, aimed at making the larger EU more efficient. Meanwhile, many Europeans remained ambivalent about the European Union, while others were patently hostile. The global economic downturn of 2007–10 added new problems to the mix, emphasizing the remaining economic weaknesses and vulnerabilities of Europe, and testing the performance of the euro.

Postwar Europe

The European Union was born out of the ruins of the Second World War. Before the war, Europe had dominated global trade, banking and finance, its empires had stretched across the world and its military superiority had been unquestioned. But Europeans had often disagreed, their conflicts undermining the prosperity that cooperation might have brought. Pacifists hoped that the Great War of 1914-18 would have offered final proof of the futility and brutality of armed conflict, but it would take the Second World War to convey the message to a wider audience: the war left more than 40 million dead and widespread devastation in its wake; every country involved sustained heavy casualties and physical damage; cities lay in ruins, agricultural production was halved, food was rationed, and communications were disrupted. The war also dealt a near-fatal blow to Europe's global power and influence, heralding the beginning of the end of the great European empires, and clearing the way for the emergence of the United States and the Soviet Union as superpowers.

The western postwar economic agenda had been set at a meeting held in July 1944 at Bretton Woods, New Hampshire, and attended by representatives from 44 countries. All agreed to an Anglo-American proposal to promote free trade, non-discrimination and stable exchange rates, and supported the view that Europe's economies should be rebuilt and placed on a more stable footing. However, it soon became clear that reconstruction needed substantial capital investment, the readiest source of which was the United States, which saw Europe's progress as essential to its own economic and security interests, and made a large investment in the future of Europe through the Marshall Plan (see Box 3.1).

The second postwar priority was the security of Europe, from itself and from external threats, and once again the United States was to play a critical role. Winston Churchill had warned in his famous 1946 speech of an iron curtain descending on Europe, and in March 1948 the governments of Britain, France, and the Benelux countries created a Western Union under which they pledged to provide all possible military aid in the event of an attack from outside. Three months later the three western occupying powers in Germany agreed to combine their zones into a new West German state, with a new currency. The Soviets responded with a blockade around West Berlin, prompting a massive western airlift to supply the beleaguered city. The United States had quickly withdrawn its troops from Europe after the war, but now felt that it had no choice but to return in order to counterbalance the Soviets. In 1949 the North Atlantic Treaty Organization (NATO) was created, by which the United States agreed to help its European allies 'restore and maintain the security of the North Atlantic area'. But while NATO members agreed that an attack on one of them would be considered an attack on all of them, each agreed only to respond with 'such actions as it deems necessary'.

The Western Europeans now overreached themselves with a 1950 proposal for the creation of a European Defence Community (EDC), and a coincidental European Political Community (EPC) that would offer a fast-track to a European federation. But while the EDC had the support of the governments of West Germany, France, Italy and the Benelux states, it lacked the essential support of Britain, and many in France were nervous about the idea of German rearmament so soon after the war. A critical blow came in May 1954 with the humiliating defeat of French troops at Dien Bien Phu in French Indochina. Reeling from the effects of wounded national pride, the French National Assembly voted down the EDC treaty in August, which also meant an end to plans for the EPC. The security focus now shifted back to the Western Union, which was renamed the Western European Union (WEU), and whose founding members were joined by West Germany and Italy. Within days of the launch of the WEU in May 1955 and the coincidental admission of West Germany into NATO, the Soviet bloc created the Warsaw Pact. The lines of cold war Europe were now clearly defined, and its implications illustrated by the breaking of the Suez crisis.

In July 1956, seeking funds to help him build a dam on the Nile, Egyptian president Gamal Abdel Nasser nationalized the Suez Canal, still owned and operated by Britain and France. Their governments

Box 3.1   The Marshall Plan

US policy after 1945 was to withdraw its military forces as quickly as possible from Europe. However, it soon became clear that Stalin had plans to expand the Soviet sphere of influence, and the US State Department began to realize that it had underestimated the extent of Europe's economic destruction: despite a boom in the late 1940s, sustained growth was not forthcoming. When an economically exhausted Britain ended its financial aid to Greece and Turkey in 1947, President Truman argued the need for the United States to fill the vacuum in order to curb communist influence in the region.

US policy makers also felt that European markets needed to be rebuilt and integrated into a multilateral system of world trade, and that economic and political reconstruction might help forestall Soviet aggression and the rise of domestic communist parties (Hogan, 1987: 26–7). Thus Secretary of State George Marshall argued that the United States should provide Europe with assistance to fight 'hunger, poverty, desperation and chaos'. The original April 1947 State Department proposal made clear that one of the ultimate goals of the plan was the creation of a Western European federation (quoted in Gillingham, 1991: 118–19).

The European Recovery Programme (otherwise known as the Marshall Plan) provided just over $12.5 billion in aid to Europe between 1948 and 1951 (Milward, 1984:94) (about $115 billion in 2011 terms, adjusted for inflation). Disbursement was coordinated by the Organization for European Economic Cooperation (OEEC), a new body set up in April 1948 with headquarters in Paris. Governed by a Council of Ministers made up of one representative from each member state, the OEEC's goals included the reduction of tariffs and other barriers to trade, and consideration of the possibility of a free-trade area or customs union among its members. Opposition from several European governments (notably Britain, France, and Norway) ensured that the OEEC remained a forum for intergovernmental consultation rather than becoming a supranational body with powers of its own (Wexler, 1983:209; Milward, 1984:209–10).

Although the effects of the Marshall Plan are still debated, there is little question that it helped underpin economic and political recovery in Europe, and helped bind more closely the economic and political interests of the United States and Western Europe. It was a profitable investment for the United States, in both political and economic terms, but it also had critical influence on the idea of European integration: as Western Europe's first venture in economic cooperation, it encouraged European governments to work together and highlighted the interdependence of their economies (Urwin, 1995: 20–2). It also helped liberalize intra-European trade, and helped ensure that economic integration would be focused on Western Europe.

immediately conspired with that of Israel to launch an invasion of the canal. Coincidentally, the Hungarian government announced the end of one-party rule, the evacuation of Russian troops, and withdrawal from the Warsaw Pact. Just as Britain and France were invading Egypt, the Soviets were sending tanks into Hungary. The United States wanted to criticize the Soviet use of force, but obviously could not while British and French paratroopers were storming the Suez Canal. In the face of US hostility, Britain and France were ostracized in the UN Security Council and the attempt to regain the canal was abandoned. The effects were profound (see Hourani, 1989): Britain and France finally recognized that they were no longer world powers capable of significant independent action; both embarked on a concerted programme of decolonization; Britain began to look to Europe for its economic and security interests; and it became obvious to Western Europeans that the United States was the dominant partner in the Atlantic Alliance.

First steps towards integration (1948–55)

For many Europeans, the major obstacles to peace were nationalism and the nation state, both of which had been discredited by the war. Economic reconstruction and military security were critical to the future of the region, but Europeans also needed a greater sense of unity and common purpose than they had ever been able to achieve before. The spotlight fell on Britain, which had taken the lead in fighting Nazism and was still the dominant European power. In 1942–43, Winston Churchill had suggested the development of 'a United States of Europe' operating under 'a Council of Europe' with reduced trade barriers, free movement of people, a common military and a High Court to adjudicate disputes (quoted in Palmer, 1968:111). He made the same suggestion in a speech in Zurich in 1946, but it was clear that Churchill felt this new entity should be based around France and Germany and would not necessarily include Britain – before the war he had argued that Britain was 'with Europe but not of it. We are interested and associated, but not absorbed' (Zurcher, 1958:6).

National pro-European groups decided to organize a conference focused on the cause of regional unity. The Congress of Europe, held in The Hague in May 1948, agreed the creation of the Council of Europe, founded with the signing in London in May 1949 of a statute by ten Western European states. But the Council would never be more than a loose intergovernmental organization, and was not the kind of body that European federalists wanted. Among those looking for something more substantial were the French entrepreneur and bureaucrat Jean Monnet (1888–1979) and French foreign minister Robert

Schuman (1886–1963). Both felt that practical steps needed to be taken that went beyond the broad statements of organizations such as the Council of Europe, and agreed that the logical starting point should be the resolution of the perennial problem of Franco-German relations.

By 1950 it was clear to many that West Germany had to be allowed to rebuild if it was to play a useful role in the western alliance, but this would best be done under the auspices of a supranational organization that would tie West Germany into the wider process of European reconstruction. Looking for a starting point that would be meaningful but not too ambitious, Monnet opted for the coal and steel industries on the grounds that they were the building blocks of industry, the heavy industries of the Ruhr had long been the foundation of Germany's power, and integrating coal and steel would make sure that West Germany became reliant on trade with the rest of Europe, under-pinning its economic reconstruction while helping the French overcome their fear of German industrial domination (Monnet, 1978:292). He now proposed a new institution independent of national governments, which would be supranational rather than intergovernmental in nature.

The plan was announced by Robert Schuman at a press conference in Paris on 9 May 1950 (now celebrated each year as Europe Day). In what later became known as the Schuman Declaration, he argued that Europe would not be united at once or according to a single plan, but step by step through concrete achievements. This would require the elimination of Franco-German hostility, and Schuman proposed that French and German coal and steel production be placed 'under a common High Authority, within the framework of an organization open to the participation of the other countries of Europe'. This would be 'a first step in the federation of Europe', and would make war between France and Germany 'not merely unthinkable, but materially impossible' (Schuman, quoted in Stirk and Weigall, 1999:76).

Although membership of the new body was open to all European states, only four accepted: Italy, which sought respectability and eco-nomic and political stability, and the three Benelux countries, which were small and vulnerable, had twice in recent memory been invaded by Germany, were heavily reliant on exports, and felt that the only way they could have a voice in world affairs and ensure their security was to become part of a bigger regional unit. The other European gov-ernments had different reasons for not taking part: Britain still had extensive interests outside Europe, exported little of its steel to the con-tinent, and the new Labour government had recently nationalized Britain's coal and steel industries and did not like the supranational character of Schuman's proposal; Ireland was heavily agricultural and tied economically to Britain; for Denmark and Norway the memories of German occupation were too fresh; Austria, Finland, and Sweden wished to protect their neutrality; Portugal and Spain were dictatorships with little interest in international cooperation; and participation by Soviet-dominated Eastern Europe was out of the question.

The lines of thinking now established, the governments of the Six opened negotiations and on 18 April 1951 signed the Treaty of Paris, creating the European Coal and Steel Community (ECSC). The new organization began work in August 1952, managed by an appointed nine-member High Authority (with Jean Monnet as its first president), and decisions being taken by a six-member Special Council of Ministers. An appointed 78-member Common Assembly helped Monnet allay the fears of national governments regarding the surrender of powers, and disputes between states were to be settled by a seven-member Court of Justice.

The ECSC had limited goals and powers, but it was notable for being the first supranational organization to which European governments had transferred significant powers. It was allowed to reduce tariff barriers, abolish subsidies, fix prices, and raise money by imposing levies on steel and coal production, its job made easier by the fact that some of the groundwork had been laid by the Benelux customs union (founded in 1948). Although the ECSC failed to achieve many of its goals (notably the creation of a single market for coal and steel (Gillingham, 1991:319)), it had ultimately been created to prove a point about the feasibility of integration, which it did. But it did not go far enough for Monnet, who resigned the presidency of the High Authority in 1955, disillusioned by the political resistance to its work and impatient to further the process of integration (Monnet, 1978:398–404).

The European Economic Community (1955–86)

Efforts to promote European integration now moved on to a more ambitious plane. A meeting of the ECSC foreign ministers at Messina in Italy in June 1955 resulted in agreement to adopt a Benelux proposal 'to work for the establishment of a united Europe by the development of common institutions, the progressive fusion of national economies, the creation of a common market, and the progressive harmonization of their social policies' (Messina Resolution, in Weigall and Stirk, 1992:94). A new round of negotiations led to the signing in March 1957 of the two Treaties of Rome, one creating the European Economic Community (EEC) and the other the European Atomic Energy Community (Euratom), both of which came into existence in January 1958. The EEC had a similar administrative structure to the ECSC, with a quasi-executive appointed Commission, a Council of

Ministers with powers over decision making, and a Court of Justice. A new 142-member Parliamentary Assembly was also created to cover the EEC, ECSC and Euratom; in 1962 it was renamed the European Parliament.

The EEC Treaty committed the Six to the creation of a common market within 12 years by removing all restrictions on the internal movement of people, money and services; the setting of a common external tariff for goods coming into the EEC; the development of common agricultural, trade and transport policies; and the creation of a European Social Fund and a European Investment Bank. Action would be taken in areas where there was agreement, and disagreements could be set aside for future discussion. The Euratom Treaty, meanwhile, was aimed at creating a common market for atomic energy, but it was of real interest only to France, and Euratom was to remain a junior actor in the process of integration, focused primarily on research.

The birth and early years of the EEC have to be seen in the light of international developments. The threats posed by the Soviets were clear, as was the extent to which Western Europe had to rely on the security guarantees offered by the United States. Less often considered in the story of European integration are the effects of differences of opinion within the Atlantic Alliance. Western Europeans had wondered about American priorities and perceptions as early as the Korean War, which had sparked worries about a wider conflict being set off by American plans to invade the north. Then came the 1962 Cuban missile crisis, during which the two superpowers had briefly stood on the brink of nuclear war while the Americans made little reference to the opinions of their European allies. Finally, the 1960s saw escalation of the conflict in Vietnam, for which no European government offered open support, and which by the late 1960s had generated widespread public criticism of US policy.

Amidst these wider changes in international affairs, it had early become clear that the EEC needed to expand its membership if its effects were to reach beyond an exclusive club of six. Any European state was allowed to join under the terms of the Treaty of Rome, but non-members had mixed feelings about the Community. Most obvious by its absence was Britain, whose nostalgic view that it was still a world power above the fray of narrow European interests was dashed at Suez. Even then, Britain had doubts about the EEC and instead championed a looser exercise in cooperation known as the European Free Trade Association (EFTA), founded in January 1960 with the signing of the Stockholm Convention by Austria, Britain, Denmark, Norway, Portugal, Sweden, and Switzerland. But it had already become clear to Britain that influence in Europe lay with the EEC, and that it risked isolation if it stayed out: the EEC had made impressive

Box 3.2   Early steps on the road of integration

The early years of integration were a mix of achievements, failures, and crises, setting a pattern still found in the European Union today:

- Although the 12-year deadline for the creation of a common market was not met, internal tariffs fell quickly enough to allow the Six to agree a common external tariff in July 1968, and to declare an industrial customs union.
- Decision making was streamlined in April 1965 with the Merger treaty, which created a single institutional structure for all three communities. New authority and consistency were provided by the formalization in 1975 of regular summits of EEC leaders coming together as the European Council. The EEC was also made more democratic with the introduction in 1979 of direct elections to the European Parliament.
- A dispute in 1965 over the powers of the Commission, voting in the Council of Ministers, and the Community budget led to a boycott of meetings of the Council by France (the empty-chair crisis), resolved only when the right of national veto was affirmed.
- Integration meant the removal of the quota restrictions that member states had used to protect their domestic industries from competition from imported products, contributing to accelerated economic growth and a rapid increase in intra-EEC trade.
- In the interests of removing non-tariff barriers to the free movement of goods across borders – including different standards and regulations on health, safety and consumer protection – standards were harmonized during the 1960s and 1970s. It was not until the passage of the 1986 Single European Act, however, that a concerted effort was made to bring all EEC members into line.
- Another priority was to lift restrictions on the free movement of workers. While some limits remain even today, progress was made towards easing them during the 1960s and 1970s.
- Agreement on a Common Agricultural Policy (CAP) was achieved in 1968, creating a single market for agricultural products, and assuring EEC farmers of guaranteed prices for their produce. The CAP initially encouraged both production and productivity, but it became increasingly controversial, not least because of its cost (see Chapter 8).
- The Six worked more closely together on international trade negotiations, achieving a joint influence that would have been missing if they had worked independently. The EEC acted as one, for example, in negotiations under the General Agreement on Tariffs and Trade (GATT), and in reaching preferential trade agreements with 18 former African colonies under the 1963 Yaoundé Convention (see Chapter 9).

economic and political progress and British industry wanted access to the rich EEC market.

In August 1961, barely 15 months after the creation of EFTA, Britain applied for EEC membership, along with Denmark and Ireland, joined in 1962 by Norway. Denmark's motive was mainly agricultural: it was producing three times as much food as it needed, and the EEC represented a big market for those agricultural surpluses, as well as a boost for Danish industrial development; Norway also realized the importance of the EEC market. Ireland saw EEC membership as a way of furthering its industrial plans, and of reducing its reliance on agriculture and on Britain. With four of its members now looking to the EEC, EFTA ceased to have much purpose, so Austria, Sweden, and Switzerland all applied for associate membership of the EEC; they were followed in 1962 by Malta, Portugal, and Spain.

Negotiations between Britain and the EEC opened in early 1962, and appeared to be on the verge of success when they fell foul of President Charles de Gaulle's plans for an EEC built around a Franco-German axis. He also saw Britain as a rival to French influence in the Community, resented Britain's lack of enthusiasm for the integrationist moves of the 1950s, and felt that British membership of the EEC would give the United States too much influence in Europe. In January 1963 – without asking his EEC partners – de Gaulle vetoed the British application. Since it was part of a package with Denmark, Ireland and Norway, they too were rejected. Britain reapplied in 1967 and was once again vetoed by de Gaulle. Following his resignation as president in 1969 Britain applied for a third time, and this time its application was accepted, along with those of Denmark, Ireland, and Norway. Following negotiations in 1970–71, Britain, Denmark, and Ireland finally joined the EEC in January 1973. Norway would have joined as well but a public referendum in September 1972 narrowly went against membership.

An additional round of enlargements in the 1980s pushed the borders of the EEC further south and west. Greece had made its first overtures to the EEC in the late 1950s, but had been turned down on the grounds that its economy was too underdeveloped. It was given associate membership in 1961 as a prelude to full accession, which might have come sooner had it not been for the Greek military coup of April 1967. With the return to civilian government in 1974, Greece almost immediately applied for full membership, arguing that EEC membership would help underpin its attempts to rebuild democracy. The Community agreed, negotiations opened in 1976, and Greece joined in January 1981.

Meanwhile, a preferential trade agreement had been signed with Spain in 1970 and with Portugal in 1973, but it was only with the overthrow of the Caetano regime in Portugal in 1974 and the death of

Map 3.1   *Growth of the EU, 1952–86*

Franco in Spain in 1975 that EEC membership for the two states became a real possibility. Despite their relative poverty, problems over fishing rights, and concerns about Portuguese and Spanish workers moving north in search of work, the EEC felt that membership would encourage democracy in the Iberian peninsula and help link the two countries more closely to NATO and Western Europe. Negotiations opened in 1978–79 and both states joined in January 1986, the Ten thereby becoming the Twelve.

The doubling of membership had several important consequences for the EEC: it increased its global influence, it changed the dynamic of Community decision making, it reduced the overall influence of France and Germany, it altered the Community's relations with the United States and with developing countries, and – by bringing in the poorer Mediterranean states – it altered the internal economic balance of the EEC. Rather than enlarging any further, it was now decided to focus on deepening ties among the Twelve. Applications were made by Turkey (1987), Austria (1989), and Cyprus and Malta (1990), and although East Germany entered through the back door with German reunification in October 1990, there was to be no more enlargement until 1995.

Economic and social integration (1979–92)

By 1986 the EEC had become known simply as the European Community (EC). Its member states had a combined population of 322 million and accounted for just over one-fifth of all world trade. The EC had its own administrative structure and an independent body of law, and its citizens had direct (but limited) representation through the European Parliament. But progress towards integration remained uneven. Decisions were taken primarily by government leaders and technocrats, most ordinary Europeans having little understanding of (or interest in) what was being done in their name. The customs union was in place, but completion of the common market was handicapped by barriers to the free movement of people and capital, including different national technical, health and quality standards, and varying levels of indirect taxation. It was also clear that there could never be a true single market without a common European currency, a controversial idea because it would mean a significant loss of national sovereignty and a significant move towards political union. These issues had now begun to concern EC leaders, who responded with the two critical initiatives: the launch of the European Monetary System, and the signature of the Single European Act.

The need to encourage stable exchange rates had long been a priority, but EEC leaders disagreed about whether economic union or monetary union should come first (Urwin, 1995: 155). At a December 1969 summit in The Hague, Community leaders discussed the principle of economic and monetary union (EMU), and agreed to control fluctuations in the value of their currencies and to make more effort to coordinate national economic policies. In August 1971, however, the Nixon administration signalled the end of the Bretton Woods system of fixed exchange rates by ending the convertibility of the US dollar with gold, imposing domestic wage and price controls, and placing a surcharge on imports. This led to international monetary turbulence, made worse in 1973 by the Arab–Israeli war and the attendant global energy crisis.

In 1979, a new initiative was launched in the form of the European Monetary System (EMS). Using an Exchange Rate Mechanism (ERM) based around an accounting tool known as the European currency unit (ecu), the EMS was designed to control fluctuations in exchange rates (see Chapter 7 for more details). The hope was that the ecu would become the normal means of settling debts among Community members, psychologically preparing them for the idea of a single currency. With this in mind, in 1989 Commission president Jacques Delors took EMU a step further with the elaboration of a three-stage plan aimed at fixing exchange rates and turning the ecu into a single currency. His hopes were dashed, however, by speculation on the world's money markets, which caused Britain and Italy to pull out of the ERM, and Ireland, Portugal and Spain to devalue their currencies. Ironically the crisis deterred speculation and reinforced currency stability, and EMU was back on track by 1994.

Meanwhile there was concern that progress towards the single market was being handicapped by inflation and unemployment, and by the temptation of member states to protect their home industries with non-tariff barriers such as subsidies. Economic competition from the United States and Japan was also growing. In response, a decision was reached at the 1983 European Council meeting in Stuttgart to refocus on the original core goal of creating a single market. The result was the signing in Luxembourg in February 1986 of the Single European Act (SEA), the first major change to the treaties since the signing of the Treaty of Rome. It came into force in July 1987 with several goals, the most important of which was to complete all requirements for the single market by midnight on 31 December 1992. This involved agreeing and implementing nearly 300 new pieces of legislation aimed at the removal of all remaining physical barriers (such as customs and passport controls at internal borders), fiscal barriers (mainly in the form of different levels of indirect taxation) and technical barriers (such as conflicting standards, laws, and qualifications). This would create 'an area without internal frontiers in which the free movement of goods, persons, services and capital is assured'.

The effects of the SEA were profound:

- It created the single biggest market in the world. Many internal passport and customs controls were eased or lifted, banks and companies could do business throughout the Community, there was little to prevent EC residents living, working, opening bank accounts and drawing their pensions anywhere in the Community, EC competition policy was given new prominence, and monopolies on everything from electricity supply to telecommunications were broken down.
- It gave Community institutions responsibility over new policy areas such as the environment, research and development, and regional policy.
- It gave new powers to the European Court of Justice, and created a Court of First Instance to hear certain kinds of cases and ease the workload of the Court of Justice.

- It gave legal status to meetings of heads of government under the European Council, and gave new powers to the Council of Ministers and the European Parliament.
- It gave legal status to European Political Cooperation (foreign policy coordination) so that member states could work towards a European foreign policy and work more closely on defence and security issues.
- It made economic and monetary union an EC objective and promoted 'cohesion', meaning the reduction of the gap between the richer and poorer parts of the EC.

Despite the signing of the SEA, progress on opening up borders was variable, and there was no common European policy on immigration, visas, and asylum. Impatient to move ahead, the governments of France, Germany, and the Benelux states in 1985 signed the Schengen Agreement, under which all border controls were to be removed among signatory countries. All EU member states have since signed the agreement, along with Iceland, Norway and Switzerland, but not all have introduced truly passport-free travel (Britain has stayed out of most elements of Schengen, claiming its special problems as an island state, and Ireland has had to follow suit because of its passport union with Britain), and the terms of the agreement allow the signatories to implement special controls at any time. Nonetheless, its signature marked a substantial step towards the removal of border controls.

From Community to Union (1992–2003)

Once again, developments within Western Europe must be understood within their broader international context, where remarkable changes were taking place. Reforms instituted by the Gorbachev administration in the Soviet Union after 1985 quickly spread in unanticipated directions, leading to demands for political change in East Germany, the dismantling of the Berlin Wall in 1989, and the reunification of Germany in October 1990. Meanwhile, anti-communist movements brought change throughout Eastern Europe, the dissolution of the Soviet Union in December 1991, and the break-up of Yugoslavia and Czechoslovakia. The end of the cold war fundamentally changed life for all Europeans, but the violence in the former Yugoslavia posed an immediate security problem that the Community tried and failed to resolve, falling back once again on the Americans (who brokered the 1995 Dayton peace accords) and proving to itself and to the rest of the world just how much work remained to be done if European political cooperation was to have any real meaning.

Box 3.3   Social issues move up the agenda

With all the early focus on economic issues, social problems were often overlooked by European leaders. The Treaty of Rome provided for the development of a Community social policy, but this was left in the hands of the member states and was narrowly defined, emphasizing improved working conditions and standards of living for workers, equal pay for equal work among men and women, social security for migrant workers, and increased geographical and occupational mobility for workers. As the economic links among EEC member states tightened, however, so their different levels of wealth and opportunity became more obvious. Even in the mid-1960s, per capita GDP in the Community's ten richest regions was nearly four times greater than in its ten poorest regions. With the accession of Britain, Greece, and Ireland the gap grew to the point where the richest regions were five times richer than the poorest (George, 1996:143–4).

Cohesion policy has since focused on working to close the gaps by helping the poorer parts of Europe, revitalizing regions affected by serious industrial decline, addressing long-term unemployment, providing youth job training, and helping the development of rural areas (see Chapter 8). The Commission gives economic assistance in the form of grants from what are collectively known as structural funds. These include the European Social Fund (ESF) (which concentrates on job creation and worker mobility), the European Regional Development Fund (ERDF) (set up in response to the regional disparities that grew when Britain and Ireland joined the Community) and the Cohesion Fund (which compensates the poorest EU member states for the costs of tightening environmental controls, and provides help for transport projects). The structural funds accounted for just 18 per cent of EC expenditure in 1984, but by 2011 represented 35 per cent of EU spending.

The SEA made cohesion a central part of economic integration, the assumption being that although the single market would create new jobs, this would not be enough. New attention was drawn to social policy in 1989 with the agreement of the Charter of Fundamental Social Rights of Workers (the Social Charter), which promoted the free movement of workers, fair pay, better living and working conditions, freedom of association, and protection of children and adolescents. Social issues are now one of the core policy areas for the EU, with many of the actions taken by the governments of the member states driven by the requirements of EU law. The latter has addressed issues as varied as health and safety at work, parental leave from work, public health, and programmes to help the disabled and the elderly.

The controversial idea of political integration had long been left on the back-burner because it was felt that there was little hope of political union without economic union, and political union in turn demanded cooperation on foreign policy. False starts had been made with the European Political Community and an attempt in 1961 to draw up a political charter that would spell out the terms of political union (the Fouchet Plan; see Urwin, 1995:104–7). Agreement was reached in 1970 on European Political Cooperation (EPC), a loose and voluntary process revolving around regular meetings of the Community foreign ministers. It achieved some modest successes and was eventually given legal status with the SEA, but it was more reactive than proactive and often found European governments at odds with one another. A more substantial step was taken in 1974 with the decision to create the European Council, formalizing the periodic meetings of Community heads of government; it met for the first time in March 1975.

Seeking to reassert French leadership in the EC, President François Mitterrand had focused on the theme of political union at the Fontainebleau European Council in 1984, and a decision was taken at the June 1990 European Council to convene an intergovernmental conference (IGC) on political union. The outcome was the Treaty on European Union, agreed at the European Council summit in Maastricht in December 1991 and signed in February 1992. The treaty had to be ratified by the 12 member states before it could come into force, and although doubts were raised by lengthy political debates in Britain, France, and Germany, a shock came when it was rejected by Danish voters in a referendum in June 1992, and only narrowly accepted by a referendum in France in September. The content of the treaty was further discussed by the European Council, and following agreement that the Danes could opt out of the single currency, common defence arrangements, European citizenship, and cooperation on justice and home affairs, a second Danish referendum was held in May 1993 and the treaty was accepted, coming into force the following November.

Like the Single European Act before it, the Treaty on European Union – usually known as the Maastricht treaty – made some significant changes to the contract among the member states of the EU:

- Reflecting the lengths to which member states were occasionally prepared to go to reach compromises, three 'pillars' were created under a structure given the new label 'European Union'. The first pillar was the renamed European Community, while the second and third pillars consisted of areas in which there was to be more formal intergovernmental cooperation: a Common Foreign and Security Policy (CFSP), and justice and home affairs. Final responsibility for the

CFSP remained with the individual governments rather than being handed over to the EU. The pillar arrangement was eventually abolished under the terms of the Treaty of Lisbon.

- The Delors three-stage plan for monetary union was confirmed.
- EU responsibility was extended into new policy areas such as consumer protection, public health policy, transport, education, and (except in Britain) social policy.
- There was to be greater intergovernmental cooperation on immigration and asylum, a European police intelligence agency (Europol) was to be created to combat organized crime and drug trafficking, a new Committee of the Regions was set up, and regional funds for poorer EU states were increased.
- New rights were provided for European citizens and an ambiguous EU 'citizenship' was created which meant, for example, the right of citizens to live wherever they liked in the EU, and to stand or vote in local and European elections.
- New powers were given to the European Parliament, including a codecision procedure under which certain kinds of legislation were subject to a third reading in the European Parliament before they could be adopted by the Council of Ministers.

The Danish rejection of Maastricht and the near-miss in France were to prove significant. Even though the French result was at least in part a reflection of the declining popularity of François Mitterrand (Criddle, 1993), for the first time there were signs that ordinary Europeans were asking hard questions about what was being done in their name. The old 'permissive consensus', when few Europeans took much interest in the work of the Community, leaving key decisions to government leaders, was now being challenged. As the reach of integration expanded, and more Europeans felt its effects, so the debate about its pros and cons expanded. Unfortunately, much of that debate has taken place against substantial public confusion and misinformation, driven by the media, interest groups, and political parties with strong positions on integration (see Chapter 5 for more details). But whatever the motivations, euroscepticism – or resistance to European integration – has become a critical new factor in the debates over Europe.

Meanwhile enlargement was still on the agenda, the end of the cold war leading to a new focus on expansion to Eastern Europe. At its June 1993 meeting in Copenhagen, the European Council agreed a formal set of requirements for membership of the EU. Known as the Copenhagen conditions, they require that an applicant state must (a) be democratic, with respect for human rights and the rule of law; (b) have a viable free market economy and the ability to respond to market forces within the EU; (c) be able to take on the obligations of

Existing Members

East Germany 1990

Third Enlargement 1995

1 Armenia
2 Azerbaijan
3 Albania
4 Bosnia and Herzegovina
5 Macedonia
6 Montenegro

Map 3.2 *Growth of the EU, 1990–95*

the *acquis communautaire* (the body of laws and policies already adopted by the EU); and (d) adapt their administrative structures in order to meet the demands of integration. Deciding whether applicants meet these criteria has proved difficult, not least because of the problem – discussed in Chapter 2 – of defining 'Europe'.

Throughout the 1980s, discussions about enlargement centred on other Western European states, if only because they came closest to meeting the criteria for membership. In order ostensibly to prepare prospective members (or, in the view of Dinan (2004:268)), to fob them off), negotiations began in 1990 on the creation of a European Economic Area (EEA), under which the terms of the SEA would be extended to the seven EFTA members, in return for which they would accept the rules of the single market. The EEA came into force in January 1994, but quickly lost relevance because Austria, Finland, Norway, and Sweden had applied for EC membership. Negotiations with these four applicants were completed in early 1994, and all but Norway (where a referendum once again went against membership) joined the EU in January 1995.

Their accession left just three Western European countries outside the EU: Iceland, Norway and Switzerland. Iceland kept its distance from the EU until the 2007–10 global economic crisis set off a collapse of its banking industry, prompting it to lodge a hurried application in July 2009 to join the EU. Should it join, it would – with a population of just 320,000 – be the smallest EU member state. In Norway, much of the early opposition to EU membership - based on factors such as fear of lowered environmental standards and concern about the power of large member states – has dissipated, and Norway continues to keep pace with economic and foreign policy developments in the EU, and to be impacted by EU developments through its membership of the EEA. Switzerland, which had considered applying for EC membership in 1992, rejected the EEA that same year and in 1995 found itself completely surrounded by the EU. Demands for the Swiss to open their highways to EU trucks and intra-EU trade increased the pressure for EU membership, but further discussion ended in March 2001 when a national referendum went heavily against EU membership.

Partly in preparation for anticipated eastern enlargement, but also to account for the progress of European integration and perhaps move the EU closer to political union, two new treaties were signed in 1997–2000. The first was the Treaty of Amsterdam, which was signed in October 1997 and came into force in May 1999, and which did little more than confirm plans for eastern enlargement and the launch of the single currency, confirm plans for the CFSP (creating a new office of High Representative for the CFSP), extend EU policy responsibilities to health and consumer protection, incorporate the Schengen Agreement into the treaties, and expand the powers of the European Parliament. Equally modest was the Treaty of Nice, agreed in December 2000 and signed in February 2001, which made a few more changes to the structure of the EU institutions, including increasing the size of the European Commission and the European Parliament, and redistributing the votes in the Council of Ministers. But European leaders were taken by surprise in June 2001 when Irish voters rejected the terms of the treaty, its opponents arguing that it involved the surrender of too much national control, and being particularly concerned about the implications for Irish neutrality. A second vote was taken in Ireland in October 2002, following assurances that Ireland's neutrality on security issues would be respected, and – thanks in part to a bigger turnout – the treaty was accepted by a 63 per cent majority. Nice came into force in February 2003.

More significant in constitutional terms was the agreement under Nice to integrate into the treaties the Charter of Fundamental Rights of the European Union. Its story begins with the 1950 European Convention on Human Rights (ECHR), drawn up and maintained by the Council of Europe. Little known to most Europeans for much of its life, the ECHR applies to member states of the Council of Europe, includes a wide range of civil and political rights, and is supported by the work of the Strasbourg-based European Court of Human Rights. As respect for human rights became a precondition for entry to the EU, and issues relating to justice and home affairs began to move up the EU agenda, so the ECHR achieved a new prominence. Following a 1996 decision by the European Court of Justice that its treaties did not allow the EU to accede to the ECHR, the decision was taken to pull together a wide range of pre-existing rights in the form of the Charter of Fundamental Rights, which is now part of the legal structure of the EU.

The euro, Lisbon, and beyond

Meanwhile, there had been rapid progress on the single currency. A decision had been taken in 1995 to call it the euro, and the timetable agreed under Maastricht required participating states to fix their exchange rates in January 1999. Several so-called 'convergence criteria' were considered essential prerequisites: these included placing limits on national budget deficits, public debt, consumer inflation, and long-term interest rates. At a special EU summit in May 1998 it was decided that all but Greece met the conditions, but public and political opinion in the member states was divided on which should or would fix their exchange rates. While inflation rates were low in the member states, unemployment rates were not, and the rate of industrial growth was slowing in several. There was also considerable public resistance to the idea of the single currency in several countries, notably Britain and Germany. In the event, all but Denmark, Sweden, and the UK adopted the euro when it came into being as an electronic currency in January 1999, banknotes and coins began circulating in January 2002, and the 12 members of the eurozone abolished their national currencies in March.

But against the background of these developments there were concerns about the inability of the European marketplace to improve its rates of productivity or to create enough new jobs to meet demand. The term Eurosclerosis had been coined earlier by Giersch (1985) to describe the problem, and there was little sign of change in the late 1990s, prompting a decision by the European Council in March 2000 to launch the Lisbon Strategy. This set the goal of making the EU – by 2010 – the most dynamic economy in the world, which demanded the creation of more jobs, bringing more women into the workplace, liber-

Map 3.3   *Growth of the EU, 2004–07*

alizing telecommunications and energy markets, improving transport, and opening up labour markets. In the event, the targets proved too ambitious, and Lisbon was superseded by the Europe 2020 Strategy, focusing on innovation, education, sustainable growth, a low-carbon economy, and job creation (see Chapter 7 for more details).

In May 2004, the EU undertook its most significant enlargement when ten Eastern European and Mediterranean states joined: Cyprus, the Czech Republic, Estonia, Hungary, Latvia, Lithuania, Malta, Poland, Slovenia, and Slovakia. All their economies combined were smaller than that of the Netherlands, and they increased the population of the EU by less than 20 per cent; the real significance of the 2004 enlargement lay in the fact that the EU was no longer an exclusive club for wealthy west Europeans. The East was now included, and – for the first time – former Soviet republics (Estonia, Latvia, Lithuania) became part of the European Union. As well as providing

Table 3.1 *Prospective members of the EU*

	Application made	Status
Candidates		
Croatia	June 2004	May join 2013–14
Iceland	June 2010	Negotiations under way
Macedonia	December 2005	
Montenegro	December 2008	
Turkey	April 1987	Negotiations under way
Applicants		
Albania	April 2009	
Serbia	December 2009	
Others		
Bosnia & Herzegovina		Medium-term potential
Kosovo		Medium-term potential
Armenia		Longer-term potential
Azerbaijan		Longer-term potential
Belarus		Poor prospects without democratic change
Georgia		Longer-term potential
Moldova		Too tied to Russia
Norway		Improving potential
Switzerland		Strong internal resistance
Ukraine		Mixed prospects

Indicates status as of early 2011.

an important symbolic confirmation of the end of the cold war division of Europe, the 2004 enlargement also promised to accelerate the process of transforming the economies and democratic structures of Eastern European countries. The trends continued in January 2007 when Bulgaria and Romania joined the EU, a development widely seen as a second phase of the 2004 enlargement. Croatia, Iceland, Macedonia, Montenegro and Turkey have also been accepted as 'candidate countries' (meaning that negotiations on membership are under way) (see Table 3.1).

With all the policy and membership changes taking place, the need to rewrite the rules of the EU became increasingly pressing, as did the need to make the EU more democratic and to bring it closer to its citizens. At the Laeken European Council in December 2001 it was decided to establish a convention to debate the future of Europe, and to draw up a treaty containing a constitution designed to simplify and replace all the other treaties. The Convention on the Future of the European Union met between February 2002 and July 2003 under the presidency of former French president Valéry Giscard d'Estaing, with

105 representatives from the 15 EU member states, 13 applicant Eastern European and Mediterranean countries, the 28 national parliaments, and the European Parliament. The convention considered numerous proposals, including an elected president of the European Council, a foreign minister for the EU, a limit on the membership of the European Commission, a common EU foreign and security policy, and a legal personality for the EU, whose laws would cancel out those of national parliaments in areas where the EU had been given competence. It took two European Council meetings (December 2003 and June 2004) to reach agreement on the draft treaty, which had then to be put to public referendums or legislative votes in every EU member state.

Lithuania became the first country to ratify through a parliamentary vote in November 2004, and Spain became the first to ratify through a national referendum in February 2005. But there were already clear signs of political and public resistance in several countries, the general expectation being that the treaty was unlikely to survive a referendum in eurosceptical Britain. But it was left to the French and the Dutch – both founding members of the EU – to stop the process in its tracks, with negative votes in national referendums in May and June 2005, respectively. It is questionable how much the votes were a true reflection of popular opinion about integration, and how much they were approached by French and Dutch voters as an opportunity to comment on their home governments (both of which favoured the treaty). But in spite of widespread predictions of institutional collapse and loss of strategic direction, the EU survived and continued to function, while worried discussions were held about the next step.

The debate about the constitution took place against a background of the most serious rift in transatlantic relations in decades. Following the September 2001 terrorist attacks in the United States, the administration of George W. Bush had quickly orchestrated a multinational attack on Afghanistan, accused of being a harbour for terrorists. But then it turned its attention to Iraq, claiming that the regime of Saddam Hussein possessed weapons of mass destruction and posed a substantial security threat. European public opinion was strongly against the proposed invasion of Iraq, but EU governments were split, with France and Germany leading the opposition and Britain and Spain offering support. It seemed that all the mounting questions about American leadership of the Atlantic Alliance had now come to a head, as well as all the questions about the EU's inability to make a mark on the global stage (see Chapter 9 for more details).

Even while transatlantic tensions were playing themselves out, EU leaders were taking another look at constitutional change, and in early 2007 agreed to save as many elements as possible of the failed constitutional treaty, and to reformulate them into a new treaty designed

Table 3.2   *Key elements of the Treaty of Lisbon*

- A new president for the European Council, appointed by its members for a two-and-a-half-year term (renewable once) and approved by Parliament.
- A High Representative of the Union for Foreign Affairs and Security Policy, appointed by the European Council for five-year terms, charged with conducting the CFSP, and backed up by a new European External Action Service.
- Abolition of the pillar system introduced by Maastricht, and of the European Community.
- Equal powers for the European Parliament and the Council of Ministers over proposals for almost all EU legislation.
- Recognition of the rights laid out in the Charter of Fundamental Rights, and accession to the European Convention on Human Rights.
- More powers for the EU in the areas of energy policy, public health, climate change, crime and terrorism, commercial policy, humanitarian aid, sport, tourism, research and space.
- A new formula for qualified majority voting in the Council of Ministers from 2014: at least 55 per cent of members of the Council must be in favour representing at least 65 per cent of the population of the EU, with states representing 35 per cent of the population needed for a blocking minority.
- Expansion of the use of qualified majority voting, but the national veto to be retained for foreign and defence policy and taxation.
- A single legal personality for the EU, designed to strengthen its negotiating powers on the international stage.
- Formal recognition, for the first time, of the freedom of a member state to leave the EU.

mainly to adjust the institutional structure of the EU to account for enlargement. In fact the new Treaty of Lisbon was to be almost a replica of the constitution, several governments claiming that because it was an amendment to the treaties it did not need a national referendum for approval. But Ireland was required by law to hold such a referendum, and caused consternation in June 2008 when it once again voted against a new treaty. A protocol was negotiated that addressed Irish concerns about neutrality and tax issues, and Lisbon was approved in a second Irish referendum in October 2009. As well as ending the pillar arrangement introduced by Maastricht, it made a number of key institutional changes, including the creation of a new president for the European Council and a single legal personality for the EU (see Table 3.2).

Through all the treaty changes, the identity of the EU on the global stage has undergone something of a transformation. European leaders had been embarrassed by their failure to provide leadership in responding to the violent break-up of Yugoslavia, but EU policy succeeded in Eastern Europe, where it took the lead on post-cold war reconstruction, helping former Soviet-bloc states to make the transition to democracy and free markets. Meanwhile, the role of the United

States in EU affairs was declining, as reflected in the fallout from the 2003 crisis over Iraq, which history may eventually show to have been the event that finally pulled the EU out of the foreign policy lethargy into which it had fallen. US leaders were particularly taken aback by the openness with which their policy was criticized by hostile EU governments. More was to come with the breaking in 2007 of a global financial crisis that had its origins in the United States, where too little regulation had allowed the extension of credit to consumers patently unable to service their debts, and much of that debt had been bought up by European banks and financial institutions. The crisis expanded during 2008 and 2009, its impact on the EU deepened in 2010 by budget crises in Greece, Ireland, Spain and Portugal, the effect of which was to raise troubling questions about the future of the euro.

Conclusions

Europe has travelled a long and uneven road since the end of the Second World War. Most European states in 1945 were physically devastated, the suspicions and hostilities that had led to two world wars in the space of a generation still lingered, Western Europe found itself being pulled into a military and economic vacuum as power and influence moved outwards to the United States, and Eastern Europe came under the political and economic control of the Soviet Union. The balance of power in the west changed as an exhausted Britain and France dismantled their empires and reduced their militaries, while West Germany rebuilt and eventually became a dominant force in continental politics. Intent on avoiding future wars, and concerned about being caught in big-power rivalry, Western European leaders began considering new levels of regional cooperation, pooling the interests of their states, and helping give the region new confidence and influence.

Beginning with the limited experiment of integrating their coal and steel industries, and building on an economic foundation and security shield underwritten by the United States, six European states quickly agreed a common agricultural policy, a customs union, and the beginnings of a common market. The accession of new members in the 1970s and 1980s increased the size of the Community's population and market, pushing its borders to the edge of Russia and the Middle East. The global economic instability that followed the end of the Bretton Woods system and the energy crises of the 1970s served to emphasize the need for Western European countries to cooperate if they were to have more control over their own future rather than simply to respond to external events.

After several years of relative lethargy the European experiment was given new impetus by completion of the single market, and then by the controversial decision to stabilize exchange rates as a prelude to the abolition of national currencies and the adoption of a single European currency. At the same time, the EU showed a new face to the rest of the world, with more cooperation on foreign and trade policy (along with some embarrassing disagreements along the way), and the seeds of a European defence capacity. The effects of integration have been felt in a growing number of policy areas, including agriculture, competition, transport, the environment, energy, telecommunications, research and development, working conditions, culture, consumer affairs, education and employment.

But ordinary Europeans were in two minds about the exercise of integration, and since the early 1990s there has been growing resistance to what is being done in their name. The 2003 controversy over Iraq drew new attention to the place of the EU in the international system, while the 2004–06 eastern enlargement had an important impact on the personality of the EU, making it more truly an exercise in European integration. The failure of the European constitution proved a disappointment to many, but it had nothing like the deleterious effect on the functioning of the EU that pessimists predicted. The organizational changes anticipated by the constitution were largely addressed – albeit through the back door – by the Treaty of Lisbon. But the rising tide of doubts about the direction being taken by the EU, and the methods used to encourage its evolution, were overtaken by the global economic crisis of 2007–10 and by the breaking in 2010 of budget crises in several eurozone states.

Chapter 4

The European Institutions

As the European Union has grown, so have the powers and the reach of its institutions. But they have been designed to reflect short-term needs and compromises without much long-term sense of what the 'government' of the EU should eventually become. The result has been less a structured system of government than a changeable system of governance: decisions, laws, and policies are made without the existence of formal institutions of government. The member states are still the only formal governments, with a strong grip on the policy process, but – as we saw in Chapter 1 – the EU has gone far beyond the definition of a standard intergovernmental organization.

In a nutshell, the major institutions work as follows: the European Commission develops proposals for new laws and policies, on which final decisions are taken by the Council of Ministers and the European Parliament. Once a decision is made, the European Commission is responsible for overseeing implementation by the member states. Meanwhile, the Court of Justice works to ensure that laws and policies meet the terms and spirit of the treaties, while the European Council brings the leaders of the member states together at periodic summit meetings to guide the overall direction of European integration. Alongside the Big Five are a cluster of other institutions with more focused responsibilities, including the European Central Bank, the European Investment Bank, Europol, and a host of regulatory and executive agencies.

Comparisons can be made with the governing bodies of the member states, but only up to a point. The College of Commissioners is something like a cabinet of ministers, but not quite. The European Parliament has some of the powers of a conventional legislature, but not all. The European Commission is a bureaucracy responsible for drafting and executing the laws and regulations of the EU, but provides more leadership than most national bureaucracies. The European Council and the Council of Ministers are like nothing found in most national governments, although the latter can be compared in some ways to an upper chamber of a legislature. The Court of Justice is the only institution to directly parallel those found at the national level – it has most of the features of a typical constitutional court. Into this mix must be added the many subtle nuances of European decision making, and the many informal aspects of EU government: the influence of the member states; the key role played by interest groups, corporations, staff in the Commission, specialized working groups in the Council of Ministers, and the permanent representatives of the member states; and all the muddling through and incremental change that often characterize policy making in the EU, as in national systems of government.

This chapter looks at the major institutions of the EU, describing how they are structured, explaining what they do, and showing how they relate to each other and to the member states. It paints a picture of a system that is often complicated, occasionally clumsy, constantly evolving, and regularly misunderstood. It argues that the EU institutions are caught in a web of competing national interests, and that the tension between intergovernmental and supranational forces impacts them all. But in spite of the challenges to their identity and personality, they have taken on many of the features of a distinctive supranational European political system, and they are best understood as such.

A constitution for Europe

A constitution is a written document that describes the structure of a system of government, outlines the powers of the different governing institutions, describes limits on those powers, and lists the rights of citizens relative to government. Almost every state has one, and they are each supported by a constitutional court responsible for providing interpretation by measuring laws and the actions of government against the content and principles of the constitution. Most importantly, they are permanent documents, and provision is made for them to be amended, wholesale changes coming only on those rare occasions when a system of government has broken down and is in need of a thorough overhaul, as – for example – when France replaced the Fourth Republic with the Fifth Republic in 1958.

The European Union has no formal constitution, and has instead been guided by a series of treaties which together function as something like a constitution: Paris (now expired), the two Treaties of Rome, the Single European Act, Maastricht, Amsterdam, Nice, and Lisbon (see Table 4.1). Each has amended and built upon its predecessor, resulting in a mobile constitution, or one surrounded by talk of constitution building or the 'constitutionalization' of the EU legal order (see Snyder, 2003) without achievement of a final form. For Eriksen *et al.* (2004:4–5), the result has been a 'material constitution', meaning that the treaties are legally binding, the EU institutions amount to a political community separate from the member states, and EU law represents a constitutional legal order.

When American leaders drew up a new federal constitution for the United States in 1787, they wrote a document that had four important

Table 4.1   *The major treaties*

Year signed	Year in force	Name	Main effects
1951	1952	Treaty of Paris	Created European Coal and Steel Community
1957	1958	Treaties of Rome	Created European Economic Community and European Atomic Energy Community
1986	1987	Single European Act	Set goal of completing single market within five years
1992	1993	Treaty on European Union (Maastricht)	Cleared way for economic and monetary union, created three pillars under new European Union
1997	1999	Treaty of Amsterdam	Organizational changes and expanded EU policy responsibilities
2001	2003	Treaty of Nice	Resolved unfinished business from Amsterdam
2004	Failed	Treaty on the European Constitution	Would have replaced and consolidated all existing treaties, and made significant institutional changes
2007	2009	Treaty of Lisbon	Made most of the changes intended by the constitutional treaty

features. First, it was a contract between people and government, outlining their relative roles, powers, and rights. Second, it was short and succinct, meaning that it could easily be read and understood by almost anyone. Third, it was often ambiguous, allowing room for evolutionary change. Finally, there was provision for amendments to be made, but – by accident – loopholes ensured that the most important changes to the constitution were to come as a result of judicial interpretations provided by the US Supreme Court and new laws passed by the US Congress. These have changed many of the details of the structure of government, allowing the constitution more or less to keep up with the prevailing political, economic, and social mood.

The EU treaties have none of these qualities. Instead of being contracts between people and government, they have been contracts among governments, drawn up by their representatives meeting in intergovernmental conferences (see Box 4.1). Instead of being short, they have been long and often complex, sometimes confusing even the legal experts. Instead of being ambiguous, the focus on making sure that there is minimal room for misunderstanding has produced documents that have often gone into great detail on the powers of EU institutions, the policy responsibilities of the EU, and the rights of citizens.

Box 4.1 Intergovernmental conferences

The extent to which decision making in the EU is still intergovernmental rather than supranational is reflected in the way that many of the biggest decisions of recent years have come out of intergovernmental conferences (IGCs), convened outside the formal framework of the EU's institutions to allow negotiations among representatives of the governments of the member states. Even as the powers of those institutions have grown, so the IGC has become a common event on the EU calendar; there have been about a dozen IGCs since 1950, eight of which have been held since 1985. While there is nothing in the founding treaties about IGCs, they have become a normal part of the calendar of European integration.

The first opened in May 1950, was chaired by Jean Monnet, and led to the signing of the Treaty of Paris and the creation of the ECSC. The second opened at Messina in April 1955, and led to the creation of the EEC and Euratom and the signing of the Treaties of Rome. Perhaps because national leaders were focused on building the three Communities and the common market, because of the intergovernmental nature of Community decision making in the early years, and because of the fallout from the energy crises of the 1970s, it was to be another 29 years before another major IGC was convened. Concerned about the lack of progress on integration and Europe's declining economic performance in relation to the United States and Japan, an IGC launched in September 1985 had – by December – outlined the framework of what was to become the Single European Act.

Two more IGCs met during 1991 to discuss political and monetary union, their work resulting in the Treaty on European Union. Conference in 1996 and 1997 had institutional reform and preparations for eastward enlargement at the top of their agenda, and drafted the Treaty of Amsterdam. Institutional reform was also on the agenda of the IGC that led to the 2000 Treaty of Nice, widely regarded as a disappointment. The eighth major IGC in 2003 reviewed the draft of the new European constitution, which was itself designed to 'promote new forms of European governance'. The ninth IGC in 2007 finalized the details of the Treaty of Lisbon.

And instead of being changed only by formal amendments, by judicial interpretation, or by changes in EU law, wholesale revisions have been introduced as a result of new treaties.

The European constitutional convention that met in 2002–03 might have taken the opportunity to undertake some spring-cleaning, producing a short, readable, and flexible American-style document that would replace the treaties and give Europeans a better sense of what integration meant. But where the authors of the US constitution were designing a virtually new political system from scratch, had relatively few opinions to take into account, and were dealing with just 13 largely homogeneous American states, the authors of the EU constitution were faced with the challenge of summarizing an accumulation of 50 years' worth of treaties, and had to account not only for the views of 15 member states with often different values and priorities, but also for those of more than a dozen candidate member states from Eastern Europe. The result was a draft treaty that was long (well over 300 pages), detailed, and controversial – all factors in its eventual demise at the hands of French and Dutch voters in 2005. Most of its key provisions were revived in 2007 in the form of the new Treaty of Lisbon, which came into force in 2009.

The EU still does not have a formal constitution, and the fatigue generated by more than 20 years of often controversial proposals for – and votes on – new treaties means that it is unlikely that any new treaties will be proposed any time soon. But this may not matter; the Treaty of Lisbon brought the rules of the EU up to date, and for Moravcsik (2007: 23, 24, 47), the process of integration has achieved 'a stable constitutional equilibrium' that is 'likely to endure, with incremental changes, for the foreseeable future'. It is no longer necessary, he argues, for the EU to move forward to consolidate its achievements: 'When a constitutional system no longer needs to expand and deepen in order to assure its own continued existence, it is truly stable. It is a mark of constitutional maturity.'

The European Council

The European Council – which functioned on the edge of the EU system of governance until it was formally confirmed as a full institution by the Treaty of Lisbon – is something like a steering committee or a board of directors for the EU: it discusses broad issues and goals, leaving it to the other EU institutions to work out the details (Werts, 2008). Sharing the Justus Lipsius building with the Council of Ministers in the European Quarter of Brussels, it consists of the heads of government of the EU member states. This group meets at least four times each year at summit meetings chaired by an appointed president, and provides strategic policy direction for the EU. The Council also has a key role in making appointments, nominating its own president, the president of the European Commission, and the High Representative for foreign and security affairs.

The Council was created in 1974 in response to a feeling among some European leaders that the Community needed better leadership, and a body that could take a more long-term view of where the

Community was headed. It immediately became an informal part of the Community decision-making structure, its existence being finally given legal recognition only with the Single European Act. Maastricht elaborated on its role, but did not provide much clarity beyond noting that the Council would 'provide the Union with the necessary impetus for its development and shall define the general political guidelines thereof'. With Lisbon its job description was described thus: 'The European Council shall provide the Union with the necessary impetus for its development and shall define the general political directions and priorities thereof. It shall not exercise legislative functions.'

The Council has been an important force for integration, with many of the most important initiatives of recent years coming out of Council discussions, including the launch of the European Monetary System in 1978, and the discussions that led to all the most recent European treaties. Council summits have also issued major declarations on international crises, reached key decisions on institutional changes (such as the 1974 decision to begin direct elections to the European Parliament), and given new clarity to EU foreign policy. But the Council has also had its failures, including its inability to speed up agricultural or budgetary reform, or to agree common EU responses to crises in Iraq and the Balkans.

Until Lisbon, the Council was chaired by the head of government of the member state holding the presidency of the Council of Ministers. But in order to help provide more sustained leadership, it was decided to have an individual appointed to the job by the heads of government for a term of two and a half years, renewable once. In the lead-up to the first vote, in 2009, there was speculation that the Council would opt for a high-profile international leader such as Tony Blair, but in the end they opted for the incumbent prime minister of Belgium, Herman van Rompuy, who was all but unknown outside his native country. The leaders did not want someone in the job who would outshine them or prove too powerful, opting instead for someone with a reputation as a conciliator and consensus-builder.

The European Council makes the key decisions on the overall direction of political and economic integration, internal economic issues, foreign policy issues, budget disputes, treaty revisions, new member applications, and institutional reforms. It does this through a combination of brainstorming, intensive bilateral and multilateral discussions, and bargaining. The results depend on a combination of the quality of organization and preparation, the leadership skills of the president, and the ideological and personal agendas of individual leaders. The interpersonal dynamics of the participants is also important: for example, the political significance of the Franco-German axis was long a key part of the mechanics of decision making (although less so since eastward enlargement has diluted the voting and political power of the Big Two). Leaders who have been in office a long time or who have a solid base of political support at home or who have a record of progressive positions on Europe will be in a different negotiating position from those who do not.

Regular summits of the Council are held four times each year, with additional meetings held when necessary. They once took place in the capital of the member state holding the presidency of the Council of Ministers, or in a regional city or town, but they now all take place in Brussels. The agenda is driven in part by the ongoing priorities of the EU, but also by emergencies or by unfinished business from previous meetings. Some issues (especially economic issues) are routinely discussed at every summit, while the European Commission may also promote issues it would like to see discussed. The goal is to agree a set of Conclusions, an advanced draft of which is usually awaiting the leaders at the beginning of the summit, and provides the focus for discussions.

Much symbolism is attached to the outcomes of the summits, the level of failure or success reflecting on the whole process of European integration and on the abilities of European leaders. For example, the failure of December 2003 summit intended to reach agreement on the draft constitution was seen in part as a reflection on the erratic Italian presidency and the leadership of prime minister Silvio Berlusconi. By contrast, when the German presidency was able to broker agreement at the June 2007 European Council on the treaty that would replace the failed constitution, it reflected well on the new influence of the Merkel government.

The European Commission

The European Commission is the executive-bureaucratic arm of the EU, responsible for developing proposals for new laws and policies, for overseeing the execution of those laws and policies once they are adopted, and for promoting the general interests of the EU. Its headquarters are in the Berlaymont building in Brussels, and its staff work in multiple buildings around the city, and in regional cities around the EU and national capitals around the world. It is the most supranational of the EU institutions, working to promote EU interests and acting as the driving force behind key EU policy initiatives.

While it is the best known of the major EU institutions, the Commission is also the most misunderstood. Critics charge that it is big, expensive, and powerful, that it meddles in the internal affairs of member states, that its leaders are not elected, and that it has too little public accountability. But the criticism is often misguided:

- Far from being big and expensive, it has just under 40,000 staff, only two-thirds of whom work actively on policy. This makes it smaller than the administration of a mid-sized European city, and its administrative costs account for just over 2 per cent of the EU budget, or about €3.3 billion in 2011.
- It is not particularly powerful, being less a decision-making body than a servant of the member states, charged with translating the goals of integration into specific proposals for action. Decision-making power rests with a combination of the Council of Ministers, which is firmly under the control of the governments of the member states, and the European Parliament, elected by the voters of the EU.
- Although European Commissioners are not elected, they are nominated by elected national government leaders and confirmed by the elected European Parliament.
- It may sometimes appear secretive and anonymous, but its record is no worse than that of national bureaucracies, and in some ways is better. It has so few staff and resources that it must rely heavily on input from outside agencies.

The Commission is headed by a College of Commissioners with 27 members, one from each of the member states, which serves a five-year term beginning six months after elections to the European Parliament. Each commissioner has a portfolio for which he or she is responsible (ranging from competition to trade, economic and monetary affairs, the environment, transport, and enlargement), and collectively they make the final decisions on which proposals for new laws and policies to send on for approval. Commissioners are nominated by their national governments, but must swear an oath of office saying that they will renounce any defence of national interests. Nominees are discussed with the Commission president, and must be acceptable to other governments and to the European Parliament (see Spence, 2006:34–8).

The dominant figure in the Commission is the president, usually the most publicly visible person in the EU hierarchy. Although no more than the chief bureaucrat of the EU, the president can influence the appointment of other commissioners, has sole power over distributing portfolios, drives the agenda for the Commission, can launch new policy initiatives, chairs meetings of the College, can reshuffle portfolios mid-term, and represents the Commission in dealings with other EU institutions and national governments. There are few formal rules regarding how the president is appointed (see Nugent, 2001:63–8), the normal procedure being for the leaders of the member states to decide the nominee at the European Council held in the June before the term of the incumbent Commission ends, settling on someone acceptable to all of them and who can win confirmation by the European

Parliament. Appointed for renewable five-year terms, the president will usually be someone with a strong character and proven leadership abilities, but not so strong as to become too independent.

As with all such positions, the powers of the office depend to some extent on the personality of the office holder (see Table 4.2). Without question the most influential was former French economics minister Jacques Delors (1985–94), who centralized authority, had firm ideas about a strong, federal Europe asserting itself internationally, and used this vision to champion the single-market and single-currency programmes (see Ross, 1995). He was succeeded by Jacques Santer, former prime minister of Luxembourg, who avoided bold new initiatives, focusing instead on improving the implementation of existing laws and policies. The Santer College resigned en masse in January 1999 following charges of nepotism and incompetence directed against some of its members.

Santer was replaced by former Italian prime minister Romano Prodi, who witnessed the passage of the treaties of Amsterdam and Nice, the fallout over Iraq, the holding of the constitutional convention, the arrival of the euro, and the 2004 enlargement. Prodi was replaced in late 2004 by José Manuel Barroso, the incumbent prime minister of Portugal, who was faced with fighting public apathy towards the EU, improving relations with the US, dealing with the collapse of the constitutional treaty, and responding to the breaking of the global economic crisis. He was confirmed to a second term in 2009.

Below the College, the Commission is divided into 38 directorates-general (DGs) and services, the equivalent to national government ministries. Every DG is tied to a commissioner, has its own director-general, and deals with a specific area of policy. The Commission also works closely with a series of several hundred advisory, management, and regulatory committees made up of national government officials (in a phenomenon known as comitology), and with expert committees made up of national officials, specialists appointed by national governments, corporate interests, and special interest groups.

The general task of the Commission is to ensure that EU policies are advanced in light of the treaties (for details, see Edwards and Spence, 1997: ch. 1). It does this in five ways.

- *Powers of initiation.* The Commission makes sure that the principles of the treaties are turned into laws and policies (see Box 4.2). Proposals can come from a commissioner or a staff member of one of the DGs, may be a response to a ruling by the Court of Justice, may flow out of the requirements of the treaties, or may come out of pressure exerted by member-state governments, interest groups, the

Table 4.2   *Presidents of the European Commission*

Term	Name	Ideology	Member state
1958–67	Walter Hallstein	Christian Democrat	West Germany
1967–70	Jean Rey	Centrist	Belgium
1970–72	Franco Maria Malfatti	Christian Democrat	Italy
1972	Sicco Mansholt	Social democrat	Netherlands (interim)
1973–76	François-Xavier Ortoli	Conservative	France
1977–80	Roy Jenkins	Social democrat	Britain
1981–84	Gaston Thorn	Socialist	Luxembourg
1985–94	Jacques Delors	Socialist	France
1995–99	Jacques Santer	Christian Democrat	Luxembourg
1999	Manuel Marin	Socialist	Spain (interim)
1999–2004	Romano Prodi	Centrist	Italy
2004–	José Manuel Barroso	Centrist	Portugal

European Council, the European Parliament, and even private corporations. Proposals will be drafted by officials in one of the DGs and will then work their way through the different levels of the DG, being discussed with other DGs and with outside parties, such as interest groups or corporations. Drafts will finally reach the College of Commissioners, which can accept or reject them, send them back for redrafting, or defer making a decision. Once accepted, proposals are sent to the European Parliament and the Council of Ministers for a decision. The process can take anything from months to years, and Commission staff will be involved at every stage.

- *Powers of implementation.* Once a law or policy is accepted, the Commission must make sure that it is implemented by the member states. It has no power to do this directly, but instead works through national bureaucracies, using its power to collect information from member states, to issue written warnings, and to take to the Court of Justice any member state, corporation, or individual that does not conform to the spirit of the treaties or follow subsequent EU law. The Commission adds to the pressure by publicizing progress on implementation, hoping to embarrass laggards into action.
- *Acting as the conscience of the EU.* The Commission is expected to rise above competing national interests and to represent and promote the general interest of the EU. It is also expected to help smooth the flow of decision making by mediating disagreements between or among member states and other EU institutions.
- *Management of EU finances.* The Commission makes sure that all EU revenues are collected, plays a key role in drafting and guiding the EU budget through the Council of Ministers and Parliament, and administers EU spending.

- *External relations*. The Commission represents the EU in dealings with international organizations such as the United Nations and the World Trade Organization (Smith, 2006), is a key point of contact between the EU and the rest of the world, and vets applications for EU membership from aspirant states, and oversees negotiations with an applicant. Beginning in 2010, the new European External Action Service took over some of the Commission's responsibilities, such as running its overseas delegations.

The Commission has been at the core of European integration since the beginning, and while it is subject to the same problems as any other large organization, it has – on the whole – been a productive source of initiatives for new laws and policies, and is more accessible and open than, say, the Council of Ministers. Eurosceptic media and politicians like to use the Commission as one of the key targets of their criticism, but the Commission has no formally independent powers, and can do no more than it is allowed by the treaties.

The Council of Ministers

The Council of Ministers is the key decision-making arm of the EU, sharing responsibility with the European Parliament for voting on new proposals for EU law. Headquartered in the Justus Lipsius building in Brussels, the Council is one of the least-known of the major EU institutions: its meetings attract little media coverage, it has been the subject of much less academic study than the Commission or Parliament, and critics of the EU often forget how much power still lies in the hands of the Council, which is one of the most intergovernmental of EU institutions. When Europeans think about the activities of the EU, they tend to first think of the Commission, forgetting that the Commission can only propose, while it is up to the Council of Ministers and the European Parliament to dispose. In many ways, their powers make the Council and Parliament 'co-legislatures' of the EU.

The Council of Ministers (formally the Council of the European Union, but usually known simply as 'the Council') consists of national government ministers, who meet in one of ten technical councils (or 'configurations'), the membership depending on the topic under discussion. The most important of these is the General Affairs Council (GAC), which prepares – and follows up on – meetings of the European Council. Foreign Affairs brings together EU foreign ministers to deal with external relations and trade issues, while economics and finance ministers meet together as the Economic and Financial Affairs Council (Ecofin), agriculture ministers as the Agriculture and Fisheries Council, and so on. The relevant European commissioner will also

Box 4.2 European Union law

A key difference between the EU and a conventional intergovernmental organization is that the EU has a body of law which is applicable in all its member states, which supersedes national law in areas where the EU has responsibility, and which is backed up by rulings from the Court of Justice. The creation of this body of law has involved the voluntary surrender of powers by the member states in a broad range of policy areas, and the development of a new level of legal authority to which the member states are subject.

The foundation of the EU legal order is provided by the treaties, which are the primary sources of EU law (Lasok *et al.*, 2001: ch. 4), out of which come the secondary sources, the most important of which are the thousands of individual binding laws adopted by the EU, and which take three main forms:

- *Regulations* are the most powerful, and most like conventional acts of a national legislature. They are directly applicable in that they do not need to be turned into national law, they are binding in their entirety, and they take immediate effect on a specified date. Usually fairly narrow in intent, regulations are often designed to amend or adjust an existing law.
- *Directives* are binding in terms of goals, but it is left up to the member states to decide what action they need to take to achieve those goals. For example, a 2006 directive on equality for men and women in the workplace mandated equal access to employment, and equality in regard to pay, promotion, working conditions, and social security schemes, but left it up to the member states to decide individually how to meet those targets. Directives usually include a date by which national action must be taken, and member states must tell the Commission what they are doing.
- *Decisions* are also binding, but are usually fairly specific in their intent, and aimed at one or more member states, at institutions, or even at individuals. Some are aimed at making changes in the powers of EU institutions, some are directed towards internal administrative matters, and others are issued when the Commission has to adjudicate disputes between member states or corporations.

The EU has several other administrative tools which, because they are not binding, cannot be considered laws even though they can result in policy change. *Recommendations* and *opinions* are sometimes used to test reaction to a new EU policy, but they are used mainly to persuade or to provide interpretation on the application of regulations, directives, and decisions. Meanwhile, *white papers* and *green papers* are documents published by the EU that test the waters by making suggestions for new policies, the latter more detailed and specific than the former.

attend in order to make sure that the Council does not lose sight of broader EU interests. How often each council meets depends on the importance of its policy area. The GAC, Ecofin, and the Agriculture and Fisheries Council meet monthly because of the amount of work on their agendas, but the councils dealing with other issues meet perhaps only two to four times each year. Most meetings last no more than one or two days, and are held in Brussels.

Between meetings of ministers, national interests in the Council are further protected and promoted by Permanent Representations, or national delegations of professional diplomats, which are much like embassies to the EU. Expert staff from the delegations meet regularly in the powerful Committee of Permanent Representatives (Coreper), whose critical role in EU policy making is often overlooked. Coreper acts as a link between Brussels and the member states, conveys the views of the national governments, and keeps capitals in touch with developments in Brussels. Most importantly, it prepares Council agendas, oversees the committees and working parties set up to sift through proposals, decides which proposals go to which council, and makes many of the decisions about which proposals will be accepted and which will be left for debate by ministers (see Hayes-Renshaw and Wallace, 2006:72–82).

Direction is given to the deliberations of the Council and Coreper by the presidency of the Council of Ministers, which is held not by a person, but by a member state. Every EU member state has a turn at holding the presidency for a spell of six months, the baton being passed in January and July each year (see Table 4.3). The state holding the presidency sets the agenda for, and arranges and chairs meetings of the Council of Ministers. It had more authority until Lisbon, one of the effects of which was to create a new appointed president for the European Council, who took over many of the responsibilities held until then by the presidency of the Council. At the same time, the High Representative of the Union for Foreign Affairs and Security Policy became chair of the Foreign Affairs Council.

There are both advantages and disadvantages to the rotating presidency. It allows the governments of the member states to convene meetings and launch initiatives on issues of national interest, to bring those issues to the top of the EU agenda, and – if they do a good job – to earn prestige and credibility. It also helps make the process of European integration more real to the citizens of the country holding the presidency. But as the EU has grown, so has the workload of the presidency, and some of the smaller states struggle to offer the necessary leadership. As membership of the EU has expanded, so has the cycle of the presidency. With the founding six member states, each had a turn at the helm once every three years, but with 27 members the rotation has grown to thirteen and a half years.

Table 4.3   *Rotation of presidencies of the Council of Ministers*

	First half	Second half
2010	Spain	Belgium
2011	Hungary	Poland
2012	Denmark	Cyprus
2013	Ireland	Lithuania
2014	Greece	Italy
2015	Latvia	Luxembourg
2016	Netherlands	Slovakia
2017	Malta	UK
2018	Estonia	Bulgaria
2019	Austria	Romania

Once the European Commission has proposed a new law, it is sent to the Council of Ministers and Parliament for debate and for a final decision on adoption or rejection. The more complex proposals will usually go first to one or more specialist Council working parties, which will look them over in detail, identifying points of agreement and disagreement, and responding to suggestions for amendments made by Parliament (for more detail, see Hayes-Renshaw and Wallace, 2006). The proposal will then go to Coreper, which looks at the political implications, and tries to clear as many of the remaining problems as it can, ensuring that the meeting of ministers is as quick and as painless as possible. The proposal then moves on to the relevant Council for a final decision. Unanimity was once required, but votes are now rarely called, and where they are there are two options: a simple majority is used for procedural issues in the case of select number of specific policy issues, all other business being put to a qualified majority vote (QMV).

Under this arrangement, each minister is given several votes roughly in proportion to the population of his or her member state (see Table 4.4), for a total of 345. To be successful, a proposal must win at least 255 votes (just under 74 per cent of the total) and the support of ministers from at least 14 states that are collectively home to at least 63 per cent of the population of EU. This arrangement both reduces the power of big states and encourages states to form coalitions. With effect from November 2014, the qualified majority will be 55 per cent of the votes in the Council, from 15 member states containing at least 65 per cent of the population of the EU. A blocking minority will also be available, requiring states representing 35 per cent of the population of the EU, plus one member. Once a proposal has been voted on by the Council, it then goes to the European Parliament and the two institutions may pass it back and forth, with amendments, as many as three

Table 4.4   *Votes in the Council of Ministers*

Germany	29	Czech Republic	12	Finland	7
UK	29	Belgium	12	Ireland	7
France	29	Hungary	12	Lithuania	7
Italy	29	Portugal	12	Latvia	4
Spain	27	Austria	10	Slovenia	4
Poland	27	Bulgaria	10	Estonia	4
Romania	14	Sweden	10	Cyprus	4
Netherlands	13	Slovakia	7	Luxembourg	4
Greece	12	Denmark	7	Malta	3
				Total	345

times. In the event of a failure to agree, the proposal is sent to a Conciliation Committee made up of 27 representatives from each institution, with Commission staff also being present.

Because the Council of Ministers is a meeting place for national interests, the keys to understanding how it works are terms such as *compromise*, *bargaining*, and *diplomacy*. The ministers are often leading political figures at home, so they are motivated by national political interests. Their views are also ideologically driven, and their authority will depend to some extent on the strength and stability of the governing party or coalition at home. All these factors combine to pull ministers in different directions, and to deny the Council the kind of structural regularity enjoyed by the Commission.

The European Parliament

The European Parliament (EP) is the quasi-legislative arm of the EU: unlike conventional legislatures it cannot introduce laws or raise revenues (powers that rest with the Commission), instead sharing the tasks of amendment and decision with the Council of Ministers. Directly elected by the voters of the EU since 1979, it is the most clearly democratic of the EU institutions, and yet few EU citizens know what it does, and they have not developed the same kinds of psychological ties to the EP as they have to their national legislatures. In spite of this, Parliament has shrewdly used its powers to play a more active role in running the EU (see Rittberger, 2005: chs 5, 6), and has been entrepreneurial in suggesting new laws and policies to the Commission. Where it once mainly reacted to Commission proposals and Council votes, it has become more aggressive in launching its own initiatives and making the other institutions pay more attention to its opinions. It has also won more powers to amend laws and to check the activities of the other institutions, with the result that it now has equal standing

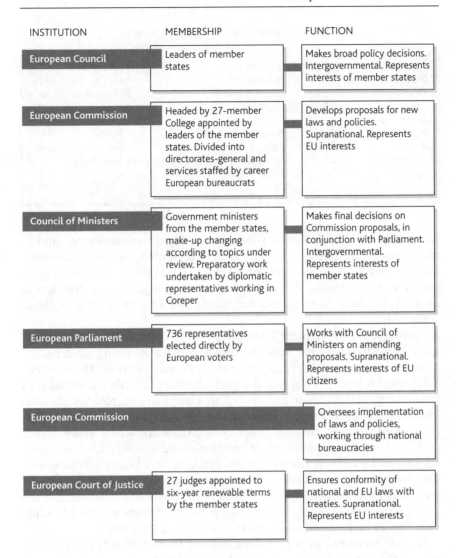

INSTITUTION | MEMBERSHIP | FUNCTION

European Council — Leaders of member states — Makes broad policy decisions. Intergovernmental. Represents interests of member states

European Commission — Headed by 27-member College appointed by leaders of the member states. Divided into directorates-general and services staffed by career European bureaucrats — Develops proposals for new laws and policies. Supranational. Represents EU interests

Council of Ministers — Government ministers from the member states, make-up changing according to topics under review. Preparatory work undertaken by diplomatic representatives working in Coreper — Makes final decisions on Commission proposals, in conjunction with Parliament. Intergovernmental. Represents interests of member states

European Parliament — 736 representatives elected directly by European voters — Works with Council of Ministers on amending proposals. Supranational. Represents interests of EU citizens

European Commission — Oversees implementation of laws and policies, working through national bureaucracies

European Court of Justice — 27 judges appointed to six-year renewable terms by the member states — Ensures conformity of national and EU laws with treaties. Supranational. Represents EU interests

Figure 4.1 *The institutional structure of the EU*

with the Council of Ministers on deciding which proposals for new laws will be enacted and which will not.

The European Parliament is the only directly elected international legislature in the world. It has a single chamber, and the 736 Members of the European Parliament (MEPs) are elected by universal suffrage by all eligible voters in the EU for fixed, renewable five-year terms. The number of seats is divided up among the member states roughly on the basis of population, so that Germany has 99 while Malta has just five

Table 4.5   *Seats in the European Parliament*

Germany	99	Belgium	22	Finland	13
United Kingdom	72	Portugal	22	Ireland	12
France	72	Czech Republic	22	Lithuania	12
Italy	72	Hungary	22	Latvia	8
Spain	50	Sweden	18	Slovenia	7
Poland	50	Austria	17	Estonia	6
Romania	33	Bulgaria	17	Cyprus	6
Netherlands	25	Slovakia	13	Luxembourg	6
Greece	22	Denmark	13	Malta	5
				Total	736

(see Table 4.5). This formula means that bigger countries are under-represented and smaller countries over-represented, so while Germany, Britain, and France each have one MEP per 835,000–845,000 citizens, the ratio for Belgium, the Czech Republic, Hungary, and Portugal is about 1:425,000 citizens, and for Malta and Luxembourg it is about 1:80,000.

Absurdly, the Parliament's buildings are divided among three cities: while the administrative headquarters are in Luxembourg, and parliamentary committees meet in Brussels for about two to three weeks every month (except August), the parliamentary chamber is situated in Strasbourg, and MEPs are expected to meet there in plenary sessions (meetings of the whole, or part-sessions) for about three or four days each month except August. Since committees are where most of the real bargaining and revising takes place, and since 'additional' plenaries can be held in Brussels, attendance at Strasbourg plenaries can sometimes be sparse. This arrangement comes courtesy of the French government, which stubbornly insists that Strasbourg must remain the site for plenary sessions, undermining the credibility of the EP while inflating its budget (see Judge and Earnshaw, 2008:148ff.)

The EP is chaired by a president, elected from within Parliament for renewable five-year terms to preside over debates during plenary sessions, decide which proposals go to which committees, and represent Parliament in relations with other institutions. The president would normally come from the majority political group, but since no party or group has ever won a majority of seats (see Chapter 5), a semi-permanent arrangement has been worked out by which the job is rotated between the two major groups (conservatives and socialists) for half the life of a Parliament. To help with the task of dealing with many different political groups in Parliament, the president works with the chairs of the different groups in the Conference of Presidents, which draws up the agenda for plenary sessions and oversees the work of parliamentary committees.

Like most national legislatures, the EP has 20 standing committees and a variable number of temporary committees which meet in Brussels to consider legislation relevant to their area or to carry out parliamentary inquiries (see Judge and Earnshaw, 2008: 177–96). The committees range in size between two dozen and six dozen members, and have their own hierarchy, which reflects levels of parliamentary influence over different policy areas: among the most powerful are those dealing with the environment and the budget. Seats on committees are distributed on the basis of a mixture of the balance of party groups, the seniority of MEPs, and national interests. For example, there are more Irish and Polish MEPs on the agriculture committee than on committees dealing with foreign and defence matters.

The concern of member states with preserving their powers over decision making in the Council of Ministers has resulted over the years in several changes to parliamentary rules. Parliament initially had a *consultation procedure* under which it was allowed to give a non-binding opinion to the Council of Ministers before the latter adopted a new law in selected areas, but this is now rarely used. The SEA introduced a *cooperation procedure* which gave Parliament the right to a second reading for certain laws being considered by the Council of Ministers, notably those relating to the single market. Maastricht created a *codecision procedure* under which Parliament was given the right to a third reading on bills, effectively giving it equal authority with the Council. With Lisbon, this became the *ordinary legislative procedure*, which is now the standard approach to law-making, giving Parliament equal powers with the Council of Ministers.

In addition to these legislative powers, Parliament also has joint powers with the Council of Ministers over fixing the EU budget, so that the two institutions between them constitute the budgetary authority of the EU; they review the annual draft sent to them by the Commission, and the EP can ask for changes to the budget, ask for new appropriations for areas not covered (but cannot make decisions on how to raise money), and ultimately – with a two-thirds majority – reject the budget. Under the *consent procedure*, the support of Parliament is needed for the accession of new members to the EU and for the conclusion of international agreements by the EU, and Parliament also has several supervisory powers over other EU institutions, including the right to debate the annual programme of the Commission, to put questions to the Commission, and to approve the appointment of the president of the Commission and the College of Commissioners.

The most substantial of Parliament's powers is its ability – with a two-thirds majority – to force the resignation of the College of Commissioners through a vote of censure. While this power has never been used successfully, Parliament came close in January 1999 after charges of mismanagement and nepotism were directed at two members of the College. Anticipating a vote of censure, the Santer Commission resigned just before the findings of an EP investigation were published in March. In October 2004, Parliament blocked the appointment of the new Italian Commissioner Rocco Buttiglione, who had expressed controversial views on homosexuality and women, and in 2010 Bulgarian nominee Rumiana Jeleva withdrew after Parliament raised questions about her financial declaration and her abilities to be a commissioner.

The European Court of Justice

The Court of Justice is the most underrated of the five major institutions of the EU, and the one that attracts the least public and political attention (or academic political analysis). While the Commission and Parliament often become embroiled in headline-making political controversies, the Court has quietly gone about its business of clarifying the meaning of the treaties and of European law. Its activities have been critical to the progress of European integration, and its role just as significant as that of the Commission or Parliament, yet few Europeans know what it does, and its decisions rarely make the news.

Based in an expanding cluster of buildings in the Centre Européen on a plateau above the city of Luxembourg, the Court is the supreme legal authority of the EU, and the final court of appeal on all EU laws. Its job is to make sure that national and European laws – and international agreements being considered by the EU – meet the terms and the spirit of the treaties, and that EU law is equally, fairly, and consistently applied throughout the member states. It does this by ruling on the 'constitutionality' of EU law, giving opinions (preliminary rulings) to national courts in cases where there are questions about the meaning of EU law, and making judgments in disputes (direct actions) involving EU institutions, member states, individuals, and corporations. In so doing, the Court makes sure that the decisions and policies of the EU are consistent and fit with the agreements inherent in the treaties. EU law takes precedence over the national laws of member states where the two come into conflict, but only in areas of EU competence. Hence the Court does not have powers over criminal law or family law, but has instead made most of its decisions on the kind of economic issues in which the EU has been most actively involved, having less to do with policy areas where the EU has been less active, such as education and health.

It made its most basic contribution to the process of integration in 1963 and 1964 when it declared that the Treaty of Rome was not just a treaty, but was a constitutional instrument that had direct effect on member states, and had supremacy (took precedence) over national law in policy areas where the EU has responsibility. The Court has also established important additional precedents through decisions such as the *Cassis de Dijon* case [1979], which simplified completion of the single market by establishing the principle of mutual recognition: a product made and sold legally in one member state cannot be barred from another (see Chapter 7). Other Court rulings have helped increase the powers of Parliament, strengthened individual rights, promoted the free movement of workers, reduced gender discrimination, and helped the Commission break down the barriers to competition.

The Court of Justice has 27 judges, each appointed for a six-year renewable terms. In order to keep the work of the Court running smoothly, appointments are staggered so that about half the judges come up for renewal every three years. The judges are theoretically appointed by common agreement among the governments of the member states, so there is technically no national quota. However, because every member state has the right to make one nomination, all 27 are effectively national appointees. Apart from being acceptable to the other member states, judges must be independent, must be legally competent, and must avoid promoting the national interests of their home states. Some judges have come to the Court with experience as government ministers, some have held elective office, and others have had careers as lawyers or as academics; whatever they have done in their previous lives, they are not allowed to hold administrative or political office while they are on the Court. They can resign from the Court, but they can only be removed by the other judges (not by member states or other EU institutions), and then only by unanimous agreement that they are no longer doing their job adequately (Lasok, 2007:7–8).

The judges elect one of their own to be president by majority vote for a three-year renewable term. The president presides over Court meetings, is responsible for distributing cases among the judges and deciding the dates for hearings, and has considerable influence over the political direction of the Court. Despite his or her critical role in furthering European integration, the president – Vassilios Skouris of Greece was elected to a third term in 2009 – never becomes a major public figure in the same mould as the president of the Commission.

To speed up its work, the Court is divided into chambers of three, five, or 13 judges which make the final decisions on cases. To further ease the workload, the judges are assisted by eight advocates-general, advisers who review each of the cases as they come in, and deliver a preliminary opinion on what action should be taken and on which EU law applies. The judges are not required to agree with the opinion, or even to refer to it, but it gives them a point of reference from which to reach a decision. Although advocates-general are again appointed in theory by common accord, one is appointed by each of the Big Five member states, and the other three are appointed by the smaller states. One of the advocates-general is appointed First Advocate-General on a one-year rotation.

The Court of Justice has become busier as the reach of the EU has widened and deepened. In the 1960s it was hearing about 50 cases per year and making about 15–20 judgments, but it now hears several hundred cases each year, and makes as many as 200 judgments. As the volume of work grew during the 1970s and 1980s, it was taking the Court up to two years to reach a decision on more complex cases. To move matters along, a subsidiary Court of First Instance was created in 1989 (since renamed the General Court), to be the first point of decision on less complicated cases. If cases are lost at this level, the parties involved may appeal to the Court of Justice. There are 27 judges on the General Court – one from each member state – and it uses the same basic procedures as the Court of Justice. To further ease the workload, the EU Civil Service Tribunal was created in 2004 to take over from the General Court any cases involving disputes between the EU institutions and their staff. It has seven judges appointed for six-year renewable terms.

The work of the Court comes under two main headings:

- *Preliminary rulings.* These make up the most important part of the Court's work, and account for about 40–60 per cent of the cases it considers. If a matter of EU law arises in a national court case, the national court can ask for a ruling from the European Court on the interpretation or validity of that law. Members of EU institutions can also ask for preliminary rulings, but most are made on behalf of a national court, and are binding on the court in the case concerned.
- *Direct actions.* These are cases where an individual, company, member state, or EU institution brings proceedings against an EU institution or a member state. For example, a member state might have failed to meet its obligations under EU law, so a case can be brought by the Commission or by another member state. Private companies can also bring actions if they think a member state is discriminating against their products. Direct actions can also be brought against the Commission or the Council to make sure that EU laws conform to the treaties, and to attempt to cancel those that do not, and against an EU institution that has failed to act in accordance with the terms of the treaties.

Unlike all the other EU institutions, where English is becoming the working language, the Court works mainly in French, although a case can be heard in any official EU language at the request of the plaintiff or defendant. Court proceedings usually begin with a written application, describing the dispute and the grounds on which the application is based. The President assigns the case to a chamber, and the defendant is given one month to lodge a statement of defence, the plaintiff a month to reply, and the defendant a further month to reply to the plaintiff. The case is then argued by the parties at a public hearing before a chamber of judges. Once the hearing is over, the judges retire to deliberate, and – having reached a conclusion – return to Court to deliver their judgment.

Court decisions are supposed to be unanimous, but votes are usually taken by a simple majority. All decisions are secret, so it is never publicly known who – if anyone – dissented. The Court has no direct powers to enforce its judgments, so implementation is left mainly to national courts or the governments of the member states, with the Commission keeping a close watch (Conant, 2002). Maastricht gave the Court of Justice new powers by allowing it to impose fines, but the question of how the fines would be collected was left open, and the implications of this new power are still unclear.

Specialized institutions

As the EU has grown, so has the number of institutions and specialized agencies created to deal with different aspects of its work. They have been created mainly according to need, without an overall plan or template, the result being that they vary considerably in terms of their political reach, their administrative powers, and their internal structure. The best known is the European Central Bank (ECB), created in 1998 with the job of helping manage the euro by ensuring price stability, setting interest rates, and managing the foreign reserves of the eurozone states. With the global economic crisis that broke in 2007, and the subsequent debt problems of Greece, Ireland, Portugal, and Spain, the ECB became more active and the pressure to give it more powers over monetary policy grew. New regulatory bodies were created in the wake of the global economic crisis, including the European Systemic Risk Board, the European System of Financial Supervisors, the European Banking Authority, and the European Securities and Markets Authority. These joined a pre-existing network of other specialized agencies, including permanent regulatory agencies (nearly 30 in all) with mainly technical and informational responsibilities, advisory bodies such as the Committee of the Regions, temporary executive agencies responsible for policy implementation, and agencies dealing with aspects of the Common Security and Defence Policy (see Table 4.6). The ad hoc nature of the way they have been created has recently sparked a debate over the need for a more structured approach to their management and responsibilities (European Commission, 2008).

Table 4.6 *Specialized EU institutions (selected)*

- *European Investment Bank* (Luxembourg, 1958). An autonomous institution that encourages 'balanced and steady development' by granting loans and giving guarantees.
- *European Centre for the Development of Vocational Training* (Thessaloniki, Greece, 1975). Promotes vocational training in the EU.
- *Court of Auditors* (Luxembourg, 1977). The EU's financial watchdog, charged with carrying out annual audits of the accounts of EU institutions.
- *European Environment Agency* (1990, Copenhagen). Collects information which is used to help develop environmental protection policies, and to measure the results.
- *Committee of the Regions* (Brussels, 1994). Allows representatives of local units of government to meet and discuss matters relating to regional and local issues.
- *European Agency for Safety and Health at Work* (Bilbao, Spain, 1995). Provides information in support of improvements in occupational safety and health.
- *European Medicines Agency* (London, 1995). Evaluates and supervises medicines for human and veterinary use.
- *Office for Harmonization in the Internal Market* (Alicante, Spain, 1996). Responsible for the registration and administration of EU trademarks and designs.
- *European Central Bank* (Frankfurt, 1998). Ensures monetary stability by setting interest rates in the euro zone.
- *European Police Office (Europol)* (The Hague, 1999). Promotes EU police cooperation by managing a system of information exchange targeted against serious forms of international crime.
- *European Food Safety Authority* (Parma, Italy, 2002). Provides independent scientific advice on issues relating to food safety.
- *Eurojust* (The Hague, 2002). Encourages interstate judicial cooperation.
- *European Aviation Safety Agency* (Cologne, 2003). Helps Commission draft new rules on civil aviation safety.
- *European Railway Agency* (Valenciennes, France, 2004). Promotes an integrated and competitive European rail network.
- *European Agency for the Management of Operational Cooperation at the External Borders* (Warsaw, 2004). Coordinates cooperation among member states on the management of the EU's external borders.
- *European Centre for Disease Prevention and Control* (Stockholm, 2005). Works to strengthen Europe's defences against infectious disease.
- *Community Fisheries Control Agency* (Vigo, Spain, 2005). Monitors the uniformity and effectiveness of enforcement of the Common Fisheries Policy.
- *European Chemicals Agency* (Helsinki, 2007). Manages the registration and evaluation of chemicals.
- *European Fundamental Rights Agency* (Vienna, 2007). Provides help and expertise on the implementation of EU fundamental rights law and policy.
- *European Institute for Gender Equality* (Vilnius, Lithuania, 2010). Information clearing house.

Conclusions

The European Union has built a wide network of administrative bodies since its inception. Among them, they are responsible for making general and detailed policy decisions, developing and adopting laws, overseeing the implementation of laws and policies by the member states, ensuring that those laws and policies meet the spirit and the letter of the treaties, and overseeing activities in a variety of areas, from environmental management to transport, consumer protection, drug regulation, and police cooperation. In many ways they fit the standard definition of a confederal system of administration: a general system of government coexisting with the governments of the member states, each with shared and independent powers, but with the balance in favour of the member states. Except for the European Parliament, EU citizens do not have a direct relationship with any of the EU institutions, instead relating to them through their national governments.

Despite concerns in some of the member states about the federalization of Europe, the institutions still lack many of the features of a conventional federal government: there is no European army or air force, no elected European president, no European tax system, no European foreign and defence policy, and no single postal system. Furthermore, much of the focus of decision making still rests with the European Council and the Council of Ministers, both of which are intergovernmental rather than supranational. Finally, the European Union is still ultimately a voluntary arrangement, and lacks the powers to force its member states to implement European law and policy. The withdrawal of one of its members would not be regarded as secession.

Nonetheless, while debates rage about the finer points of the decisions reached by the EU institutions, the national governments of the member states have transferred significant powers to these institutions. Particularly since the passage of the Single European Act, the activities of the Commission, the Council of Ministers, Parliament, and the Court of Justice have had a more direct impact on the lives of Europeans, and government in Europe is no longer just about what happens in national capitals and regional cities, but also about what happens in Brussels, Luxembourg, and Strasbourg.

The relationships among the five major institutions – and between them and the governments of the member states – change constantly as the balance of power is adjusted and fine-tuned. Out of a combination of internal convenience and external pressure is emerging a new form of governance that is winning more powers as the member states cautiously transfer sovereignty from the local and national levels to the regional level. In the next chapter we will see what this has meant for the citizens of Europe.

Chapter 5

The EU and its Citizens

The Maastricht treaty famously claimed that the goal of European integration was to create 'an ever closer union among the peoples of Europe, in which decisions are taken as closely as possible to the citizen'. But even the most enthusiastic supporters of the EU concede that it has been less a popular movement for change than a process begun and sustained by elites. The argument that the average European has few opportunities directly to influence the work of the EU has been serious enough to earn its own label: the democratic deficit.

'What about us?' the European public might reasonably ask. 'Does anyone in Brussels or our national capitals care what we think?' It sometimes seems as though the work of the EU goes on despite public opinion, which is often confused, sometimes doubtful, and in some cases actively hostile towards integration. Many of the key decisions on Europe are taken as a result of negotiations among national political leaders, who often refuse to put those decisions to a democratic test through a national referendum. Popular control over the European Commission and the European Court of Justice is only indirect, and although voter interests are directly represented in the European Parliament, declining turnout at EP elections suggests that most Europeans are not engaged with its work.

At the heart of the problem is the prevailing confusion about the European Union. Its character and personality are hard to pin down, there is no easy answer to the question 'What is the EU?', it is engaged on a journey to an unknown destination, the media often misrepresent the way it works, most academic writing on the EU makes the European project sound dull and legalistic, and most Europeans neither know how the EU works nor understand what difference it has made to their lives. The European Council decided as long ago as 1984 to promote 'a people's Europe' aimed at making Europe more real to its people, and changes to the treaties have made the EU institutions more transparent, but the argument that popular enthusiasm can be generated by public policy is fundamentally flawed.

But there is a counter-argument to all this: as we saw in Chapter 4, the interests of citizens are represented by their national governments in the meeting rooms of the European Council and the Council of Ministers, and the powers and influence of the European Parliament are growing. The European Commission is no less transparent or responsive than national bureaucracies, and is so short-staffed that it makes more use of input from ordinary citizens, interest groups, and corporations than do most of its national counterparts. And in many respects the democratic deficit in the EU is not so different from that found in the member states, where citizens often complain that they are insufficiently consulted.

This chapter asks what integration has meant for Europeans, and for the nature of democracy in the European Union. It begins with an assessment of public attitudes towards integration, examining the relationship between public opinion and the decisions taken by national leaders, and discussing euroscepticism, the knowledge deficit, and the democratic deficit. It then looks at the channels through which Europeans can express their opinions on EU policy – including elections, referendums, and interest groups – and asks how effective they have been, and what drives the ways in which ordinary Europeans engage with the European project and make their decisions on European issues.

Public opinion and Europe

The EU has a survey research programme known as Eurobarometer, which measures public opinion on a wide variety of topics relating to European integration, ranging from views on the general process to those on specific policies. Surveys over the last 30 years have found a waxing and waning of enthusiasm: support grew from 50 per cent in 1980 to a peak of 71 per cent in 1990, but fell in Germany after reunification, and then more widely throughout the EU in the wake of the controversy over Maastricht. In the period 2001–09, only about 53–55 per cent of Europeans thought that membership was a 'good thing', ranging from a low of 48 per cent in 2003–04 to a high of 58 per cent in 2007 (Eurobarometer poll 72, 2009:143).

There has also been something of a roller-coaster in the number of people who believe that their country has benefited from membership, from 58 per cent in 1990 to 47 per cent in 2004, 59 per cent in 2007, and back down to 53 per cent in 2010. Among those most convinced of the benefits are the majority of Eastern European member states (Bulgaria, Hungary, and Latvia excepted) and older member states that had – at least until the 2007–10 global economic crisis – most clearly seen the economic benefits of membership, such as Ireland, Greece, and Spain (which also, as it happens, were hit hardest by global and eurozone economic problems in 2009–10). Eurosceptical Denmark is surprisingly enthusiastic (with four out of five Danes seeing benefits), stalwarts France and Germany are surprisingly lukewarm (barely half of respondents feel there have been benefits), and Britain brings up its accustomed place at the rear (see Figure 5.1).

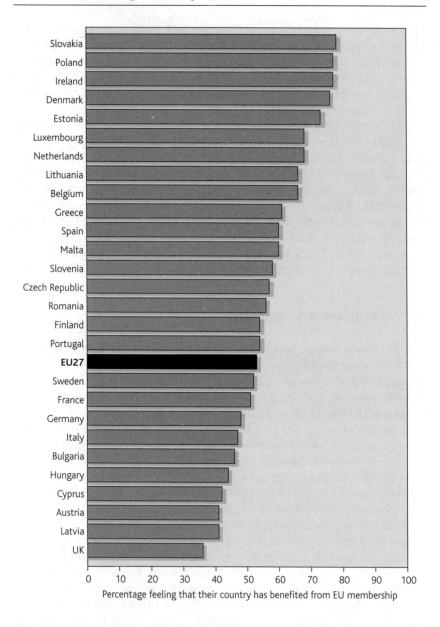

Figure 5.1   *Public opinion on EU membership*
Data from *Eurobarometer* 73, Spring 2010.

There are several possible explanations for the mixed opinions. First, integration is still a relatively new issue for the average European. True, the Treaty of Rome was signed back in 1957, and work was under way on the construction of the common market in the 1960s and 1970s, but it has only been since the early 1990s that the effects of integration have really begun to have much of a direct impact on the lives of Europeans, who have been slow to appreciate its implications, and have only recently begun to think in much depth about the costs and benefits of integration, to take a more European view of policy issues, or to learn more about how the EU works. As they have, so the reaction against integration has hardened – see Box 5.1.

Second, the actions of national and EU leaders are often at odds with the balance of public opinion. Take the issue of enlargement, for example: only 44 per cent of EU citizens supported the idea in 2000 while 35 per cent were opposed, and only 26 per cent saw it as a priority for the EU while 62 per cent did not. Undeterred, the Commission continued to negotiate with aspirant members, and 12 of them joined in 2004–07. In a similar vein, support for the euro strengthened in the lead up to the final switch in 2002, but it was still lukewarm, with only 55 per cent in favour, 37 per cent against, and 8 per cent undecided. Equally undeterred, the leaders of 12 member states gave up their national currencies and switched to the euro, in every case failing to put the issue to a public referendum. In those two states where referendums *were* held – Denmark in 2000 and Sweden in 2003 – majorities came down against adoption.

Third, the effort to explain the implications, costs, and benefits of integration – whether by national leaders, European institutions, the media, or academic experts – has been less than perfect. To be fair, integration is a complex process whose rules regularly change, and its implications have not always been fully understood even by policy makers; every new treaty has produced unanticipated effects and the switch to the euro was a leap into the unknown. But there has been no constitution to which citizens can refer for clarification, the treaties confuse as much as they illuminate, analysts often seem to be more interested in what is wrong with the EU than what is right with it, and coverage in the eurosceptic media misleads by emphasizing the negative at the expense of the positive.

The final problem is the sheer confusion of ordinary Europeans, who mostly admit to knowing little about how the EU functions or what it does (see Box 5.2), which raises questions about the credibility of the views of many of those surveyed by Eurobarometer or other polls. There have been several cases where polls have found initial majority opposition to an initiative, only to find it later replaced by majority support. Take, for example, the debate over the euro. Two years after its adoption, Europeans still had mixed views (47 per cent support and

Box 5.1 Euroscepticism

Public and political opinion on European integration and on the work of the European institutions is divided, but this is no surprise: all political endeavours in democratic systems have their supporters and their opponents. While there is majority support for integration and for the benefits of EU membership, there are many Europeans who have become eurosceptics. Although the scale of criticism has not increased much in recent years, the eurosceptic debate has become more visible thanks in part to its growing prominence in media debates about Europe, and it has played a greater role both in domestic politics – with the rise of political parties opposed to European integration, and splits over Europe within mainstream parties – and in the broader debate about integration, where it has had a critical role in opposition to treaty reforms, enlargement, and new policy initiatives.

Euroscepticism is far from monolithic, with views ranging from reform of the process to its wholesale rejection. The arguments put forward by eurosceptics vary by issue, time, and member state, but they have included some or all of the following:

- The European institutions are elitist, have become too powerful, and lack adequate transparency or democratic accountability.
- Integration is leading to the creation of a federal European superstate that is out of touch with citizens.
- The EU is promoting unpopular policies. For the political left, for example, this means too much of an emphasis on free markets, and for the political right it means too much power in the hands of workers.
- Too many decisions are taken by European leaders without sufficient reference to citizens.
- National sovereignty and identity are threatened by integration.
- The demands of Europe are unsustainable for more fragile economies.
- In more extreme cases, some believe that there is a conspiracy among European leaders to move ahead without reference to citizens (Booker and North, 2005).

Euroscepticism is less a well-defined ideology than a set of related positions based on opposition to European integration. Taggart and Szczerbiak (2004) distinguish between hard and soft forms, the former based on principled objections to the transfer of power to European institutions, being relatively easy to see, and being most obvious in the case of those who argue for the withdrawal of their countries from the EU, and in the case of political parties whose platform is opposition to the EU, such as the People's Movement in Denmark and the UK Independence Party in Britain. Meanwhile, soft euroscepticism is based on opposition to the direction being taken by the EU and a further expansion of its powers, and is both harder to see and more widespread.

Box 5.2 The knowledge deficit

No matter how much the European Commission tries to make Europe seem more real to its citizens, and no matter how often the European Council talks about the importance of transparency, one critical reality remains: the average European knows little about how the EU works. (True, the average European also knows little about how national systems of government work, but their levels of familiarity with the EU are much weaker.) The problem is reflected in the results of Eurobarometer surveys, in which respondents since the early 1990s have been asked how much they think they know about the EU, its policies, and its institutions. The results for 2000–06 consistently showed that only about a quarter knew 'a lot' or 'quite a lot' while about half knew 'a bit' and one in five knew 'almost nothing' (see Figure 5.2).

Those who feel they know the most include managers, university graduates, people who use the media regularly, and those in the age range of 25–54. Those with the lowest levels of knowledge include manual workers, retirees, and people with a high-school education or lower. In descending order, Luxembourgers, Danes, the Dutch, Austrians, Slovakians, and Swedes felt they knew the most in 2006, while those who scored themselves lowest were Italians, Belgians, Bulgarians, French, Spaniards, Hungarians, and Britons. It is interesting to note that eurosceptic Danes scored themselves so high, while the French admitted to knowing relatively little.

People are also occasionally tested on their knowledge, the results generally supporting the prevailing confusion. In one Eurobarometer survey in 2004, for example, 55 per cent of respondents incorrectly thought that the EU was created just after the First World War, 50 per cent did not know that Members of the European Parliament were directly elected by voters, and 48 per cent incorrectly thought that the president of the European Commission was elected to that position. Meanwhile, nearly one in three Europeans had never even *heard* of the Council of Ministers, and about one in five had never heard of the European Commission, the Court of Justice, or the European Central Bank. Meanwhile, reflecting popular prejudices, one in four Europeans thought that the biggest item on the EU budget was the cost for officials, meetings, and buildings. (As we will see in Chapter 6, administration actually accounts for just under 6 per cent of EU spending, while cohesion and agriculture account for 66 per cent.) (All results from Eurobarometer 61, Spring 2004.)

These are not encouraging figures. It will be difficult for Europeans to develop a sense of belonging to the European Union if they continue to know so little about it, and as long as they know so little, they will continue to misunderstand its work and open themselves to manipulation by supporters and opponents of integration. The knowledge deficit also raises questions about just how far the results of polling on the EU can be relied upon, and perpetuates the elitist qualities of EU decision making.

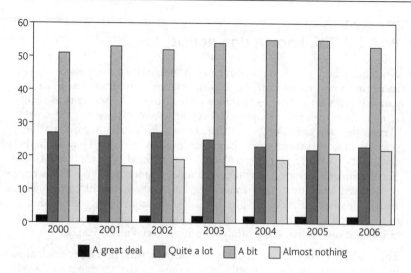

Figure 5.2 *How much do Europeans know about the EU?*
Data from *Eurobarometer* 66, September 2007, page 147. Data are for autumn waves only.

44 per cent opposition). However, by 2006 there had been a switch to 60 per cent support, and nowhere was the change of heart more clear than in Germany: polls in the mid-1990s found that more than 60 per cent of Germans were opposed to the euro and unwilling to surrender the deutschmark, but by 2006 two-thirds of Germans supported the euro (Eurobarometer, Flash EB 153, November 2003; Eurobarometer 66, December 2006). On some issues at least, the EU's political leaders can reasonably claim to be ahead of public opinion.

The democratic deficit

Much of the criticism about the EU has focused on the issue of the democratic deficit. This has been defined as 'the gap between the powers transferred to the Community level and the control of the elected Parliament over them' (Williams, 1991:162) and as 'the shift in decision-making powers from the national to the EU level, without accompanying strengthening of parliamentary control of executive bodies' (Archer, 2000:58). These definitions imply that the democratic deficit could be narrowed by giving the European Parliament greater powers, or by giving national legislatures greater control over EU institutions, but the problem is much broader, and a better definition of the democratic deficit might be the gap between the powers of European institutions and the ability of European citizens to influence their work and decisions.

The deficit takes several forms:

- The leaders of the member states, meeting as the European Council, reach decisions on important policy matters without always referring to their electorates. Less than half the original EU-15 member states asked their citizens whether they wanted to join the European Community or the European Union, for example (in contrast to the newest eastern and Mediterranean members, where referendums were held in nine of the 12 countries). The Maastricht treaty was negotiated largely behind closed doors, poorly explained to the European public and – despite the important changes it made to the structure and goals of the EU – was put to the test of a referendum in only three member states (Denmark, France, and Ireland), one of which (Denmark) said no, and another of which (France) said yes only by a narrow margin. Amsterdam and Nice were equally poorly explained, and equally poorly tested.
- Despite its powers over proposing and developing new European laws, the Commission is subject to little direct or even indirect public accountability. Appointments to the College of Commissioners must be approved by Parliament, but otherwise they are made without reference to voters (much the same, it must be said, as appointments to senior positions in domestic bureaucracies). The president of the Commission is appointed as a result of a game of musical chairs run by the leaders of the member states, represents the views of the EU in several international forums without a mandate from the people, and has tenure that is subject to the whims of national leaders rather than the opinions of European citizens (other than through the European Parliament). Furthermore, there is little opportunity for citizens to take part in or contribute to the deliberations of the Commission, and only limited (albeit improving) opportunity for the European Parliament to hold it accountable for its initiatives and decisions.
- Most meetings of the Council of Ministers and the permanent representatives in Brussels are closed to the public, despite the fact that many important decisions on the content of new laws and policies, and on their acceptance or rejection, are taken there. Ministers and representatives take the kinds of decisions that – at the national level – are taken by members of elected assemblies, who are held accountable for their actions at elections, by the media, and in the court of public opinion.
- The European Parliament – the only democratically elected institution in the EU system – cannot raise revenues or introduce new laws, and it has only a limited ability to hold the Commission accountable for its decisions. It has worked hard to win new powers for itself, but most of the important decisions on EU law and policy are still taken elsewhere.

- The Court of Justice is the institution that best champions the cause of individual Europeans, being the final court of appeal for anyone who feels they have been hurt by European law, by its non-appliance, or by contradictions between European and national law. However, Europeans have no direct or indirect say in appointments to the Court, nor will they until the kind of legislative confirmation that is used for courts in many member states is adopted by the EU, and nominees to the Court of Justice and the General Court are investigated and confirmed by the European Parliament.
- The formal rights of Europeans relative to the EU institutions are modest: they can vote in European elections, petition Parliament or the European ombudsman (see below) if they feel their rights or interests have been violated, access the documents of EU institutions (within certain limits), and can request diplomatic representation outside the EU by any member state, provided their own country has no local representation.

The democratic deficit has contributed to a psychological barrier between Europeans and the EU, undermining the development of the ties that must exist between leaders and citizens in order for a system of government to work. True, most national systems of government also suffer from their own forms of democratic deficit, but the perception (at least) is that the problem is significantly worse in the EU, and that it has helped create a troubling distance between Europeans and the EU institutions. It is hardly surprising that the anti-European media are able to generate public distrust and resentment towards these institutions, which often appear distant and mysterious. This is most obvious in the case of the European Commission, which is often portrayed (wrongly) by eurosceptics as powerful, overpaid, unaccountable, and secretive. The Commission is well aware of the problem, and made some candid admissions in a White Paper published in 2001 on the issue of governance:

> Europeans ... increasingly distrust institutions and politics or are simply not interested in them. The problem ... is particularly acute at the level of the European Union. Many people are losing confidence in a poorly understood and complex system to deliver the policies that they want. The Union is often seen as remote and at the same time too intrusive ... [The EU] must start adapting its institutions and establishing more coherence in its policies so that it is easier to see what it does and what it stands for. A more coherent Union will be stronger at home and a better leader in the world ... . Reform must be started now.

The paper also defended the work of EU institutions, noting that there is a perception that the EU cannot act effectively where a clear case exists (such as on unemployment, food-safety scares, and security concerns on EU borders), that even where the EU acts effectively it rarely gets fair credit for its actions, that people do not see that improvements in their quality of life often come from European rather than national initiatives, 'that "Brussels" is too easily blamed by member states for difficult decisions that they themselves have agreed or even requested', and that many Europeans 'do not know the difference between the [EU institutions, and do not] understand who takes the decisions that affect them and do not feel the Institutions act as an effective channel for their views and concerns' (European Commission, 2001a: 3, 7).

The democratic deficit has been the topic of a scholarly debate dating back many years (see, for example, Andersen and Eliassen, 1995; Chryssochoou, 2000), but opinion is divided on whether or not it is the problem it seems. Franklin (1996:197) once described the lack of proper democratic accountability in the EU as 'a crisis of legitimacy', and this is a view still widely held. But Moravcsik (2002) argues that the EU institutions are constrained by constitutional checks and balances, including 'narrow mandates, fiscal limits, super-majoritarian and concurrent voting requirements and separation of powers'. On balance, he concludes, 'EU policy-making is, in nearly all cases, clean, transparent, effective and politically responsive to the demands of European citizens', and 'the EU redresses rather than creates biases in political representation, deliberation and output'. Much depends upon how the EU is understood. If it is a federation, or has aspirations to become one, then the necessary links between citizens and EU institutions are indeed weak. But if it is a confederation, then the links are unusually strong. As we saw in Chapter 1, representation in a confederation is expected to be no more than indirect: national governments answer to their citizens, and in turn represent them in the meeting chambers of the central authority. Except in the case of the European Parliament, this is much how the EU institutions work.

The people's Europe

Reflecting the elitist qualities of the EU, it took more than thirty years for political leaders to begin paying much attention to the question of how ordinary Europeans related to the process of integration. A report was drawn up in 1975 at the request of the European Council by Leo Tindemans, prime minister of Belgium, looking into what might be done to achieve a more integrated Europe that was 'closer' to its citizens. But little changed until June 1984, when the Fontainebleau meeting of the EEC heads of government briefly turned its attention to the idea of a 'people's Europe'. Pietro Adonnino, a former Italian

MEP, was hired to chair a committee to put forward suggestions on how the EEC might be brought more closely in touch with its citizens.

The committee endorsed arrangements that had already been made for a European passport: national passports were phased out after 1986 and replaced by a standardized burgundy-coloured European passport bearing the words 'European Community' (later 'European Union') in the appropriate national language, and the name and coat of arms of the holder's home state. It also endorsed arrangements for a European flag, adopting the design developed and used since 1955 by the Council of Europe: a circle of 12 gold stars on a blue background. The flag quickly became a potent symbol of Europe, visible on public buildings, shops, and hotels throughout the EU, and omnipresent at meetings of EU leaders. Meanwhile the European Commission created an annual 'Europe Day' (9 May, the anniversary of the Schuman Declaration), and adopted as the official European anthem the 'Ode to Joy' by Friedrich von Schiller, sung to the final movement of Beethoven's Ninth Symphony.

The Single European Act incorporated more of the Adonnino recommendations, the most important of which was the easing of restrictions on the free movement of people. At the time of the Treaty of Rome it was understood that an open labour market would be an essential part of a single market, but while all Community citizens were given the right to 'move and reside freely' within all the member states, this was subject to 'limitations justified on grounds of public policy, public security or public health'. Since integration in the early days was economically driven, priority was given to making it easier for people who were economically active to move from one state to another. Limits were placed on migration, initially because governments wanted to protect themselves against the possibility of a shortage of skilled workers, and then because of the lack of opportunities in the target states (Barnes and Barnes, 1995, p. 108). Changes under the SEA allowed residents of the EU-15 to move and live anywhere in the EU, provided they were covered by health insurance and had enough income to avoid being a 'burden' on the welfare system of the country to which they moved (see Chapter 7 for more discussion).

Migration has been made easier by another element of the Adonnino report that was formalized by the SEA: arrangements for the mutual recognition of professional qualifications. The Commission at first tried to work on each profession in turn, to reach agreement on the requirements, and then propose a new law. But this was time-consuming, and in 1991 a general systems directive was adopted by which the member states agreed to trust the adequacy of qualifications that required at least three years of professional training in other member states. The list of mutually recognized professions has since grown, and now includes accountants, librarians, architects, engineers, and lawyers. The Commission has meanwhile published a comparative guide to national qualifications for more than 200 occupations, helping employers work out equivalencies across the member states.

An important element in worker mobility has been education, and while education policy still remains the preserve of the member states, efforts have been made by the EU to encourage educational exchanges and the transferability of credits and degrees (see Walkenhorst, 2008). The Lifelong Learning Programme (LLP), which in 2007 replaced an earlier programme called Socrates, helps promote cross-border education through sub-programmes called Comenius (primary and secondary school partnerships), Erasmus (higher education), Leonardo da Vinci (vocational education), and Grundtvig (adult education). Since 1999 the Bologna process (championed by the Council of Europe) has encouraged the standardization of university education, working to create a European higher-education area within which university education is compatible, comparable, and transferable, and to make European higher education more attractive and internationally competitive. Bologna includes a European Credit Transfer and Accumulation System (ECTS) under which study at any university in the EU is translated into a common credit system, thus helping open up the educational options available to students in Europe. Nearly 50 countries have now signed on to the process.

The inability to speak other languages poses a practical barrier to the free movement of workers, and also stands as a potent reminder of the differences among Europeans. In addition to the 23 official languages of the EU – Bulgarian, Czech, Danish, Dutch, English, Estonian, Finnish, French, German, Greek, Hungarian, Irish, Italian, Latvian, Lithuanian, Maltese, Polish, Portuguese, Romanian, Slovak, Slovene, Spanish, and Swedish – Europeans must also deal with many local languages and dialects, and languages spoken within the EU by large numbers of nationals from non-EU states (notably Turks and Arabs). Almost all secondary school pupils in the EU learn at least one foreign language, although some have a better record than others. The rise of English as the lingua franca of Europe has been notable and inexorable, helped by its use in international commerce, entertainment, and sport; an estimated 85 per cent of secondary school pupils in the EU-25 were learning English as a second language in 2004, the most active English learners being in Austria, Denmark, Finland, France, Germany, Greece, Latvia, the Netherlands, Spain, and Sweden (where more than 95 per cent of students take English classes). Meanwhile, only 23 per cent of Germans are learning French, and only 18 per cent of French students are learning German (Eurostat, 2007: 91).

While tourism, the removal of technical barriers to movement and the promotion of language training all contribute to free movement, integration will never be able to do much about the social and psychological barriers posed by differences in the routine of daily existence. Americans can readily travel from one state to another in search of jobs or to improve the quality of their lives, and will find their daily routine changing little; they will find the same shops, the same banking system, the same money, the same programmes on television, and so on. By contrast, Europeans not only face different languages, but must also deal with a host of new norms and rules, including everything from different social customs to different sets of road signs and traffic regulations, different procedures for renting or buying a home, taking out car insurance, or opening a bank account, and a new array of products on the shelves of unfamiliar local supermarket chains. It is psychologically difficult enough for an American family to uproot itself and move hundreds of kilometres away, but the challenge of acculturation in the EU is much greater. An Italian moving to Denmark or a Swede moving to Hungary may eventually learn how things are done locally, but there is a limit to how much new EU laws and policies can help.

Another of the changes introduced by Maastricht was the promotion of European citizenship, although this is not what it seems. Citizenship in democracies is usually defined as full and responsible membership of a state, and has been described by some social scientists as including the right to equality before the law, the right to own property, the right to freedom of speech, and the right to a minimum standard of economic and social welfare (see Heater, 2004). But these are all rights that legal non-citizens of democracies also enjoy. What usually makes a citizen different from a non-citizen in practical terms is that a citizen can vote and run for elective office in his or her home state, can serve on a jury in that state, is eligible to serve in the armed forces of that state (although some countries allow non-citizens to serve), cannot be forcibly removed from that state to another, has the right to receive protection from the state when outside its borders, is recognized as a subject of that state by other governments, and must usually obtain the permission of other governments to travel through or live in their territory. More intangibly, citizens feel a sense of 'belonging' to their home state.

According to Lisbon, 'every person holding the nationality of a Member State shall be a citizen of the Union', but this is less substantial than it sounds, and the treaty goes on to note that 'citizenship of the Union shall be additional to and not replace national citizenship' (Article 20). For now, citizenship of the EU means that citizens of a member state finding themselves in need in a non-EU country where their home state has no diplomatic representation can receive protection from the diplomatic and consular authorities of any EU state that has a local office. It also means that citizens of one member state living in another can vote and stand for municipal and European Parliament elections (but not for national elections). But until such time as citizens of an EU member state have the right of unrestricted movement throughout the EU, and the same rights as local wherever they live, and can exchange their state passports for an EU passport, the idea of European citizenship will always be limited.

Participation and representation

The efforts made under the People's Europe programme have been helpful, but probably more meaningful to the development of a sense of Europeanness is the idea that EU institutions work in the interests of ordinary Europeans, who can participate directly in EU decision-making and have their needs and opinions represented. As 'Europe' becomes a more important issue in national politics, as more Europeans take advantage of the removal of internal borders and travel restrictions, and as voters add policies on Europe into their calculations about choosing among competing national political parties and leaders, so 'Europe' becomes more real. These kinds of connections are being given more substance by four channels through which Europeans can influence the outcome of EU-level policy decisions: voting in European elections and referendums, supporting the work of interest groups, and using the European ombudsman and the citizen initiative.

European elections

Held every five years since 1979, elections to the European Parliament (EP) give Europeans the opportunity to decide the make-up of the EP, which has had an increasingly effective role in making European law. Voters must be 18 years of age, must be citizens of one of the EU member states, and can vote – and even to run for the EP – in whichever country they have legal residence. The minimum age for candidates varies from 18 to 25 years, depending on the country of residence, and there are also different rules on how candidates qualify; some member states do not allow independent candidates, some require candidates to pay deposits, others require them to collect signatures, and so on.

Every member state uses multi-member districts and variations on the theme of proportional representation (PR), either treating their entire territory as a single electoral district (Germany, Spain, Poland, and most of the smaller EU states) or dividing it up into several Euro-constituencies (Britain, France, Italy, Belgium, and Ireland). Seats are then divided among parties according to their share of the vote. PR has the advantage of reflecting more accurately the proportion of the vote given to different parties, but it also results in many small parties being elected to Parliament. Also, PR leads to voters being represented by a

Box 5.3   Political groups in the European Parliament

European elections bring dozens of different parties to the EP, many of which consist of as few as one or two members. Since there is little that these parties can achieve alone, it is in their interests to build alliances with other parties, and thus they have habitually formed cross-European political groups. Some of these have been marriages of convenience, but most have built more consistency and focus with time (for details, see Bardi, 2002; Corbett *et al.*, 2005: ch. 5). Moving from left to right on the ideological spectrum, the groups in 2011 were as follows:

- *European United Left–Nordic Green Left (GUE–NGL)*. The main left-wing group in the EP, critical of the elitist and market-oriented policies of the EU.
- *Progressive Alliance of Socialists and Democrats (PASD)*. Currently the second largest group in the EP, ranging from ex-communists on the left to more moderate social democrats, with members from every EU state.
- *Alliance of Liberals and Democrats for Europe (ALDE)*. Consistently the third largest group in the EP, most of its members sitting in or around the centre, and its biggest national blocs coming from Germany and the UK.
- *Greens–European Free Alliance (Greens–EFA)*. A confederation of green parties and those representing national minorities, pursuing a variety of issues related to social justice.
- *European People's Party (EPP)*. The major right-wing group in Parliament, which overtook the socialists in 1999 to become the biggest political group, with MEPs from every EU member state except the UK.
- *European Conservatives and Reformists (ECR)*. A new group set up in 2009 to bring together parties opposed to European federalism and in favour of stronger controls on immigration. More than half its members come from the UK and Poland.
- *Europe of Freedom and Democracy (EFD)*. The most eurosceptic political group, opposing further integration and demanding that all new treaties be put to national referendums.

group of MEPs of different parties, and constituents may never get to know or develop ties with a particular MEP.

Once elected, MEPs sit not in national blocs but in cross-national political groups with similar goals and values. By the rules of the EP, a group must have at least 25 members from at least one-quarter of member states. No one party group has ever had enough seats to form a majority, so groups must work together in order to achieve a majority. The balance of power and the order of business is also affected by frequent changes in the number and make-up of political groups. Three groups have developed a particular consistency over time – the Socialists on the left, the Liberals on the centre-right, and the European People's Party on the right – but they have always had to share power with a cluster of smaller parties with a variety of values and opinions (see Box 5.3).

Turnout at EP elections is low, compromising the credibility and political influence of Parliament. From a modest peak of 63 per cent in 1979, figures fell to just under 57 per cent in 1994, then took a relatively sharp fall to just over 49 per cent in 1999, tailing off to 43 per cent in 2009 (see Figure 5.3). Belgium and Luxembourg usually have the highest turnout (more than 90 per cent), but in most member states fewer than half of all voters now cast ballots. Several countries started out on a high note upon joining the EU, only to see their voters lose enthusiasm: thus Portugal fell from 72 to 37 per cent, Austria from nearly 70 to a low of 42 per cent, and Finland from 60 to 40 per cent. Optimists expected that the figures in 2004 for new members in their first flush of membership would be high, but they turned out to be among the worst ever: less than 42 per cent turned out in most countries, and just one in five in Poland and Slovakia.

There are several explanations for this state of affairs, the most compelling of which is the relative significance of 'first-order' and 'second-order' elections (Reiff and Schmitt, 1980), the rankings depending on the issues at stake. National elections are considered first-order because they determine who controls the national executive and legislatures, which in turn make the decisions that are most immediate and relevant in the lives of citizens. National elections are also hard-fought and attract the most media attention. By contrast, European elections are seen as second-order because there is less at stake; there is no potential change of government involved, they draw less media attention, and most Europeans either know very little about what Parliament does, or are confused or badly informed about European issues.

Among the other explanations for low turnout (see discussion in Judge and Earnshaw, 2008:77–80):

- EU voters have developed relatively few psychological ties to the European Parliament, which still seems anonymous and distant to most.
- MEPs do not become well-known political figures, so there is little of the personality politics at the European level that often sparks voter interest and turnout in national elections.
- Low turnout mirrors a general downward trend in national elections in many EU member states. Where turnout at EP elections fell by 13 per cent between 1979 and 1999, it fell by 10–14 per cent over-

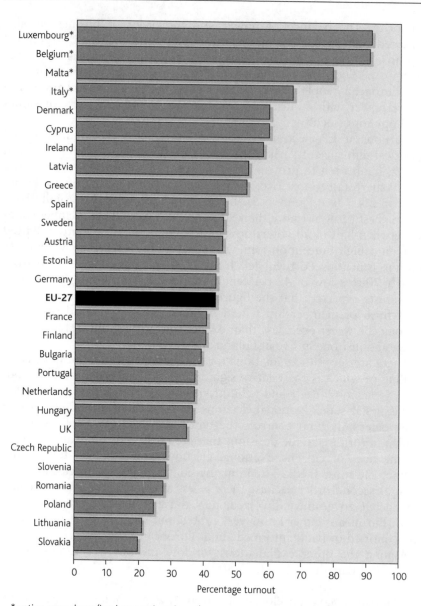

* voting compulsory (but laws rarely enforced)

Figure 5.3　*Turnout at European Parliament elections, 2009*
Data from European Parliament website, http://www.europarl.europa.eu

roughly the same period in (for example) France, Germany, Ireland, and the Netherlands (Corbett, 2001).

A notable quality of European elections is that they are contested by national political parties running in 27 separate sets of elections. The result is that they are not only fought more on the basis of national than of European issues, but voter turnout – and the choices made by voters – is often a reflection of how voters view their home governments and national political issues, and many will use their vote to send a message to national politicians (Heath *et al.*, 1999). Party activity at the European level has been encouraged by a growth in the number of European party organizations and confederations, which have improved coordination among like-minded national parties. The oldest of these date back to the 1970s, but it has only been since 2002 that there has been real growth in the number of European parties. They are still evolving and have not made much of a mark on the consciousness of the European voter, but they have become more adept at coordinating policy and at building links between party leaders at the national and European levels (Hix, 2005:192). What effect this will have over the longer term on party politics and voter turnout remains to be seen.

Referendums

National referendums allow European voters to express their opinions on narrow (but usually important) topics. Not every country uses them, and they have only been used for selected issues, but they have come to play an increasingly important role in the process of European integration, and there has been increased moral and political pressure for their use. Some have been little more than tools for political manipulation, as when Britain held a referendum in 1975 that was ostensibly about whether or not Britain should stay in the Community following renegotiation of the terms, but was actually designed to settle a division of opinion about Europe within the government (Nugent, 2006:483). Others have had a significant impact on the course of European integration, as when the opposition of 33 million French voters (the number of eligible voters who voted no) in 2005 was enough to stop the constitutional treaty dead in its tracks.

Most referendums have fallen into one of two major categories (see Table 5.1). First, there have been votes on whether or not to join the Community/EU. The first such votes were held in Denmark, Ireland, and Norway in 1972. A majority of Danes and Irish approved, but a majority of Norwegians disapproved, and said no in a second referendum in 1994. The Swiss also said no to EU membership in a referendum in 2001. All three countries that joined the EU in 1995 held referendums, as did nine of the ten countries that joined in 2004 (the exception was Cyprus). The results were all positive for membership, but levels of enthusiasm varied: the Slovaks, Lithuanians, and Slovenians were the most supportive, with 90–92 per cent majorities in favour, while in Finland, Sweden, and Malta, bare majorities of just over 50 per cent said yes. The only example of a territory leaving the EU came in 1982, when the 53,000 voters of Greenland – which had joined in 1973 as part of Denmark – voted to leave.

Second, there have been votes on whether or not to accept a new treaty. These have only been a recent phenomenon, and only in a select few countries. Denmark held a vote on the Single European Act in 1986, mainly because the government wanted to outmanoeuvre parliament, which had voted against ratification. Most Danes (more than 60 per cent) said yes on that occasion, but in 1992 Denmark became the first member state ever to turn down a new treaty when a bare majority of 50.7 per cent rejected Maastricht, and 54 per cent of Irish voters turned down the Treaty of Nice in 2001. The negative votes gave Europeans pause for thought, and resulted in changes to the treaties and new referendums in both countries that went in favour of the treaties. Referendums were also held in 1998 in Denmark and Ireland on the terms of the Amsterdam treaty, and both were positive. Undoubtedly the most politically significant referendums to date were those in the Netherlands and France in 2005 on the constitutional treaty, when – respectively – 61 per cent and 55 per cent voted no. The French vote was particularly newsworthy, given that France has been a staple of European integration from the beginning.

Just as important as the result of some of these votes has been the symbolism often attached to the *absence* of referendums. The issue of adopting the euro was particularly controversial, and was put to a vote in just two countries, Denmark and Sweden, where the outcomes were both negative. Meanwhile, none of the 17 governments that have adopted the euro have held a referendum, often for fear of a similar result. The Blair administration in Britain promised a referendum when the time was right, but never did, again mainly for fear of a negative vote; the Eurobarometer 61 poll (2004) found 61 per cent of Britons opposed to adopting the euro. Soon after coming to office, Gordon Brown found himself in trouble over the issue of the Lisbon treaty, claiming that it was significantly different from the constitutional treaty and thus did not merit a referendum, but he failed to convince his critics.

Interest groups

While national leaders promote national agendas, non-governmental organizations (NGOs) – or interest groups – have cut across national

Table 5.1   *National referendums on EU issues (selected)*

Year	Country	Issue	Outcome
1972	Denmark, Ireland	Join EEC	Yes
	Norway	Join EEC	No
1975	UK	Continued membership of EEC	Yes
1982	Greenland	Continued membership of EEC	No
1986	Denmark	Single European Act	Yes
1987	Ireland	Single European Act	Yes
1992	Denmark I	Maastricht treaty	No
	Ireland, France	Maastricht treaty	Yes
1993	Denmark II	Maastricht treaty	Yes
1994	Austria, Finland, Sweden	Join EU	Yes
	Norway	Join EU	No
1998	Ireland, Denmark	Treaty of Amsterdam	Yes
2000	Denmark	Adopt euro	No
2001	Ireland I	Treaty of Nice	No
2002	Ireland II	Treaty of Nice	Yes
2003	Malta, Slovenia, Hungary, Lithuania, Slovakia, Poland, Czech Republic, Estonia, Latvia	Join EU	Yes
	Sweden	Adopt euro	No
2005	Spain,	Constitutional treaty	Yes
	France, Netherlands	Constitutional treaty	No
	Luxembourg	Constitutional treaty	Yes
2008	Ireland I	Treaty of Lisbon	No
2009	Ireland II	Treaty of Lisbon	Yes

frontiers to promote the shared sectional interests of groups of people in multiple member states. In addition to the EU bodies that represent these interests, such as the European Economic and Social Committee and the Committee of the Regions (see Box 4.3), the last 20–25 years have seen the growth of hundreds of NGOs that represent the views of a large number of groups of people with a stake in EU policy and law. Many are an outgrowth of pre-existing national groups, others have been set up specifically to respond to European issues, and many have opened offices in Brussels in order to be close to the Commission and the Council of Ministers. A recent study (Balme and Chabanet, 2008) suggests that there are more than 850 groups working to influence decisions taken at the European level, many of which date back to before 1980.

The growth in interest group activity at the European level has paralleled the growth in the power and influence of the EU institutions, or the 'Europeanization' of policy areas that were once the preserve of national governments (Mazey and Richardson, 1996:200). The groups have not always simply followed the evolution of the EU, going wherever new opportunities for influence have presented themselves, but have often been actively involved in pushing the EU in new directions. Business leaders, for example, were champions of the single market, arguing that competition among European corporations was a handicap to their ability to take on the Americans and the Japanese. At the same time, the European Commission has encouraged interest group activity; it uses groups as a source of expert knowledge and to test the viability of new laws, and also uses them to monitor the compliance records of member states: most groups are only too happy to blow the whistle on their home governments if they are not implementing EU law.

Historically, business and labour groups have been the most active, mainly because the process of integration was for so long driven by economic issues (Greenwood, 2003). As the EU won new powers over competition policy, mergers, and the movement of workers, so business and labour groups made greater efforts to influence the Commission and the Council of Ministers. Not only are individual corporations represented either directly or through lobbying firms in Brussels, but several cross-sectoral federations have been created to represent the interests of a broader membership. These include Business Europe (formerly the Union of Industrial and Employers' Confederations of Europe (UNICE)), which represents 40 national business federations from 33 countries, the European Round Table of Industrialists (which brings together the chief executives of major European corporations such as British Airways, Renault, Fiat, Philips, Volvo, and Nokia), and EUROCHAMBRES (the Association of European Chambers of Commerce and Industry), which represents national associations in 45 countries.

Labour is also represented in Brussels, notably through groups such as the European Trade Union Confederation (ETUC), whose membership consists of more than 80 European-level industry federations and national labour federations from 36 countries, including Britain's TUC, France's CGT, and Germany's DGB. Professional interests are represented by groups such as the Council of European Professional and Managerial Staff (EUROCADRES), and by associations representing everything from architects to dentists, journalists, opticians, and vets. Several Brussels-based interest groups include member organizations from outside the EU, a reflection of how much the EU has come to matter to business and labour throughout Europe.

Groups representing public interests, such as consumer issues and the environment, have also become more active as the EU has become more involved in matters about which they care. Until the 1970s, environmental groups focused their attentions on national governments, because they had different priorities, and because most environmental policy in Western Europe was still made at the national level. As the Community became more active on the environment in the mid-1980s (see Chapter 8), it became a more profitable target for interest group pressure. The new emphasis given to EU-level activities was reflected in the opening of offices in Brussels by such groups as Friends of the Earth, Greenpeace, and the World Wide Fund for Nature, while many other groups employed full-time lobbyists. As environmental groups became more active, so did groups representing the industrial perspective on environmental issues, such as the European Chemical Industry Council (Cefic), Eurelectric (representing national electricity supply associations), and the European Crop Protection Association.

Increased access to EU policy makers led in turn to a more systematic approach among environmental groups to lobbying at the European level, and a clear trend towards approaching domestic environmental problems as EU-wide problems. The complexity of those problems encouraged domestic groups to work more closely together and to form transnational coalitions, the best known of which – in the environmental field – is the European Environmental Bureau (EEB). Founded in 1974 with the encouragement of the Commission, the EEB is an umbrella body for national interest groups in the EU, and acts as a conduit for the representation of those groups in the EU institutions, particularly the Commission. The Bureau now claims to represent more than 140 national environmental groups from 31 countries.

The methods that European-level groups use are similar to those used by groups at any level: promoting public awareness in support of their cause, building membership numbers in order to increase their influence and credibility, representing the views of their members, forming networks with other interest groups, providing information to the EU institutions, meeting with EU lawmakers in an attempt to influence the content of law, and monitoring the implementation of EU law at the national level. As the reach of the EU has expanded, so Brussels has witnessed another phenomenon usually associated with national capitals: the rise of the think tank. These are policy institutes set up to undertake research and to influence decision-makers through the publication of reports, the generation of public debate, and the organization of conferences and seminars. They now include among their number the Centre for European Policy Studies, the European Policy Centre, and the European Enterprise Institute.

Aspinwall and Greenwood (1998) argue that the representation of interests at the European level has become more diversified and specialized, and that European groups are becoming protagonists: they now try to influence policy rather than simply to monitor events, using increasingly sophisticated means to attract allegiance. A symbiotic relationship has developed between the Commission and interest groups, with the former actively supporting the work of many groups and giving them access to its advisory committee meetings, and the latter doing what they can to influence the content and development of policy and legislative proposals as they work their way through the Commission.

The activities of interest groups have helped offset the problem of the democratic deficit and the relative weakness of political parties working at the European level by offering Europeans channels outside the formal structure of EU institutions through which they can influence EU policy. They have also helped focus the attention of the members of interest groups on how the EU influences the policies that affect their lives, have helped draw them more actively into the process by which the EU makes its decisions, and have encouraged them to bypass their national governments and to focus their attention on European responses to shared and common problems.

Other channels

Another option for representation – introduced by Maastricht – was the creation of the office of European ombudsman. If a legal resident of the EU feels that any of the EU institutions (other than the Court of Justice and the General Court) is guilty of 'maladministration', and can make a compelling case, the European Parliament must ask the ombudsman to review the complaint, and if necessary carry out an investigation. Appointed for a five-year term that runs concurrently with the term of Parliament, the ombudsman is expected to be both impartial and independent of any government. Since the first ombudsman was appointed in 1995, the Commission has been the target of most of the complaints, which have included charges that it has failed to carry out its responsibilities as guardian of the treaties, that it lacks sufficient transparency, and that it has abused its power. The number of complaints has grown over the years, which is probably less a sign that things are becoming worse than a sign that more people are becoming aware of the work of the ombudsman.

The most recent addition to the list of channels through which Europeans can express themselves on European issues is the citizen initiative introduced by Lisbon. If at least a million EU citizens from a 'significant' number of member states can be encouraged to give their support (although how that support is to be measured is not clear – presumably a petition will do), then the Commission can be invited to develop a new legislative proposal on a topic of interest to the organizers, so long as it is within the policy purview of the Commission. But the terms as they are outlined in Lisbon are vague, and until this option is tested in practice it is unclear what effect it will have.

Conclusions

The European Union has helped redefine the relationship among Europeans. Where they have long identified themselves in national terms, and have been tied politically, economically, legally, and culturally to one nation state or another, the reduction of the barriers to trade and to the movement of individuals over the past decade has encouraged Europeans to think of themselves as part of a larger entity with broader interests. Common policies have resulted in key powers over the lives of individual Europeans shifting to Brussels, so that an increasing number of Europeans feel the effect of decisions made at the EU level. Personal mobility has increased and, cultural barriers aside, Europeans have taken more interest in neighbours who have long been considered as 'foreign' rivals and occasionally a direct threat to their own national interests.

However, while this horizontal integration has been taking place, the vertical ability of Europeans directly to influence the European Union has changed only slowly. Integration was long driven by the priorities and the values of the leaders of the member states, who made most of their decisions with limited reference to their citizens. The result was the creation of a European governing structure that was only indirectly accountable to the views of the people who lived within it. But much has changed since the early 1990s, with growing demands by ordinary Europeans that their opinions should be taken into account in the making of European-level policy, and new complexity being added to patterns of public opinion. Where support for integration had been growing, it began to fall in the wake of the controversy over Maastricht, such that today only about 53–55 per cent think that membership of their country is a good thing. At the same time, the majority of Europeans admit that they do not really understand how the EU works, raising troubling questions about the quality of public opinion.

As European institutions struggle to make the concept of integration more real to the citizens of the member states, they are handicapped by the paucity of effective channels of accountability, and by the perpetuation of the democratic deficit. Changes made under the people's Europe programme and as a result of new treaties have brought change, but uniform passports, a European flag, and student exchange programmes fall short of the kinds of changes needed to make Europeans feel as though they are truly connected to the EU. For now, they are left with elections to the EP, the occasional national referendum on European issues, the work of interest groups, and other more limited channels for the expression of their opinions. The shift away from the elitism of the 1960s and 1970s is happening only slowly, and while the construction of a European political space is under way, most Europeans relate more directly to national politics, even using their views on what is happening in the national arena to guide their opinions on how to relate to Europe.

Chapter 6

The EU Policy Process

Enough responsibility for making policy has been transferred from the exclusive domain of national governments to the EU institutions that the EU has taken on some of the features of a European superstate. EU institutions are at the heart of discussions about policy priorities, many of the actions of national governments are determined by new laws adopted by the EU, and in some areas – notably trade and agricultural policy – the member states now take part in the policy process as a collective. The EU institutions, and the representatives of the member states working within those institutions, have become powerful and productive policy entrepreneurs and policy makers – certainly more powerful than can be said of the administrations of any conventional intergovernmental organization.

It is debatable just how much the EU member states can still do alone, and how far national interests still drive the work of the EU institutions, but there has been a clear loss of policy independence – and of sovereignty – by the member states. Even without the intermediary of the EU, it is quite likely that the pressures of international trade and monetary policy would have pushed European states far along the road to cooperation, with a resulting loss in policy independence. Many Europeans are unclear about what integration has meant for their home states, and continue to champion the cause of separate state identities and residual powers for their home governments. But there are others who argue that the pooling of powers has been beneficial and efficient, and not a cause for concern: state identities and interests can be preserved, and even promoted, in the face of common policies and joint institutions.

However we now understand the EU, its member states relate to each other quite differently from the way they did before the process of European integration began. As they have integrated their economies, agreed universal standards and regulations, and developed common policies on a wide range of issues, so the differences among them have declined and the effects of integration have become deeper and more complex. But just what this has meant for Europe poses a puzzle for Europeans and non-Europeans alike. The EU member states may still occupy individual seats in the United Nations and the World Trade Organization, for example, but they usually agree joint positions on important foreign policy issues, and vote together. True, they still fight

123

rearguard actions at home in the interests of preserving state sovereignty, but whatever the doubts about the wisdom and consequences of integration, the EU states have been pushed irresistibly by internal and external pressures into making policy together on a wide range of issues.

The previous chapters looked at how the European institutions work and at how ordinary Europeans participate in the decision-making system. This chapter develops that story by looking at the EU policy process: at the changing balance of policy responsibilities between the EU and the member states, at the key qualities of the EU policy process, at the underlying pressures involved in that process, and at how the policy process has changed the relationship between the parts and the whole. It then looks at the political implications of the EU budget, before ending with some general conclusions about the impact of integration on the member states of the EU.

The changing balance of authority

European society – like all societies – is in a constant state of flux. Political, economic, and social relationships among Europeans undergo continuous alteration, the pressures for change coming from different sources; where once it was war, economic competition, and political alliances, more recently it has been regional integration and changes in communications, technology, and economic activity. As noted in Chapter 1, the state system with which we are all familiar today dates back barely three centuries, and was preceded by political arrangements that were themselves constantly changing, and that led routinely to the redrawing of the political boundaries between different communities. A quick flick through an historical atlas of Europe shows how the boundaries of states have changed, and continue to change today: in the last quarter-century alone, Germany has reunified, Yugoslavia and Czechoslovakia have split apart, Montenegro became Europe's newest state in 2006, Kosovo declared its independence in 2008, and questions remain about the future political status of Belgium, Scotland, and the Basque country.

Before the Second World War, Europe held the balance of global political, military, and economic power, and the world's major powers included Britain, Germany, and France. The international system was defined in large part by the competition among mainly European powers for political, economic, and military advantage. This all changed after 1945, when Europe found itself squeezed militarily and ideologically between the two superpowers and saw the focus of economic power shifting to new centres, notably the United States and Japan. As we saw in Chapter 3, the need to save Europe from itself combined with the need to build economic and military security in the postwar world to encourage Western European elites to call for a new regional community, and for cooperation rather than competition. Where the relationship among European states before the war had been driven by competition, now it was driven by cooperation.

As late as the 1960s and 1970s, European states still related to each other as sovereign states with strong and independent national identities. They had their own bodies of law, they pursued their own distinctive sets of policies, and travellers (a good deal fewer of them then than now) were reminded of the differences when they crossed national borders and had to show their passports. There were controls and limits on the movement of people, money, goods, and services, and citizens of one state who travelled to another felt very much that they were 'going abroad' and could not stay indefinitely without permission. The nation state was dominant, and was both the focus of mass public loyalty and the source of primary political and administrative authority. Italians were clearly Italians, the Dutch were clearly Dutch, and Poles were clearly Poles – at least this is what most Europeans wanted to believe, or were encouraged to believe by circumstances.

The situation today is quite different, and the relationship between the EU and its member states has been transformed. There has been a shift, a pooling, or a transfer (various terms have been used) of authority from the member states to the European Union, and an agreement to share the exercise of power in multiple policy areas. The member states have remained the essential building blocks in this process, but they have moved far beyond the simple cooperation normally associated with intergovernmental organizations, and have built a new layer of powerful institutions underwritten by a common body of laws, a process driven by its own distinctive principles (see Box 6.1).

Two critical and competing influences have come to bear on the process. On the one hand, spillover has pushed the EU into an expanding set of policy interests, starting from a base of promoting economic integration and moving into a network of related areas, ranging from transport to communications, labour relations, judicial and police cooperation, research and development, education, financial services, the environment, and foreign and security policy. On the other hand, the brakes have been applied by the ongoing debate about subsidiarity, first raised in the European context in 1975 when the European Commission – in its response to the Tindemans report (see Chapter 5) – argued that the Community should be given responsibility only for those matters that the member states were no longer capable of dealing with efficiently. There was little further discussion until the mid-1980s, when member states opposed to increasing the power of the Commission began quoting the principle. It was finally brought into the mainstream of discussions about the EU by the Maastricht treaty.

Box 6.1   Principles of the EU policy process

The formal division of powers is summarized by four principles contained in the treaties (specifically Article 5):

- *Competence* is another term for authority, and describes the areas of policy for which the EU is responsible. For example, it has a high level of competence in the fields of competition and trade, but much less over education and taxation.
- *Conferral* is the principle that the EU can act only where it has been given authority by the member states to achieve objectives set out in the treaties, and that any areas of competence not specifically listed in the treaties default to the member states.
- *Subsidiarity* is the principle that decisions should be taken at the lowest level possible for effective action. In other words, the EU should only do what it does best.
- *Proportionality* is the principle that the EU should not go beyond taking the action needed to achieve the objectives of the treaties.

In those policy areas where the governments of the member states have agreed to provide the EU with competence, national leaders now reach most key decisions through negotiation with their counterparts in the other member states, typically in the meeting rooms of the Council of Ministers and the European Council. The trend has been for national leaders to work towards multinational compromises and towards a European consensus. As this has happened, so it has become more difficult for those leaders to define and pursue the distinctive interests of their home states, assuming that state interests can always any more be clearly distinguished from European interests. At the same time, ordinary Europeans are reminded less often of their differences, and the borders that once divided the member states – and were often fought over so bitterly in one war after another – have become so porous that in some places they have become little more than a line on a map or a sign by the side of the road.

Of course, it is a matter of opinion whether the member states or the EU deal better or more efficiently with any given area of policy. But whatever the answer, the gradual shift of powers to the European level has left national legislatures weaker and more marginalized in a process that has sometimes been described (pejoratively) as 'creeping federalism'. National legislatures once had almost complete authority to make laws as their members saw fit, within the limitations created by constitutions, public opinion, the powers of other government institutions, and the international community. They now find themselves limited to those policy areas in which the EU is less active, while reacting in other areas to the requirements of EU law and the pressures of regional integration. At the heart of the debate has been the troubling question of sovereignty, too much of which – argue critics of the EU – has been transferred to the EU institutions behind the backs of the ordinary European.

At first, the only powers transferred from the member states were those agreed under the terms of the European Coal and Steel Community. But even in this limited area there was the promise of change to come: the Treaty of Paris gave the ECSC the power to ensure the rational use of coal resources (a precursor to environmental policy), to promote improved working conditions (a precursor to social policy), and to promote international trade (a precursor to trade and foreign policy). The logic of spillover was clearly at work from the outset, and with the near-completion of the single market and the launch of the euro, there are now few areas of economic policy in which the EU does not have at least some influence. In some, such as competition and trade policy, EU competence is now exclusive, while at the other end of the scale the member states still have the bulk of control over tax policy.

On international issues, the EU still has some way to go before it can claim a common foreign policy, and the member states still have much freedom in their relationships outside Europe and in the way they define and express their security interests. But the EU is becoming a more distinctive actor on the world stage, and its effects are now measured jointly as much as individually, even if sceptics still like to point to its failures and its disagreements (see Chapter 9). In several areas of non-economic domestic policy there has also been a clear shift towards the EU, or at least towards interstate cooperation. In many of these areas, the logic of policy integration has been clear: building of trans-European transport and energy networks makes economic sense, environmental problems are often better dealt with by member states working together rather than in isolation, and the pressures of the single market have led to cooperation on employment policy, worker mobility, education, regional policy, and justice and home affairs. In some key areas of policy, such as taxation, health care, education, and policing, the balance of power still lies clearly with the member states, but the list is becoming shorter (see Table 6.1).

The policy environment

Public policies are the deliberate actions (or inactions) of government in response to the needs of society. When political parties or political leaders run for office, they do so on a platform of explanations about what they see as the most important problems and challenges facing

Table 6.1   *The division of policy authority*

Exclusive EU competence	Shared competence	Responsibility of member states
Competition	Agriculture	Broadcasting
Customs	Civil protection**	Citizenship
Fisheries conservation	Cohesion	Criminal justice
Monetary policy	Consumer protection	Defence
(euro zone)	Culture**	Education
Trade	Development cooperation	Elections
	Economic policy*	Health care
	Employment policy*	Land use
	Energy	Local transport
	External relations	Policing
	Environment	Postal services
	Fisheries	Tax policy
	Freedom, security, justice	
	Human health**	
	Humanitarian aid	
	Industry**	
	Public health	
	Research and development	
	Single market	
	Social policy	
	Space policy	
	Tourism**	
	Trans-European networks	
	Transport	
	Vocational training**	

*   EU has some powers of coordination
**   EU has powers to support, coordinate or supplement actions of member states

Data from Articles 3–6 of the Treaty on the Functioning of the EU.

society, and of what they will do in response. The actions they take while in office, and those they opt to avoid, collectively constitute their policies. Putting it another way, if the different pressures on government – such as public opinion, economic change, and external influences – are the inputs into the political process, then policies are the outputs.

Policies exist at many different levels, from the local community to towns, cities, counties, states, and even at the multinational and international levels. Policies are adopted and pursued not just by governments, but by political parties, the media, lobbies, and individual government institutions. Within every policy community there are multiple sub-communities with their own separate and often conflicting sets of policy interests, and this is no less true at the EU level than at the state level; European policy is influenced by international pressures and the demands of non-European states, the major EU institutions (such as the Commission, Parliament, and the Council of Ministers), the directorates-general within the Commission, the regional policy interests of groups of member states with shared goals, the national policy interests pursued by individual member states, and the cross-national policies pursued by groups with shared interests, such as the environmental lobby, farmers, corporations, workers, labour unions, and parties within the European Parliament.

The details of EU policies can be found in several places, beginning with the broad goals outlined in the treaties (the so-called primary rules), the body of several thousand laws adopted by the EU (secondary rules), and the multitude of action programmes, strategies, declarations, green papers, and white papers issued by EU institutions (tertiary rules). But this implies that policy is always formal, which it is not – policy is often made up on the fly in response to crises and emergencies. Wallace (1990:54–5) offers a good working definition of the difference between formal and informal actions: the formal involve the deliberate actions taken by policy makers to create and adjust rules, to establish and work through common institutions, to regulate, encourage, or inhibit social and economic flows, and to pursue common policies, while informal integration consists of patterns of interaction that develop without the intervention of deliberate government decisions, following the dynamic of markets, technology, communications, and social exchange, or the influence of mass movements. He also distinguishes between proactive and reactive integration, the former having deliberate and explicit political aims, while the latter reacts to economic and social change.

If all EU member states had similar political agendas, similar economic and social structures, similar levels of wealth and productivity, and the same sets of standards and regulations, integration would be relatively straightforward and would lean towards the formal and the proactive. However; the member states have different structures, policies, and levels of wealth, so they approach integration from different perspectives. Concerned with avoiding a multi-speed Europe, national leaders have often had to react to the unforeseen effects of integration, and so have found themselves being driven by informal pressures. For example, while the process of integration has been focused on harmonizing standards, laws, and regulations, it has also obliged European leaders in some areas to agree to proceed through mutual recognition (if something is good enough for one state, it is good enough for them all).

The influences that create and impact policies at the national level are many and complex, but at the level of the EU those complexities are compounded, coming from sources that are internal and external to the EU institutions, formal and informal, predictable and unpredictable, expected and unexpected, and structured and unstructured. They include the following:

- *Treaty obligations.* The treaties outline the general goals and principles of European integration, as well as some of the more specific tasks and roles of the EU institutions. So, for example, Maastricht said that the general goals of the EU were (among others) to 'promote economic and social progress ... the strengthening of economic and social cohesion ... [and] to assert its identity on the international scene'. These are broad and ambiguous goals, but they set the foundations for policy, which must be turned into specific actions, mainly in the form of new laws.
- *Pressures to harmonize.* The need to bring national policies into alignment has been central to reducing the economic and social differences among member states, and to ensuring the smooth functioning of the single market. It accounted, for example, for most of the early initiatives on environmental policy, designed to remove the barriers to the single market created by different environmental standards.
- *Legislative pressures.* Policy is impacted by the requirements or assumptions built into EU law. This is certainly the case with laws that include an obligation for amendment or review after a specified period of time, and is particularly true of the EU's framework directives, which set general goals with the assumption that more laws – known as daughter directives – will be developed later that will provide more detail and focus.
- *Policy evolution and spillover.* Policy is rarely static, and the principles and goals of EU policy are constantly redefined as greater understanding emerges about the causes and effects of problems, as technological developments offer new options for addressing old problems, as problems with existing policies demand adjustments and new approaches, as the balance of interests changes within the member states, and as the political, economic, and social priorities of European integration evolve.
- *Institutional pressures.* While the Commission has a monopoly over the development of new proposals for policy and law, it is subject to various formal and informal pressures, including suggestions from the European Council regarding the broad goals of EU policy, 'invitations' from the European Parliament (EP) and the Council of Ministers to develop new proposals, suggestions or demands from the EP or the Council of Ministers for changes in Commission proposals, and the impact of rulings by the Court of Justice on the content and nature of EU law.
- *International agreements.* The EU as a unit has signed numerous international treaties on behalf of the member states, most of which

impose specific policy obligations on the EU. This means the development of new laws and policies to respond to those obligations, and the development of common positions taken during negotiations on the progress of implementation.

- *Political initiatives.* Individual national leaders, working alone or in combination with others, have always been at the core of important policy initiatives. Thus the early steps on building a European foreign policy came out of a decision by European leaders to organize regular meetings among the foreign ministers of the member states, much of the headway on security policy in the late 1990s was made because of initiatives taken by Tony Blair of Britain and Jacques Chirac of France (see Chapter 9), and it was agreement among European leaders in early 2007 that led to the revival of the defunct constitutional treaty as the Treaty of Lisbon.

- *Public opinion.* Although the EU is often described as elitist and undemocratic, neither the EU institutions nor the leaders of the member states have been able to ignore public opinion. It has been important, for example, in the development and agreement of new treaties, and even if voters have not always been able to express their opinions through national referendums, the unwillingness of governments to hold referendums has itself drawn attention to public opinion and has often sparked vigorous debates about Europe.

- *Internal pressures.* As integration has proceeded, so problems have presented themselves that have been internal to Europe, common to multiple member states, and potential barriers to successful integration. These have included, for example, ongoing concerns about unemployment, which have exercised EU governments for many years, or the need to monitor the movement of criminals around the EU, which has been behind an active programme of policy responses in the field of justice and home affairs.

- *External pressures.* Problems and demands have also come from outside the EU, and have often demanded the concerted and united response of all member states. In addition to the sometimes obvious and sometimes more subtle impact of pressures from the EU's major allies (such as the United States) and its competitors (such as China), policy has also responded to changes in the economic climate (at no time was this more true than during the economic downturn of 2007–10), to trade imbalances and disputes, or to disagreements with other countries.

- *Emergencies or crises.* These have been a part of the policy calendar from the beginning, ranging from the collapse of the European Defence Community to the empty-chair crisis, the dispute over the budget in the 1980s, the EU's failures in the Balkans in the 1990s, the 2003 fallout with the United States over Iraq, the collapse of the constitutional treaty, and the problems in the eurozone in 2009–11.

Each event has been followed by much hand-wringing, but has also ultimately drawn new attention to policy needs.

These multiple influences have created a complex and sometimes disorderly policy environment in which it is often difficult or impossible to be sure of the provenance of policy initiatives, or of the key actors involved in the development and implementation of policy initiatives.

The policy cycle

In an ideal world, public policy would be developed rationally, problems would be prioritized, options would be carefully researched and weighed, spending would be carefully planned, and the best solutions would be implemented, monitored, and evaluated. But modern society is too complex to allow a meaningful cost-benefit analysis of the options available, political pressures skew the outcomes of policy, and studies of policy routinely emphasize the scarcity of real organization. The result is that policy is often driven by compromise and opportunism, and – in the words of a classic 1959 study of policy (Lindblom) – is often a matter of muddling through from one problem to another. In an attempt to impose some order on the complexity, it is common to approach policy analysis using a process model involving a cycle of actions. This implies that there is much more order to the policy process than exists in reality (see Young, 2010), but at least it offers a guide through the maze.

Problem identification and agenda-setting

Before a policy choice can be made, there must be political agreement on the existence and definition of a problem, and a decision must be made to add that problem to the list of policy concerns that are considered part of the remit of government. In a democracy, the development of the policy agenda is normally driven by a combination of the individual preferences and priorities of elected officials and their advisers, the struggles for power among political institutions (mainly the executive and the legislature), and the combined pressures of public opinion and media attention.

To the extent that there is a European agenda (see Peters, 2001), it is formed and driven mainly by the European Council, which outlines broad policy goals and occasionally sparks new policy initiatives. It is the Council, for example, that has been behind the decision to develop every new treaty since the Single European Act, that has issued major declarations on international crises, that has reached key decisions on EU institutional changes, and that has given new momentum to EU

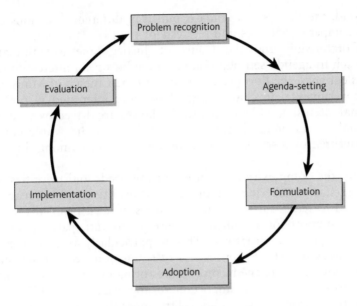

Figure 6.1 *The policy cycle*

foreign policy. But it must be remembered that the 27 prime ministers, chancellors, and presidents who meet as the Council are ultimately national political leaders, and that they are torn between pursuing national and European interests. In this they are subject to numerous pressures: treaty obligations, recommendations from consultative committees, the initiatives of other leaders, tensions among member states, the need to harmonize laws, international treaty requirements, discussion papers, specialist reports, and changes in the wider world.

There are at least three important differences between agenda-setting at the national and at the European level. First, elected leaders at the national level often add issues to the policy agenda in response to public and media opinion, or – more cynically – in order to win legislative votes or build support for the next national election. At the EU level, however, there is no European 'public' in the sense that there is a large body of citizens demanding change at the European level. Furthermore, there is no elected European government that is constantly looking to its standing in the polls or to the outcome of an election. Thus policy is heavily driven by pressures internal and external to the process of European integration, and by leaders rather than by citizens. This leads to the common – and sometimes reasonable – assertion that the EU policy process is elitist. But this is a charge that applies equally to policy making at the national level (see Dye and Zeigler, 2000).

Second, the European agenda is pulled in different directions by the often competing motives and interests of the EU institutions. So while the Commission and the Court of Justice take a supranational approach to agenda-setting, looking to the European interest (however that is defined), the European Council and the Council of Ministers are intergovernmental in character (and so more interested in protecting national interests), while Parliament's choices are driven by voter interests and the ideological leanings of MEPs, and the whole edifice is underwritten by a struggle for power and influence among the institutions.

Third, the complexity and variety of the needs and priorities of the member states make it more difficult to identify pan-European problems and to tease out the common causes of such problems, to build political support for a unified response, or to anticipate the potential effects of policy alternatives. This is particularly true in regard to policy issues on which there is less of a European consensus, such as foreign policy, where the member states bring different values and priorities to bear. It is also important to appreciate that while we may talk of the 'European agenda', it is little more than the accumulation of narrower agendas being pursued by all the actors with an interest in the European policy process. Each of these in their own way will limit, redirect, or broaden the cumulative policy interests of the European Union.

Formulation and adoption

Once a problem or a need has been recognized, a response must be formulated and adopted. In the case of the EU, this usually involves debating the options at meetings of the European Council, developing proposals for new laws and new budgetary allocations in the Commission, drafting work programmes or action programmes, publishing discussion papers, or making public announcements. Whichever response is chosen, it might be reasonable to expect that some kind of methodical analysis would be conducted in which the causes and dimensions of a problem are studied and all the options and their relative costs and benefits are considered before the most efficient policy alternative is chosen (see Dye, 2002:17). However, this rational policy model rarely works in practice, because understanding of the value preferences of Europeans is incomplete, as is the information about policy alternatives and about costs and benefits. As a result, most EU policy is designed and applied incrementally, intuitively, or in response to emergencies or changes in public opinion.

In the member states, policy is usually formulated by the executive, the legislature, or government departments. In the case of the EU, the major focus of policy formulation is the Commission, which not only has a monopoly on the drafting of new laws and policies, but also has a pivotal position as a broker of interests and a forum for the exchange of policy ideas (Mazey and Richardson, 1997). The Commission does not function in a policy vacuum, however, and its proposals are routinely amended as a result of lobbying by interest groups or national governments, as a response to internal and external emergencies and crises, and as they are discussed by consultative committees, the Council of Ministers, and the European Parliament. An approach used with increased frequency since the early 1990s has been the open method of coordination, which eschews the 'hard' setting of binding legal norms in favour of a 'soft' approach based on cooperation, reciprocal learning, and the voluntary participation of member states (see Heidenreich and Bischoff, 2008). According to the Commission's own calculations, about 30 per cent of its proposals come in response to the international obligations of the EU, about 20–25 per cent come as a follow-up to resolutions or initiatives from the other European institutions, about 20 per cent involve the updating of existing EU laws, and 10–15 per cent arise out of obligations under the treaties or secondary legislation (European Commission, 2001b:6).

Once a new law or policy has been proposed by the European Commission, it must formally be adopted before it goes into effect. The final say over adoption comes out of a complex interplay involving Parliament, Coreper, the Council of Ministers, the Commission, and the member states, with the Court of Justice providing legal interpretation when necessary. As we saw in Chapter 4, changes introduced by the Single European Act and by the Maastricht, Amsterdam, and Nice treaties have provided new powers to Parliament, which – in most areas – has now become a 'co-legislature' with the Council of Ministers.

Implementation

Arguably the most important step in the policy cycle is implementation, the point at which the goals and objectives of government result – or fail to result – in real change for the governed. Unfortunately, implementation has so far proved a relatively weak part of the EU policy process, and several structural problems have made it difficult always to be sure about the extent to which EU laws and policies are actually implemented in the manner in which they were intended by their authors, or make a difference in the lives of Europeans. This has been a matter of growing concern for EU institutions, within which there has been an expanding debate on how to improve implementation. The Commission itself blames nonconformity between national and EU law on the existence of two or more legal systems in several member states (notably those with a federal structure), and the difficulties that arise in amending national laws because of the effect they have on provisions in a variety of other areas, such as agriculture, transport, and industry (European Commission, various years).

Within member states, implementation is normally left to bureaucracies. However, the bureaucracy of the EU – the Commission – is small and has no powers directly to enforce European law, and so must work instead to ensure implementation through national bureaucracies. The Commission occasionally convenes meetings of national representatives and experts to monitor progress, and also carries out its own investigations using its contacts in national government agencies. Most of the time, however, the Commission must rely on other sources, including the governments of member states (who will occasionally report on other governments that are not being as aggressive as themselves in implementing law), whistleblowing by interest groups, the media, and private citizens, the European Parliament (which since 1983 has required that the Commission submit annual reports on the failure of member states fully to implement Community legislation), and the European ombudsman (who has the power to conduct inquiries into charges of bad administration against Community institutions, except the Court of Justice and Court of First Instance).

In cases where implementation is slow, the Commission has three options available to it. First, it can issue a Letter of Formal Notice giving a member state time (usually about two months) to comply. Second, it can issue a Reasoned Opinion explaining why it feels there may be a violation. Finally, it can take the member state (or an individual, corporation, or other institution if they are the responsible parties) to the European Court of Justice for failure to fulfil its obligations. The Commission also adds pressure by publicizing progress on implementation; the data on the number of time member states are taken to the Court of Justice for failures to fulfil their legal obligations have shown over time that Greece and Italy have the worst records (see Figure 6.2), a reflection of their relatively slow and inefficient bureaucracies.

Evaluation

The final stage in the policy cycle is to determine whether or not a law or policy has worked. This is difficult unless specific goals were set from the outset and unless national bureaucrats report accurately to the Commission on the results of policies. In many cases it is almost impossible to know which actions resulted in which consequences or whether the results are being accurately reported. This is particularly true in the case of the EU, where it is difficult always to distinguish the effects of national and local government actions from those of EU law. Nonetheless, evaluation in the EU is conducted by a combination of the Commission, the Council of Ministers, the European Council, the

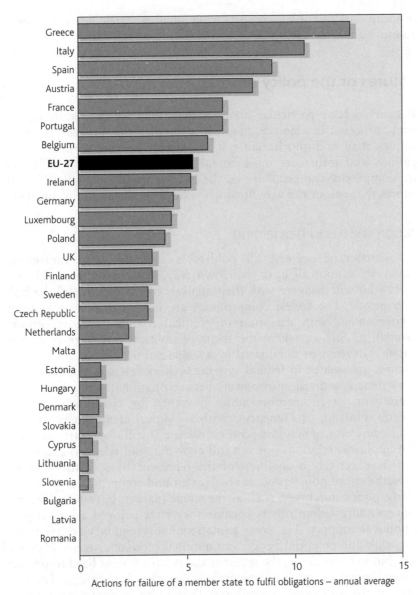

Actions for failure of a member state to fulfil obligations – annual average

Figures calculated by author from data in Annual Report of European Court of Justice, http://curia.europa.eu (retrieved January 2010). Figures show annual average for each member state since joining EEC/EU.

Figure 6.2   *Infringements of EU Law, 1952–2008*

European Parliament, and reports from member states, interest groups, and individuals.

Features of the policy process

All societies have particular qualities that influence the nature of the policy process. In democracies, for example, the process is more complex than in authoritarian systems, simply because so many more opinions and influences must be taken into consideration. With its own complexity and peculiarities, the EU has a unique combination of features that colour the way in which policy is made and implemented.

Compromise and bargaining

In a democratic society, all politics is a matter of compromise. Individuals cannot all have their own way, because there are always others who will disagree with their analysis of a problem and the best prescriptions. The fewest compromises are needed in unitary systems of government with majoritarian political parties (such as Britain, Portugal, or Spain), where the focus of political power rests with a national government dominated by a single political party. More compromises are needed in federal systems such as Belgium and Germany, where there is a division of powers between national and sub-national government, or in member states governed by coalitions (such as Bulgaria, Finland, or Hungary). With a political arrangement such as the EU, however, where the power structure is still not clearly defined, where political relationships are still evolving, and where the 'government' is effectively a coalition of the representatives of the member states, the entire policy process revolves around compromise.

Some policy initiatives, such as the single market, have been less difficult to address than others because they have enjoyed a high degree of political support. The costs to national sovereignty were relatively low, while the potential benefits to national economies were relatively high. But in other areas, the member states have fought hard to protect national interests, forcing sometimes unhappy compromises. The creation of the Common Agricultural Policy, for example, was based around compromise, with France winning concessions on agriculture in return for concessions given to West German industry. Similarly, the negotiations leading up to Maastricht were riddled with compromises and package deals, notably over the timetable for the development of the euro. The adoption of the euro was itself a compromise, with every member state given the option of either joining or not, and the rules on joining – and on managing economies once states were in the eurozone – often fudged (see Chapter 7).

Political games

A major approach to public policy analysis is offered by game theory, which focuses on situations in which two or more actors compete against each other for influence, their positions being influenced by what they think other actors will do. In the process of seeking compromises, runs the argument, politics is typically reduced to a struggle for power and influence, with one person or group trying to win concessions from – or pressing their views on – others. Such struggles take place even in the smallest and most local of human communities, but they are magnified in the EU by its sheer size and by the extent to which member states and institutions compete with each other, unconstrained (so far) by the presence of a constitution. Peters (1992:106–7) describes three sets of interconnected games in the EU:

- A national game among member states trying to extract as much as possible from the EU while giving up as little as possible. This was the case even with the six founding members, but as the EU has expanded in size, so the game has become more complex and intense, because the stakes and the payoffs have been much greater, while the EU has become more politically, economically, and socially diverse.
- A game played out among EU institutions trying to win more power and influence relative to each other. Once just an experiment in combining coal and steel industries, European integration has spilled over into almost every area of policy, and the EU has grown to cover almost all of Europe. As the stakes have been raised, so the EU institutions have jockeyed with each other for a greater role.
- A bureaucratic game in which the directorates-general in the Commission have their own organizational cultures and are competing for policy space. Again, this has been driven in large part by the growing policy responsibilities of the EU, the new resources available to the Commission, and the natural inclination of bureaucracies to justify their importance and to compete for influence.

Multi-speed integration

Jean Monnet was a champion of the Community method, a process by which all the member states would proceed at the same pace and would adopt and implement the same laws and policies (see Lindberg and Scheingold, 1970). But this incorrectly assumed that all the member states would be in agreement on how to proceed, which they never were, and an indication of this has been the advent of what is variously known as 'multi-speed' integration, Europe *à la carte*, variable geometry, or (formally) enhanced cooperation. These are terms for arrangements that either allow a limited number of member states to move ahead with more cooperation in a specific area within EU structure, or to opt out of different elements of European policy. (At a more detailed level, member states can also negotiate derogations, by which they are excused from implementing a particular part of a law or treaty which they have problems, are allowed to apply it differently, or are given a longer deadline.)

Britain was famously allowed to opt out of the Social Charter (see Chapter 8), only 17 member states have so far made the switch to the euro, not all member states have removed border controls as planned under the Schengen Agreement, traditionally neutral states such as Ireland and Finland have preferred not to participate in attempts to build a common European defence policy, and several Eastern European countries were given longer to meet some of the targets on free movement or people, goods, and services, and of the requirements of EU competition law. The Treaty of Amsterdam imposed conditions that limited the scope of the application of enhanced cooperation, while Nice required a minimum of eight member states to take part in any plan, removed the right of each member state to veto the plan, and provided for the possibility of enhanced cooperation in foreign policy. Lisbon provided for its extension to defence matters.

Incrementalism

Policy making in a democratic society is inevitably cautious, because neither public nor political opinion will typically tolerate radical change, and many competing views and interests have to be taken into account. Lacking the time and resources to investigate all the options available, policy makers tend to build on precedent, adjusting and fine-tuning what has gone before rather than bringing about whole-sale change (Lindblom, 1959). This has been particularly true at the European level, driven by concerns over the loss of national sovereignty, the absence of a consensus about the wisdom of European integration, and the need for compromise. The EU has occasionally agreed relatively dramatic policy initiatives (such as the Single European Act, Maastricht, the launch of the euro, and eastern enlargement), but none of these changes have come without much deliberation and debate, and most EU policy making is based on the development and elaboration of existing policies. Because there are so many counterweights and counterbalances in the policy process, member states and EU institutions can rarely take the initiative without conferring first with other member states or EU institutions. For the most ardent supporters of integration, the process has sometimes slowed to a crawl; for eurosceptics, meanwhile, it has usually been moving much too quickly.

Box 6.2   Europeanization

The term *public policy* is often associated with national government responses to national issues, and yet policy is made at many different levels. Of particular interest since the 1970s has been the internationalization of public policy, through which national governments have been influenced by pressures coming out of international relations, most notably by trade and globalization. Nowhere has the process of internationalization gone as far as it has in the EU, where the harmonization of European law and policy has given rise to the phenomenon of Europeanization, which has in turn spawned a large number of new analytical studies of the EU policy process.

Europeanization is usually defined as the process by which laws and policies in the member states have been brought into alignment with EU law and policy. One key set of assessments of Europeanization (Graziano and Vink, 2007:7–8) defines it as 'the domestic adaptation to European regional integration', or the process whereby administrations in the member states adapt to the requirements of EU law and policy, or the process of integration 'feeds back' into national political systems. The changes have seen differences in national laws and regulations being reduced by the agreement of European laws and regulations (see Page, 2003). But it is more than just about laws and policies; it can also be applied to understanding the meaning of 'Europe', to the new opportunities made available to interest groups by changing administrative structures and processes, to the general project of unifying Europe, and even to our understanding of the borders of Europe.

Opinion is divided on just how far the process of Europeanization has gone, and it is not always clear how far the pressures that have led to policy change have been clearly European, as opposed to coming out of initiatives driven by the member states or out of international pressures such as globalization. Opinion is also divided as to whether the concept is all that useful, or whether it has simply become fashionable to employ it. Part of the problem is that there is no universally accepted definition, and it is routinely reinterpreted to fit with the arguments made by individual scholars and analysts. But this is a problem common to most concepts in the social sciences. For now, at least, Europeanization is an important tool for understanding the EU policy world.

Spillover

Critics of the EU have charged that it has tried to become involved in too many policy areas, and that institutions such as the Commission have become too powerful and even somewhat imperious. What they often fail to realize, though, is that the EU institutions have often been driven by forces beyond their control: functionalists have argued that an 'invisible hand' of integration has been at work, the launch of new initiatives often revealing or creating new problems or opportunities, which in turn can lead to pressures for additional supporting initiatives. This policy spillover has been one of the enduring features of policy making in the EU, the prime example coming from efforts to complete the single market. The task of removing barriers to the free movement of people, money, goods, and services could not be achieved either easily or quickly, and involved making many of the adjustments – anticipated or not – that opened up the European market. This meant moving into new areas of policy that were never anticipated by the founding treaties, including social issues, working conditions, and the environment.

This combination of features has created a policy process that is complex, constantly changing, and still not yet fully understood. New attention has been paid by scholars and commentators in the last two decades to trying to better understand the different institutions of the EU, and the EU's activities in specific areas of policy. (Interestingly, there has been an something of inverse relationship between the attention paid to a policy area and its achievements on the ground; thus there have been more studies of foreign and security policy, where the EU record has been mixed, than of agricultural and trade policy, where the impact of the EU has been more substantial.) But there are still few studies of the broader policy process and of the ways in which policy making at the European level has changed the relationship among member states, and between member states and Europe as a whole (for one notable exception, see Richardson, 2006). At least part of the fault for this can be laid at the dominating influence of international relations (IR) theory in attempts to understand the EU. Scholars of IR are not typically interested in public policy, but focus instead on alliances and the balance of power. As the methods, models, and approaches coming out of comparative politics and public policy play a greater role in attempts to understand the EU, so – presumably – will our understanding of the European policy process.

The EU budget

The budget is one of the biggest influences on policy at any level of government, because the choices that a government makes regarding how and where to raise and spend money affect both the policy choices it makes and the effectiveness of the policies it pursues. It is typically less a question of how *much* is raised and spent than of *how* and *where* that money is raised and spent. The revenue and spending of the

European Union is no exception, and the budget has frequently set off controversies that have resulted in member states being at odds with one another and with the EU institutions. The level of controversy is surprising considering the relatively small size of the EU budget: just under €143 billion ($180 billion) in 2011, or just over 1.2 per cent of the combined gross domestic product (GDP) of the member states (or roughly €290 per person in the EU). Furthermore, it must be balanced – unlike the case with many of the member states, there is no EU debt and no budget deficit. Given recent debt and deficit problems in several member states, they could probably stand to learn something from the rules they themselves agreed for the EU budget.

In spite of this, the EU budget has been the source of often heated political battles over the years (see Box 6.3), most centring on the relative amounts given and received by each member state, and on the balance between national contributions and the EU's own resources (independent sources of revenue) (see Laffan and Lindner, 2010:214ff.). To the extent that the EU has had to rely on national contributions, it has been more subject to political leverage by the member states. To the extent that it has been able to develop its own sources of revenue, the EU institutions have been able to build more independence. The accumulation of reforms to the budget has resulted in the structure we find today:

- The budget cannot be greater than 1.24 per cent of the combined GDP of the member states, and cannot be in deficit.
- About 76 per cent of revenues come from national contributions based on national GDP levels, with each member state paying a set amount in proportion to its GDP.
- Revenues from customs duties on imports from non-member states and from agricultural levies account for just under 12 per cent of revenues.
- Just over 11 per cent of revenues come from VAT.

In terms of spending, the EU budget has raised a separate set of political problems. Like almost every budget, EU expenses consist of a combination of mandatory payments over which it has little or no choice (such as agricultural price supports) and discretionary payments (such as spending on regional or energy policy) regarding which there is more flexibility. EU spending is about equally divided between the two:

- In 2011, about 35 per cent of spending went on cohesion policy: development spending on poorer regions of the EU, including spending under the European Social Fund aimed at helping offset the effects of unemployment, and investments in agriculture. The pro-

Box 6.3   Battles over the budget

The European Economic Community – like most international organizations – was originally funded by national contributions. Each member state made a payment roughly in proportion to the size of its population, thus France, Germany, and Italy each contributed 28 per cent of the budget, Belgium and the Netherlands 7.9 per cent, and Luxembourg 0.2 per cent. In an attempt to win more independence for itself, in 1965 the Commission suggested that the revenue from tariffs placed on imports from outside the EC should go directly to the Community, thereby providing it with its own resources. At the same time, Parliament began pushing for more control over the budget as a means of gaining more influence over policy. Charles de Gaulle thought that the Commission already had too much power, and it was these proposals (combined with France's opposition to reform of the Common Agricultural Policy) that led to the 1965 empty-chair crisis when France refused to take part in EEC business (see Dinan, 2004:104–5).

Pressure for budgetary reform persisted regardless, and changes in the early 1970s led to an increase in the proportion of revenues derived from the Community's own resources: customs duties, levies on agricultural imports, and a small proportion of value-added tax (VAT). But there were two problems with this formula: it took little account of the relative size of the economies of member states, and the amounts raised were insufficient to meet the needs of the Community, which was not allowed to run a deficit or to borrow to meet shortfalls. By the early 1980s, the Community was nearly bankrupt, and it was obvious that either revenue had to be increased or spending had to be restructured or cut.

portion of EU expenditures in this area has almost tripled since the mid-1970s.
- About 31 per cent of spending went to agricultural subsidies, and a further 11 per cent to rural development, supports to fisheries, and the environment. Thanks to reforms in agricultural policy (see Chapter 7), the proportion of EU spending that goes to agriculture has fallen substantially from its peak during the 1970s, when it accounted for nearly 75 per cent of the budget.
- Just under 6 per cent went to administrative costs for the EU institutions. Critics of the EU routinely and misguidedly argue that the EU institutions spend far more than they actually do, and this has become one of the great myths of euroscepticism. Recent Eurobarometer polls have found that between one-quarter and one-third of Europeans think that administrative overheads are the single biggest item on the EU budget.

Matters came to a head over the insistence by the then new British prime minister, Margaret Thatcher, that Britain's contributions be recalculated. Arguing that Britain bore an unfair share of the Community budget, and received an inadequate amount in return, she generated alarm at her first European Council appearance in 1979 by bluntly telling her Community partners that she wanted a reformation of the budget (expressed colourfully but inaccurately as 'I want my money back'). Her campaign continued through the early 1980s, tied to her demands for a reform of the Common Agricultural Policy. After much acrimonious debate, a complex deal was reached in 1984 by which Britain's contributions were cut, its rebates were increased, and the overall budget was recalculated in preparation for the accession of Spain and Portugal.

The long-term effect of the changes has been to make the richer states the biggest net contributors, and poorer states the biggest net recipients. When the Commission published its Agenda 2000 proposals in 1997, aimed at preparing for eastward enlargement and reform of the Common Agricultural Policy and the regional funds, it stirred up a new hornets' nest of debate: several countries that were net contributors – including Austria, Germany, the Netherlands, and Sweden – began pressing for a re-examination of the budget, suggesting that contributions be capped at 0.3 per cent of national income. This caused particular nervousness among net recipients such as Greece and Spain, which were concerned that they would have to take on a greater burden of funding rebates.

- Most of the balance (about €9 billion, or 7 per cent of the total) went to all the other policy areas in which the EU was active, including external policies, transport, energy, consumer policy, research and development, and education.

The EU budget is only partly a reflection of the policy areas in which the member states have agreed to transfer competence to the EU institutions. Looking at the figures, one could easily conclude that Europe was not much more than an exercise in social, agricultural, and regional development. But it must be remembered that much of the work of the EU involves little or no operational cost; for example, the entire single market programme has been based largely on the development of new laws and policies. The same is true of competition policy, trade matters, and fiscal policy. It must also be remembered that the member states have their own domestic budgets to invest in agriculture

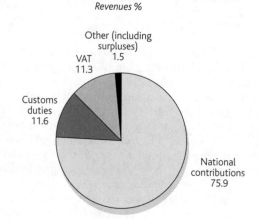

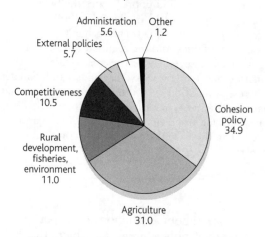

Figure 6.3   *The European Union budget*

Data from European Commission at http://ec.europa.eu/budget (retrieved August 2010).

and in the kind of development supported by EU cohesion policy. So, in this sense, the EU budget is little more than a complement to the work of the member states.

Conclusions

While debates rage about the powers and nature of the European Union, with both support for and resistance to the expansion of EU powers and responsibilities, there is no question that its member states have ceded powers to the EU and now have less policy independence than they did even twenty years ago. Integration has changed the relationship among EU member states at several levels: there has been a reduction in social differences, a harmonization of standards, laws, and regulations, and removal of the physical and fiscal barriers that have differentiated the member states from one another.

There is also an emerging consensus that cooperation in a variety of other areas makes better sense than independent action, which can lead to unnecessary competition and duplication of effort. It is still too early to talk about a federal relationship among the member states, and between them and the EU institutions, but the trend is undoubtedly in that direction – to the alarm of eurosceptics. Several levels of government are being created, all with independent powers. How far European cooperation will go depends on how we choose to define subsidiarity, but while this is moving higher up the agenda of EU negotiations, the definition of which issues are best dealt with at the level of the member state and which at the level of Europe remains fluid.

The member states still have a large measure of control over domestic policy, in a wide variety of important areas, from foreign policy to defence policy, tax policy, education, criminal justice, and health care. Compared, for example, to the American case, where the states now have only residual responsibilities in a modest selection of areas, and whose independence from national government in Washington, DC is largely symbolic, the member states of the EU are still powerful, independent actors. This is unlikely to last indefinitely, however. Internal political and economic pressures have meant a gradual surrender of powers by the member states, a steady accumulation of responsibilities by the EU institutions, and – increasingly – the sense that Europe is governed both from Brussels and from 27 national capitals.

External pressures are also bound to continue to tighten the definition of Europe. Most of the rest of the world has not yet woken up to the implications of European integration, and to the idea that the 27 member states of the EU can and should be seen as a political and economic unit, that is exerting its global influence ever more effectively. Non-Europeans still treat Europeans mainly as citizens of individual member states, but this is slowly changing. As it does, it will give Europeans themselves a greater sense that they can be both European *and* British or Italian or Greek or Czech or Lithuanian. This in turn will give a tighter definition to the concept of Europe.

Chapter 7

Economic Policy

Economic matters have dominated the life and work of the European Union. Beginning with the initial experiment in pooling coal and steel production, and moving through the customs union, efforts to achieve exchange rate stability, the building of the single market, the switch to the euro, and efforts to deal with the financial crises of 2007–11, the EU agenda has been driven since the beginning by matters involving trade, tariffs, markets, currencies, and competition. It has only been since the 1990s that the agenda has broadened to include a wider variety of policy issues, from external relations to the environment.

The priority given to economic integration was made clear in Articles 2 and 3 of the Treaty of Rome, which listed the goals of establishing a common market in which there would be no barriers to the free movement of people, services, and capital; the establishment of a customs union in which all obstacles to trade among EEC members would be removed and a common external tariff agreed for all goods coming into the EEC; common policies on trade, agriculture, and transport; a policy on competition; and efforts to bring the economic policies of the member states into alignment. The customs union was completed without much fanfare in 1968, but non-tariff barriers to trade among the member states persisted, including variations in technical standards and quality controls, different health and safety standards, and different rates of indirect taxation. Prospects for the single market seemed to move beyond reach in the mid-1970s as recession encouraged member states to protect their national markets. And early efforts to stabilize exchange rates as a precursor to eventual monetary union were undermined by international financial turbulence.

By the 1980s it had become clear that urgent action was needed to reverse the EC's relative economic decline, and a boost had to be given to the single market programme in order to respond to foreign competition. A first step was taken in 1985 with the signing of the Schengen Agreement, offering a fast track for the removal of border controls. In 1986 came the signature of the Single European Act, aimed at removing the final barriers to the completion of the single market by the end of 1992. Finally, the attempts to build exchange rate stability led in 1999 to the creation of the euro, which finally replaced national currencies in 12 countries in 2002.

148

The changes wrought by these ventures have redefined the character of Europe and the policy reach of the EU. There is now all but free movement of people, money, goods, and services. The EU's external security regime has expanded in response to concerns about the dismantling of internal borders. European corporations have engaged in an aggressive programme of cross-border mergers and acquisitions, while the Commission has kept a close watch for attempts to circumvent policies on competition. The EU has built a system of trans-European networks aimed at integrating the transport, energy supply, and telecommunications sectors of the member states. But the results have been mixed. The EU is the world's wealthiest marketplace and its biggest trading power, but efforts to make the EU the most dynamic and competitive knowledge-based economy in the world have fallen short, the 2007–10 global economic downturn had consequences for the entire region, and troubles in the eurozone in 2009–11 emphasized the many remaining challenges to developing a workable set of economic policies for the EU.

Completing the single market

In February 1985, the European Council agreed that it was time to refocus on one of the original goals of European integration: the completion of a single market. At the core of this project – which had been so central to the identity and the purpose of the Community that it was long known interchangeably as the Common Market – were the 'four freedoms', or the free movement of:

- *People*: legal residents of EU member states should be allowed to live and work in any other member state and have their professional qualifications recognized.
- *Money*: currency and capital should be allowed to flow freely across borders, and EU residents should be able to use financial services in any member state.
- *Goods*: businesses should be able to sell their products throughout the EU, and consumers should be free to buy those products in any member state.
- *Services*: architects, bankers, financial advisers, lawyers, and all other providers of services should be able to operate across borders.

In spite of its political prominence, little progress was at first made on the single market, mainly because member states continued to protect national markets and corporations, and worked independently on problems such as high unemployment, low investment, and slow growth. National monopolies in transport and communications more often bought services and products from local sources rather than seeking more competitive options outside their borders. Technical standards varied across the Community, adding a potent block to trade in merchandise. Member states had laws requiring foreign firms active within their borders to buy goods with local content, and a host of border and customs controls persisted, along with varying rates of value-added tax (VAT, a form of consumption tax) (see Neal, 2007:129).

When Jacques Delors became president of the Commission in 1985, movement on the single market was at the top of his agenda. Trade and industry commissioner Lord Cockfield was charged with drawing up a White Paper outlining the changes that needed to be made (European Commission, 1985), which in turn became the basis of the Single European Act (SEA), signed in February 1986 and coming into force in July 1987. Its core goal was the removal, by the end of 1992, of the remaining non-tariff barriers to the single market, which took three main forms.

First, there were physical barriers, the most obvious of which were customs and border checks. Member states still controlled the movement of people and maintained customs and immigration checks that were not only expensive, inconsistent, and time-consuming, but interfered with the free flow of people, goods, and services. The checks also posed a psychological barrier to integration, reminding Europeans that they still lived in a region of independent states. A critical step in the removal of border controls came in June 1985 when France, West Germany, and the Benelux countries signed the Schengen Agreement, named for the town in Luxembourg near which it was signed. Providing for the fast-track removal of controls, it came into force in 1995 and was incorporated into the EU treaties by the 1997 Treaty of Amsterdam. Other than Britain and Ireland, every member state has now signed and implemented Schengen, along with Iceland, Norway, and Switzerland. Britain has cited concerns about security and its special problems and needs as an island state, while Ireland has a passport union with Britain.

Second, there were fiscal barriers, notably different levels of indirect taxation, such as excise duties and VAT. These distorted competition, created artificial price differences, and posed a handicap to trade. For example, different levels of excise duties – reflecting different levels of national concern about human health – meant that French smokers in the 1980s paid nearly twice as much for cigarettes as those in Spain, Irish smokers four times as much, and Danish smokers six times as much. Agreement was reached in the 1990s on an EU-wide VAT system, but less progress has been made towards harmonizing corporation tax or the setting of minimum withholding tax on savings.

Finally, technical barriers came in the form mainly of thousands of different technical regulations and safety, health, environmental, and consumer protection standards (Neal, 2007:131). Early attempts to develop Community-wide standards proved time-consuming and tedious, and did little to discourage the common image of interfering Eurocrats. Three breakthroughs helped clear many bureaucratic and political hurdles: a 1979 decision by the Court of Justice established the principle of mutual recognition (if a product met local standards in one country, it could not be barred from another); a 1983 mutual information directive requiring member states to tell the Commission and the other member states if they planned to develop new domestic technical regulations; and a 'new approach' to technical regulation introduced by the Cockfield report, whereby instead of agreements being reached on every rule and regulation, laws would be passed setting general objectives, the details of which could then be drawn up by private standards institutes, such as the European Standardization Committee (CEN) and the European Confederation of Posts and Telecommunications Administrations (ETSI).

Effects of the single market

The Single European Act was the first new treaty since Rome in 1957, and not only accelerated the completion of the single market, but also changed the lives of every European, making economic integration more real to millions of people. And compared to what was to come later in the way of new treaties, it was also relatively non-controversial and widely welcomed. The effects have since been felt across a wide spectrum of activities, and have moved the EU into several new areas of policy activity.

Freedom of movement

The most immediate and practical effect of the single market on ordinary Europeans has been freedom of movement. With limited conditions, almost any legal resident of an EU member state can now live and work in any other EU member state, open a bank account, take out a mortgage, transfer unlimited amounts of capital, get an education, and both vote and run in local and European elections. Anyone who is a citizen of an EU member state can freely enter any other member state and stay for up to three months, and the most that they will be asked to do is to present a valid identity card or passport. For stays of more than six months, they must either have a job, have sufficient resources and health insurance to ensure that they do not become a burden on local social services, be a student engaged in a formal course of education, or be a family member of someone who meets one of these three criteria. No visas or residence permits are required, although new arrivals may be required to register with local authorities. After five years of legal residence, citizens of other EU member states can apply for permanent residence in the new country. Rights of entry and residence can only be limited or denied on the grounds of public policy, public security, or public health, and not for economic reasons. There are greater restrictions on residents of Eastern Europe, because of concerns about migration, but these are easing with time.

Migration historically has been driven by economic and political factors – people looking for better jobs, or escaping persecution and instability. In the case of the EU, flows were initially from south to north, with workers looking for higher-paying jobs and then sending for their families to join them. Immigration flows today are more complex, with many people moving not because they must but because they choose to. They may be looking to live in a new culture or a better climate, or to make a new start in a new country. With the removal of most of the physical and legal barriers to movement, those that remain are mainly psychological or linguistic (see Chapter 5). The opening of internal borders was accompanied by pressures to greater interstate cooperation on police and judicial matters, but while Maastricht spoke of the need to create 'an area of freedom, security and justice', there was political resistance because the goal touched on issues that were firmly the responsibility of states, and seemed to pose another challenge to national sovereignty (Lavenex, 2010). With pressures growing to deal with terrorism, applications for asylum, and illegal immigration, policy developments – when they came – came remarkably quickly (Monar, 2001) (see Box 7.1).

Trans-European networks

A key element in the successful operation of markets is integrated infrastructure. Realizing this, the EU has been working on the development of trans-European networks (TENs) aimed at integrating the different transport, energy supply, and telecommunications systems of the member states. Until 1987, harmonization of the transport sector was one of the great failures of the single market: little of substance had been done to deal with problems such as an airline industry split along national lines, time-consuming cross-border checks on trucks, national systems of motorways that did not connect with each other, air-traffic control systems using 20 different operating systems and 70 computer programming languages, and telephone lines incapable of carrying advanced electronic communications. Three developments have since made a difference.

Box 7.1   Justice and home affairs

There had been cooperation in Europe on dealing with terrorism and the cross-border movement of criminals as early as the 1960s and 1970s, but a new perspective was created by developments in the single market in the 1990s, the hands of governments ultimately being forced by the 2001 terrorist attacks in the United States. There is still no single policy on justice and home affairs (JHA), but it was incorporated by Lisbon into the mainstream of EU policy concerns, and there has been much institutional, legal, and procedural progress:

- Europol (the European Police Office) became fully operational in 1998, encouraging cross-border police cooperation.
- In the same year, a new European judicial network was charged with improving judicial cooperation by linking contact points in the member states. In 2002 it was strengthened with a new Judicial Cooperation Unit (Eurojust) set up to improve investigations and prosecutions involving two or more member states.
- In 2004 the Hague Programme listed ten priorities for EU policy, including a comprehensive response to terrorism, the integrated management of the EU's external borders, and the creation of a common asylum procedure.
- The European Arrest Warrant was introduced in 2004, allowing member states to request the arrest of a criminal in another state and his/her transfer to the issuing state within 90 days. It was joined in 2008 by a European evidence warrant designed to standardize methods for obtaining documents, data, and other evidence in cross-border cases.
- In 2009 the EU Blue Card (modelled on the US Green Card) was established as a single work and residence permit for skilled migrants.

The remaining challenges are substantial. Terrorism has been a headline problem in Europe since the activities of separatist and anarchist groups picked up speed in the 1970s, achieving new prominence with the added threat of Islamic extremism. The attractions of the massive European marketplace have proved irresistible to immigrants from North Africa and the Middle East, many of whom have had to use illegal means to enter the EU. Asylum applications have also grown dramatically in the wake of wars or ethnic unrest in the Middle East and many parts of Africa; according to the UN High Commissioner for Refugees (UNHCR); the EU received nearly 290,000 asylum claims in 2007–09, or two and a half times as many as those made to the US and Canada.

First, there has been a dramatic increase in tourism. In spite of concerns about terrorism and the overcrowding of its most popular attractions, Europe is the biggest tourist destination in the world; it captures about 60 per cent of the world tourist trade, with France and Spain being the two biggest tourist destinations, and Italy, Britain, and Germany all ranked in the top ten (World Tourism Organization website, 2010). Tourism and travel in 2010 employed about 22.2 million Europeans (about 10 per cent of the workforce in the EU), and contributed nearly $2 trillion to GDP, or 9.5 per cent of the total (World Travel and Tourism Council website, 2010). Travel has helped break down prejudices, made Europeans more familiar with each other, and encouraged greater cooperation on transportation by increasing the demand for cheap and easy access.

Second, rail transport has been revitalized as a cost-efficient and environmentally friendly alternative to road and air transport. The EU has plans to develop a 35,000-km high-speed train (HST) network connecting Europe's major cities, the way being led by France with its high-speed TGV, which needs special new track, and Germany with its ICE network, which can use existing track. With trains travelling at 200–300 kph (some of them with coaches finished to luxurious standards), the HST system has cut travel times considerably. Investments have been made along the way in building the tunnels and bridges needed to ensure uninterrupted travel: the completion in 1994 of the $15-billion Eurotunnel under the channel between Britain and France, in 1998 of road/rail bridges linking Denmark and Sweden, and in 2000 of the Øresund Bridge between Denmark and Sweden, were important pieces in the jigsaw.

Third, there has been pressure for the development of energy-supply networks, growing out of a combination of plans for a better integrated and interconnected internal market for gas and electricity supply, for greater liberalization of that market, and for addressing the problems connected with the EU's heavy dependence on natural gas imports from Russia (which supplies about a quarter of the EU's needs). Much of the latter comes via pipelines that run through Ukraine, which has twice in recent years been in disputes with Russia over payments, and has diverted some of the gas supply destined for the EU. When Russia cut the supply in retaliation in 2008, it was also cut off to more than a dozen other European countries. Plans are currently under way to build a supply pipeline direct from Russia to Germany via the Baltic Sea, and another from Russia to the Balkans via the Black Sea.

The European Commission has a programme aimed at improving transport links within the EU; €330 billion is projected to be spent in the period 2007–13 alone, involving the building of 70,000 km of railway track (including 22,000 km of new and upgraded track for

HSTs), and 15,000 km of new roads, mainly on the outer edges of the EU. Among the priority projects are high-speed rail links between Berlin and Palermo, between Paris and London, and across southwest and eastern Europe; transport links between Portugal/Spain and the rest of Europe; a Nordic triangle rail/road axis; rail and motorway projects in Eastern Europe; new motorways for Greece; and a 1,400-km Ireland–UK–Benelux road link. Plans are also afoot to encourage freight to be moved away from Europe's congested roads and highways to rail and water transport, and to integrate road, rail, water, and air transport networks.

The EU also has plans to develop independence of the US-operated Global Positioning System (GPS) by developing an alternative global navigation satellite system known as Galileo. GPS was developed by the United States mainly for military purposes, and because the US reserves the right to limit its signal strength, or to close public access during times of conflict, there are clear incentives for the EU to develop an alternative. Galileo is designed for civilian use and is intended to be compatible with GPS, while being capable of operating autonomously. Several non-EU countries have joined the project, including China and India, and there has been talk of several others joining in the future, including Australia, Brazil, Canada, Japan, Mexico, and Russia. Hopes of having it operational by 2010 proved overly optimistic, however: delays arose out of a failure to agree a public–private funding partnership, only one test satellite was in orbit by 2007 and only four of the projected 30 satellites needed had been ordered. It is currently scheduled for completion by 2014.

Liberalization of air travel

One of the most notable changes brought about by the single market has been the loosening of regulations on air transport (see Armstrong and Bulmer, 1998: ch. 7). Because most European states are too small to support a significant domestic industry, the majority of air traffic in Europe is international. Until the 1980s, most European countries had state-owned national carriers – Air France, Lufthansa, Alitalia, and others – which played an influential role in making national air transport policy, leaving air transport highly regulated and expensive; it was sometimes cheaper to fly from one European city to another via the United States rather than direct. Changes began in the mid-1980s when the Thatcher government privatized British Airways and negotiated bilateral agreements with several other EU member states. Meanwhile, the European Civil Aviation Conference recommended liberalization, as did a number of national and European interest groups, and the idea was incorporated into the Cockfield report. Three packages of laws and regulations worked their way through the EU institutions in

1987–92, substantially opening up and restructuring the air transport market.

In recent years there has been an increase in the number of international airline alliances (resulting in reduced costs, combined ticketing, and route consolidation), new pressure for airlines to merge (leading, for example, to the merger in 2003 between Dutch KLM and Air France and another in 2011 between British Airways and Iberia), and a growth in the number of cut-price operators such as easyJet, Ryanair, WizzAir, Transavia, and airBaltic. These changes have resulted in greater choice for consumers, who – at least until the air-fare increases of 2009–10, brought on by losses throughout the industry – found themselves able to fly more cheaply than before.

A new dimension was added in 2008 with an 'open skies' agreement between the EU and the United States aimed at liberalizing air travel across the Atlantic. The agreement allows any EU- or US-based airline to fly from any city within the United States to any city within the EU and vice versa, rather than being limited to the usual major hubs, such as London, Frankfurt, Paris, New York, Chicago, and Los Angeles. The European Commission has championed the agreement, and most European airlines and governments are in favour, the notable exceptions being Britain and British Airways, which have the most to lose: because the agreement involves ending the control that national airlines have traditionally had on their major domestic airports, more competition would be posed to London's Heathrow airport, the busiest international airport in the world.

Mergers and acquisitions

After the Second World War, European companies lost markets at home and abroad to competition, first from the United States and then from Japan. US and Japanese corporations were more dynamic, invested more in research and development, and had access to large home markets. Meanwhile, European business was handicapped in its attempts to move across borders into neighbouring states, facing merger and capital gains taxes, double taxation on profits, different legal systems, different regulations and standards, and limits on the movement of goods and services. Hence the majority of merger and takeover activity was either within individual countries or between European and non-European companies.

With competitiveness pushed to the top of the European agenda by the single market, the Commission by the late 1980s was addressing market fragmentation and the promotion by national governments of often state-owned 'national champions'. The Community also launched new programmes aimed at encouraging research in information technology, advanced communications, industrial technologies, and weapons manu-

Box 7.2   Europe and the aerospace industry

Few areas of multinational business have seen quite such dramatic change in recent decades as the aerospace industry, where rationalization, competition, and other economic pressures have cut the number of large civilian aircraft producers in the world from dozens to just two. Famous names of Western European aviation – from Vickers to Hawker Siddeley, Supermarine, Dornier, Messerschmitt, and Sud Aviation – have all gone. In Britain, alone, the 19 aircraft producers of the 1940s had been whittled down by the mid-1980s to just one, BAE Systems. Similar pressures have led to similar changes in the United States, where Lockheed now focuses on military aircraft and McDonnell Douglas was taken over in 1997 by Boeing, now the only remaining American manufacturer of large civilian aircraft.

Much of the responsibility for the changes on both sides of the Atlantic lies with the success of Airbus, a European consortium founded in 1970, and whose share of the new civil aircraft market has grown since 1975 from 10 per cent to more than 50 per cent. The Airbus consortium is owned by the European Aeronautic Defence and Space company (EADS), created in 2000 by a merger between Aérospatiale Matra of France, DaimlerChrysler Aerospace of Germany, and Construcciones Aeronáuticas (CASA) of Spain (BAE had a 20 per cent share until 2006, when it decided to sell out and focus on the US defence market). Airbus produces a line of 12 different airliners, the newest being the super-jumbo double-decker A380, the world's largest passenger aircraft, capable of carrying 500–800 passengers, depending upon the seating configuration. After some delays related to production problems, the A380 took its first commercial flight in October 2007.

The creation of both Airbus and EADS was prompted by the argument that economies of scale were giving American manufacturers an advantage over their European competitors, whose national markets were too small to sustain them. Similar arguments have encouraged transnational cooperation in Western Europe on military aircraft and missiles. Individual member states still make competitive products, but are finding that it makes better commercial sense to pool resources. Successful collaborations include production of the Tornado fighter-bomber and the Eurofighter Typhoon, both made by British–German–Italian consortiums. In April 2001, BAE, EADS, and Finmeccanica of Italy joined forces to create MBDA, the world's second largest producer of missiles after Raytheon of the United States.

facture (Tsoukalis, 1997:49–51). The single market increased the number of consumers that companies could reach, the euro made it easier for companies in search of acquisitions to borrow money and buy other companies, and the general trend towards globalization greatly increased the number of acquisition opportunities, joint ventures, and corporate mergers. One of the results has been a new growth in the number, size, and reach of European multinationals: nearly one-third of the corporations in the *Fortune* magazine Global 500 list of the world's largest (by revenue) are now European – mainly German, French, British, Italian, and Dutch (see Figure 7.1). They include Royal Dutch Shell, BP, AXA, ING, Volkswagen, BNP Paribas, Assicurazioni Generali, Allianz, Banco Santander, Siemens, HSBC, Fiat, and Peugeot.

Notable joint ventures have included those between Thompson of France and Philips of the Netherlands on high-definition television, Pirelli of Italy and Dunlop of Britain on tyres, BMW and Rolls-Royce on aero-engines, and among the members of the European Space Agency (ESA). Set up in 1973 in an attempt to promote European cooperation in space research, the ESA now has 18 members: the Czech Republic, Switzerland, Norway, and all the western EU-15 states. Europe has also offered competition to the Americans in the field of satellite launching, with ten European countries working together in Arianespace, a space-launch consortium owned by governments and state-owned companies (France has a stake of just over 60 per cent). Since the launch of the first in its series of Ariane rockets in 1979 from Kourou in French Guiana, Arianespace has taken over more than half the global market for commercial satellite launches, eating into a business long dominated by the United States.

The growth of new pan-European businesses seeking to profit from the opportunities offered by the single market, and looking to create 'world-size' companies to compete more effectively with the United States and Japan, has led to a surge in merger and acquisition activities, notably in the chemicals, pharmaceuticals, and telecommunications industries. Notable recent examples include the mergers since 1989 among a number of British, Canadian, and American pharmaceuticals companies to create GlaxoSmithKline, a string of takeovers by the French insurance company AXA (by 2010 the ninth biggest corporation in the world), several mergers and cooperative ventures in the energy market revolving around EDF and GDF Suez in France and E.ON and RWE in Germany, and rumours of mergers being considered between Porsche and Volkswagen in Germany, and between Virgin Atlantic Airlines and Delta.

The new opportunities offered at home have been accompanied by growth in the flows of foreign direct investment both into the EU, and from the EU into other countries. In the period 1994–2003, more than $3 trillion was invested in the EU-15, or more than twice the amount that was invested over the same period in the United States. Belgium,

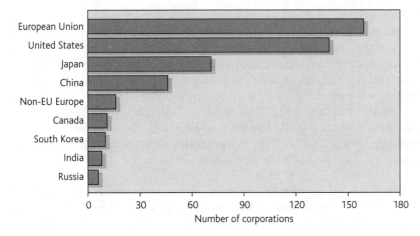

Figure 7.1 *The world's biggest corporations, by region*
Data from *Fortune* magazine, 2010.

Luxembourg, Britain, and France were the main targets, drawing in more than half the EU total among them. In terms of outflows, the EU in that period invested nearly $3.9 trillion, or nearly three times the amount invested by the United States, and nearly 15 times the amount invested by Japan. In 2006, the biggest EU spenders – in order – were France, Germany, Britain, Luxembourg, Spain, and Belgium (which together spent more than $715 billion, or more than twice as much as the United States), and the biggest EU recipients were France, Britain, Luxembourg, Spain, and Belgium (which together received nearly $400 billion, or one-third more than the United States and nearly three times as much as China) (OECD website, 2011).

The more notable examples of European companies reaching outside the EU to create large new corporations include the 1998 takeover by British Petroleum of Amoco in the United States, and the subsequent merger between BP Amoco and Atlantic Richfield; the 1999 takeover by Germany's Daimler of the US automobile manufacturer Chrysler (which came to an unhappy end in 2007, but in 2009 Fiat took a 20 per cent stake in Chrysler, with plans to exert more control as the company was reprivatized in 2011), the 2000 takeover by Germany's Deutsche Telekom of Voicestream in the United States, and the 2003 merger between Britain's P&O Princess and Carnival of the United States to create the world's largest cruise vacation group.

Competition policy

Bigger is not necessarily better in the corporate world, because takeovers can reduce competition and consumer choice by creating industries that dominate or monopolize a particular sector of the economy. The success of the single market ultimately relies on an effective competition policy, ensuring that companies do not become too big in concentrated markets, or that national governments do not give domestic companies unfair advantages through subsidies and tax breaks. Out of these concerns has come what has been described as one of the flagship policies of the EU (Cini and McGowan, 2009:1), and one in which the EU has intervened in the economic life not just of member states, but also of non-member countries. EU competition policy has four key objectives:

- Watching for restrictive practices, including conflicts of interest and the abuse of dominant positions through price-fixing, charging significantly different prices in different markets, or the existence of domestic laws that interfere with competition; thus, for example, it ordered Germany in 2003–04 to cancel a law adopted in the 1960s that prevented Volkswagen from being taken over by another company.
- Controlling mergers. The Commission monitors plans for corporate mergers and acquisitions in order to prevent the development of companies with too great a share of their particular markets, which would allow them to squeeze out smaller competitors. So, for example, it changed the terms of a 2000 merger between French oil companies TotalFina and Elf Aquitaine, and blocked the proposed takeover in 2007 by low-cost carrier Ryanair of the Irish national airline Aer Lingus on the grounds that the new company would have a near-monopoly on flights into and out of Dublin.
- Monitoring state aid. The Commission monitors the provision of subsidies, loans, grants and tax breaks to companies so as to ensure that they are not given an unfair advantage over competitors (Allen, 1996). Temporary aid is permissible in times of real need, as is aid for research and development and for regional development, but state aid must generally be in the interest of the EU as a whole.
- Promoting the competitiveness of European companies by protecting intellectual and industrial property, reducing the bureaucratic burden, providing help with research and development, and providing aid to small and medium enterprises.

Reflecting the new economic influence of the EU at the global level, recent targets of Commission investigations into mergers have even included American corporations. Thus it blocked a proposed merger in 1997 between Boeing and McDonnell Douglas, so outraging the Americans that Vice-President Al Gore threatened a transatlantic trade war (the merger went ahead after compromises were reached). It also stopped a planned takeover in 2001 of Honeywell by General Electric, which would have been the biggest corporate merger in history and would have created dominant positions in the markets for the supply of avionics and non-avionics equipment, particularly jet engines. It then made world headlines in March 2004 by imposing a record fine of €479 million (then $622 million) on the software-maker Microsoft, whose Windows operating system can be found on 90 per cent of the world's personal computers. The Commission accused Microsoft of abusing its dominant market position by bundling in its Media Player with its Windows operating system, thereby discouraging consumers from buying media players made by other companies. The Commission ordered Microsoft to begin offering within 90 days a version of Windows without the Media Player installed, and to reveal its Windows software codes so that rival companies could more easily design compatible products. Microsoft appealed the decision and lost, and finally began complying with the ruling in 2007. In late 2010 the Commission began investigating Google in light of charges that it discriminated on its website against other search engines.

Two areas in which there has been a notable lack of integrative progress have been the European energy and financial services markets. In the former, the main problem is the high level of state intervention found in member states such as France. EU goals include improving the competitiveness of the gas and electricity sectors, reinforcing security of supply, and protecting the environment, but the energy market in the EU remains fragmented, and coordination is not what it should be. Recent EU regulations have been aimed at separating production and supply from transmission, encouraging cross-border energy trade, strengthening the independence of national regulators, and encouraging greater price transparency. In the case of financial services (banking, insurance, and investment services), integration offers the benefits of stimulating competition, promoting convergence, and encouraging EU-wide pricing (Gillingham, 2003:462), but handicaps persist in the form of different tax systems, bureaucratic hurdles, and a lack of price transparency. The euro has helped by removing the barriers created by different currencies, but probably more telling influence over the short term will be changes to financial regulations flowing out of the global economic crisis of 2007–10.

A new set of challenges to the internal market was introduced with eastern enlargement, which brought greater social and economic diversity to the EU, but also widened the income gap (see Chapter 8 for details). The rural populations of Eastern European member states are typically bigger than those of the western EU-15, unemployment rates are higher, there has been less investment in infrastructure and communications, and the labour force is less educated. In the years leading up to accession, eastern states made so many changes to their trade and investment policies that – it has been argued – they had already felt most of the economic effects of enlargement before joining, they were already competing in the single market, and there was already free movement of money, goods, and services (but not labour) (Grabbe, 2004). However, improvements in competitiveness are still needed, as well as investments in infrastructure and worker education. Eastern Europe provides many market opportunities, but many challenges remain.

Meanwhile, there has been the bigger question of the place of the EU in the global marketplace. As a result of calls in the late 1990s for a new focus on modernizing the European economy, the European Council meeting in Lisbon in March 2000 set the goal of making the changes needed to finally complete the single market and to create 'the most competitive and dynamic knowledge-based economy on the planet within ten years', bringing the EU up to the levels of competitiveness and dynamism that are (or, at least, were) features of the US economy. The Lisbon Strategy called on EU governments to make a wide range of changes, including integration and liberalization of the telecommunications market, liberalization of the gas and electricity markets, rationalized road tax and air traffic control systems, lower unemployment, movement towards harmonization of EU corporate tax, and more progress towards making the EU a digital, knowledge-based economy (Wallace, 2004).

An interim report prepared in 2004 by a committee chaired by former Dutch prime minister Wim Kok argued that the Lisbon Strategy was not working: there was still too much regulation, too much protection for workers against dismissal, and not enough market liberalization or entrepreneurial freedom. The EU had also fallen behind in research and development, with expenditure as a percentage of GNP stagnating since the mid-1990s, contrasting with the much higher levels in the United States (much of it generated by the vast US defence industry), and with the high growth in Japan, China, and South Korea. There was also a tension between the continental European (or Rhenish) model of economic management, which favours more state control, and the so-called Anglo-Saxon model, which favours greater freedom for the marketplace. As a result of its problems, the Lisbon Strategy was transformed into the Europe 2020 Strategy, which moved the deadline to 2020 and focused on innovation, education, research and development, sustainable growth, a low-carbon economy, and job creation.

Inside the eurozone

In March 2002, after years of controversy and often difficult economic adjustment, 12 EU member states took one of the most far-reaching steps so far in the history of integration: they abolished their separate national currencies and replaced them with the new European currency, the euro. It was a move that was a long time coming, meeting considerable political resistance along the way and causing economic difficulties for several member states, and yet it was driven by the understanding that few barriers to the single market were as fundamental as the existence of multiple different currencies with fluctuating exchange rates. At the same time, the surrender of national currencies raised many questions about sovereignty and independence: by giving up their national currencies, the governments of eurozone states were agreeing to give up control over important domestic economic policy choices, such as the ability to adjust interest rates and to devalue their currencies. Critics also saw the adoption of the euro as another step towards the creation of a unified system of European government. There were also concerns that not all eurozone states were sufficiently prepared to adopt the euro, a problem that came home to roost in Greece in 2010 – see below.

It was understood as early as the 1950s that stable exchange rates would be an important part of the effective functioning of a single market. That stability was provided by the postwar system of fixed exchange rates, but then the system began to crumble in the late 1960s, and finally collapsed with the US decision in 1971 to end the link between gold and the US dollar. A committee headed by Luxembourg Prime Minister Pierre Werner met in 1969–70 to discuss monetary union, and concluded that the Community should work towards adopting a single currency in stages by 1980. But international currency turbulence in the wake of the energy crises of the 1970s undermined their efforts, and by 1977 only five of the 12 Community member states were still in the scheme.

A second attempt was made in March 1979 with the launch of the European Monetary System (EMS), based on an Exchange Rate Mechanism (ERM) intended to encourage exchange rate stability. An artificial currency called the European Currency Unit (ecu) was created as an anchor, its value based on a basket of European currencies, each weighted roughly according to the size of the economies of the different member states (the Deutschmark made up about 30 per cent of the ecu, the British pound about 11–15 per cent, the Italian lira about 9 per cent, and so on). Exchange rates between member states were set in ecus, and countries in the ERM undertook to make sure that those rates fluctuated by no more than 2.25 per cent either way. Although several member states found it difficult to keep their currencies stable relative to the ecu, the EMS contributed to exchange rate stability in the 1980s, and helped accustom Europeans to the idea of a single currency.

In 1989 a plan developed under the leadership of Commission president Jacques Delors proposed a staged move towards a single currency:

all member states would join the ERM, the band of exchange rate fluctuations would be narrowed and then fixed irrevocably, and the ecu would become the new single currency. Despite the near-collapse of the ERM in 1992–93 – when Britain and Italy pulled out, several other countries had to devalue their currencies, and the bands of exchange rate fluctuation had to be widened – the Maastricht treaty affirmed the basic principles behind the Delors plan. EU member states wanting to adopt the single currency had to meet several convergence criteria that were considered essential prerequisites:

- A national budget deficit of less than 3 per cent of GDP.
- A public debt of less than 60 per cent of GDP.
- A consumer inflation rate within 1.5 per cent of the average in the three countries with the lowest rates.
- A long-term interest rate within 2 per cent of the average in the three countries with the lowest rates.
- A record of keeping exchange rates within ERM fluctuation margins for two years.

At the Madrid European Council in December 1995, EU leaders decided to call the new currency the euro, and agreed to introduce it in three stages. The first came in May 1998 when it was determined which countries were ready: all member states had met the budget deficit goal, but only seven had met the debt target, Germany and Ireland had not met the inflation reduction target, and Greece had not been able to reduce its interest rates sufficiently. Maastricht, however, included a fudge clause that allowed countries to qualify if their debt-to-GDP ratio was 'sufficiently diminishing and approaching the reference value at a satisfactory pace'. In the event, despite the fact that the national debt in Belgium and Italy was nearly twice the target, all but Britain, Denmark (both of which had met all the criteria), Greece, and Sweden announced their intention to adopt the euro.

The second stage came on 1 January 1999 when the euro was officially launched as an electronic currency, participating countries fixed their exchange rates, and the European Central Bank began overseeing the single monetary policy. All its dealings with commercial banks and all its foreign exchange activities were now transacted in euros, and the euro was quoted against the yen and the dollar. Pause for thought was provided in September 2000 when, in a national referendum, Danes voted against adoption (they were followed three years later by the Swedes). Polls had also found opponents outnumbering supporters in Germany (although the balance later reversed), and opposition in Britain running at five to three in 2002, hardening to two to one by 2009. More concerns were sparked when the value of the euro against other currencies fell from an opening level of $1.18 to a low of 83

Box 7.3   The European Central Bank

Since its creation in 1998, the European Central Bank (ECB) has played an increasingly important role not just in the lives of Europeans (particularly those living in the eurozone) but has also become a key actor in the world of international monetary policy. Its role and influence (as well as some of its structural weaknesses) was most clearly on display during the crisis that came to the eurozone in 2010–11 with budgetary problems in Greece, Ireland, Spain, and Portugal.

First proposed in 1988, it was founded in 1994 as the European Monetary Institute (EMI) and finally established in June 1998 as the European Central Bank. Based in Frankfurt, its main job is to work the national banks of eurozone states, within what is called the Eurosystem, to ensure monetary stability in the eurozone, to encourage financial integration, and to manage the foreign reserves of the eurozone. It has a Governing Council consisting of the central bank governors from each participating state, and a six-member full-time Executive Board. Board members serve non-renewable terms of eight years and can only be removed by their peers or by an order from the European Court of Justice. The Bank also has links to non-participating countries through a General Council composed of the central bank governors of all EU member states. A new exchange rate mechanism (ERM II) links the euro with the national currencies of non-participating countries, and the ECB is allowed to take action to support non-participating countries so long as this does not conflict with its primary task of maintaining monetary stability among participating countries.

The structure of the ECB is an almost direct copy of the famously independent German Bundesbank. In fact, it makes the Bundesbank seem quite restricted by comparison, and the ECB was already being described in 1998 as 'the most powerful single monetary authority in the world' (*European Voice,* April 1998). But Howarth and Loedel (2005:xi) may be going too far when they describe it as 'the most important institutional creation in Europe since the institutionalization of the nation state in the seventeenth century'. Neither national nor EU leaders are allowed to try to influence the Bank, its board, or its constituent national central banks, and the only body that can play any kind of watchdog role over the Bank is the monetary subcommittee of the European Parliament, but it so far lacks the resources to be able to hold the Bank or its president particularly accountable. This makes it quite different from the United States Federal Reserve, whose chair is regularly brought to account for its policies before the banking committee of the US Senate.

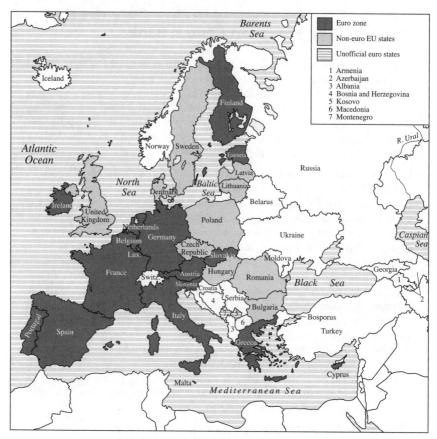

Map 7.1   *The eurozone*

cents in October 2000 (it was back up to nearly $1.60 in July 2008, and down again to $1.19 in June 2010). Nonetheless, plans for the transition proceeded, with the printing of 14.5 billion euro-banknotes and the minting of 56 billion coins. In January 2001 Greece became the twelfth member state to join the eurozone, having met the targets for reduced inflation and (so it claimed) budget deficits.

The final stage began on 1 January 2002, when euro coins and notes replaced those of participating states. The original plan had been for the euro and national currencies to be in concurrent circulation for six months, but it was subsequently decided that Europeans were to be given just two months to make the final transition from national currencies to the euro, and national currencies ceased to be legal tender in the eurozone on 1 March 2002. After (for some of them) centuries of fiscal independence, the 12 members of the eurozone made the final irrevocable step to abolish their national currencies, and

Deutschmarks, drachmas, escudos, francs, guilders, lire, marks, pesetas, punts, and schillings faded into history. In January 2007 Slovenia became the first Eastern European member state to adopt the euro, and it was followed by Cyprus and Malta in January 2008, by Slovakia in January 2009, and by Estonia in January 2011.

Opinions have been mixed on the benefits and costs of the euro, and it is probably safe to say that no one chapter in the history of European integration was approached with so much trepidation, and yet has also had so much global impact and (thanks to the economic downturn of 2007–10) caused so much public consternation and so many political headaches. Its introduction raised questions about the long-term economic effects for the EU, few of which are fully understood, even by economists. Among the benefits:

1. The euro provides monetary stability. The devaluations and revaluations of national currencies that were a feature of national monetary policy in eurozone countries in the 1970s and 1980s were initially replaced with greater stability, removing the planning problems that once came with changes in the value of currencies.
2. There is greater convenience for travellers. Instead of having to change currencies when they cross borders, and paying for goods and services with unfamiliar banknotes and coins, travellers now use the same currency wherever they go in the eurozone. This has the added psychological benefit of making them more aware of being part of the common enterprise of integration, and also makes foreign visitors more aware of the EU; they may not always understand the latter, but they cannot ignore the effect of the euro in their pocket.
3. There is greater price transparency, allowing consumers to more easily compare prices across borders. This also promotes competition thanks to pressure on businesses to make their products available at similar prices throughout the eurozone.
4. There are fewer bureaucratic barriers to the transfer of large sums of money across borders, and businesses must no longer spend time and money changing currency, thus saving them transaction costs.
5. The euro is now a world-class currency in the same league as the US dollar and the Japanese yen, providing the eurozone with a political tool that allows it to have greater international influence, rather than having to react to developments in the United States and Japan. At least until the 2010–11 crises, a growing number of analysts saw it as a substantial threat to the global dominance of the US dollar.

At the same time, the adoption of the euro has been a gamble. Never before has a group of sovereign states with a long history of independence combined their currencies on a similar scale, and the risks were significantly greater than those involved in completing the single market. Furthermore, all the key preparatory decisions about the euro were taken by European national leaders with little or no regard to public opinion, which was often hostile to the idea, and uncertain about the implications. The costs of the euro have included the following:

1. Loss of sovereignty and national identity has been a major concern. States joining the euro have given up critical tools for economic management, taking another and substantial step towards the surrender of control over domestic economic policy.
2. Loss of policy independence has been another concern. States have different economic cycles, and separate currencies allow them to devalue, borrow, adjust interest rates, and take other measures in response to changed economic circumstances. Such flexibility is no longer available to eurozone states; they no longer have national banks that can make independent judgments on interest rates, and they are more exposed than before to economic problems and mismanagement in other eurozone states. In short, the members of the eurozone must rise or fall together.
3. Some economists were concerned about the underlying weaknesses in EU economies in 1997–98, and raised questions about the extent to which figures relating to the convergence criteria were being fudged to allow countries that had not met those criteria to take part. Some feared that these weaknesses could result in a high-credibility Deutschmark being replaced with a low-credibility euro, undermining economic health throughout the EU.
4. Unless Europeans learn each other's languages and are able to move freely in search of jobs, the euro might perpetuate the pockets of poverty and wealth that already exist across the EU, thereby interfering with the development of the single market. Having a common currency in a country as big as the United States works mainly because people can move freely; this is not true of the EU, where there are still psychological and social barriers to movement.

Some of the problems inherent in the euro became clear even before it was finally adopted, with the signature in 1997 – at the insistence of Germany – of a stability and growth pact. Generated by concerns that governments in the eurozone might try to get around ECB monetary policies by increasing spending and running large budget deficits, the pact required that eurozone members keep their budget deficits to less than 3 per cent of gross domestic product, and placed a 60 per cent limit on government borrowing (Hosli, 2005:67–9). Unfortunately, recession came to most industrialized countries in 2002–03, and

France, Germany, Italy, and Portugal quickly found themselves either in breach of the deficit limit or running the danger of crossing the 3 per cent barrier; they were later joined by Greece and the Netherlands. While there was general agreement on the principle of the pact, there was criticism that it was too inflexible (in that it made no distinctions among countries with different economic bases) and that its focus on curbing inflation left it poorly equipped to deal with slow economic growth. Commission president Romano Prodi even went so far in October 2002 as to describe attempts to enforce the pact without taking heed of changing circumstances as 'stupid'.

By the second half of 2003 the European Central Bank was warning that most eurozone countries were in danger of failing to meet the target on budget deficits, thereby damaging the prospects for economic growth. In November 2003, the two biggest eurozone economies – France and Germany – both broke the limits and prevented other EU finance ministers from imposing large fines on the two countries (a decision that was annulled by the European Court of Justice in July 2004). Its ministers, along with their British counterpart, argued that the rules of the pact were too rigid and needed to be applied more flexibly if they were to work. By December the pact had all but collapsed and new rules were being explored to promote fiscal stability in the eurozone, including the granting of permission to selected countries in difficulties to temporarily carry larger deficits.

Then came the global economic downturn of 2007–10, set off in the United States by a combination of lax financial regulation and the extension of too much credit to consumers unable to manage debt. Many of the so-called 'toxic assets' of US banks and financial institutions were bought by their European counterparts, such that when the effects began to be felt in 2007, they reached around the world. After some initial indecision, EU governments bailed out banks and other financial institutions whose collapse might have posed systemic risks to the EU financial system, and supported a stimulus package proposed by the European Commission. The ECB meanwhile cut interest rates, and calls were made for a complete overhaul of the EU financial system.

But the downturn exposed problems in several eurozone states, notably in Greece, which had been borrowing heavily since switching to the euro, had been hiding its true financial situation, and now found itself weak and exposed. When a national debt crisis broke there in late 2009 it not only threatened to spread throughout the eurozone but also tested the abilities of eurozone leaders to make decisions, and threatened the international standing of the euro. Economic problems later emerged in Ireland, Spain, and Portugal, and many other EU states found themselves having to make severe budgetary adjustments. By mid-2010, there was widespread speculation that the euro was in such deep trouble that it faced complete collapse. A critical structural problem confirmed by the crisis was that while the ECB had a high degree of control over eurozone monetary policy (controlling the money supply and the setting of interest rates), it – and the other EU institutions – had little direct control over fiscal policy (the management of budgets). The Greek debt crisis underlined the importance of EU leaders working together on core economic issues and building confidence by giving financial markets a better idea of who is in charge. Clearly, substantial change is in order.

Conclusions

Although the work of the European Union has been driven most obviously by economic factors – and particularly by the goal of free trade in a single market – European leaders have found, through neofunctionalist logic, that economic integration has had a spillover effect on many other policy areas. Most notably, they have found that completion of the single market was a more complex notion than originally expected. The primary objective of the single market was the removal of tariffs and non-tariff barriers to trade; while tariff barriers were relatively easy to identify, the seeming innocuousness of the term 'non-tariff barriers' hid a multitude of problems, handicaps, and obstacles.

Among other things, economic integration has meant removing cross-border checks on people and goods, controlling the movement of drugs and terrorists, agreeing standard levels of indirect taxation, harmonizing technical standards on thousands of goods and services, agreeing regulations in the interests of consumer safety, reaching agreement on professional qualifications, allowing Europeans to take capital and pensions with them when they move to another EU state, opening up (but also keeping a close eye on) the European market for joint ventures and corporate mergers, developing trans-European transport and energy supply networks, providing the means by which Europeans can communicate with each other electronically, developing common approaches to working conditions, establishing common environmental standards, promoting the development of poorer rural and urban areas in order to avoid trade distortions, and creating an equitable and efficient agricultural sector.

In a sense, however, everything that was agreed during the 1960s, the 1970s, and the 1980s – the thousands of decisions taken by prime ministers, chancellors, presidents, ministers, and European bureaucrats, and the thousands of directives, regulations, and decisions developed and agreed by the different EU institutions – was but a prelude to the biggest project of all, the conversion to a single currency. In March 2002, 12 of the 15 member states abolished their national currencies and adopted the euro, while three – Britain, Denmark, and Sweden – opted to remain out, at least temporarily. Many questions remained about the wisdom of the positions taken both by the champions and the opponents. Were the former too hasty in their decision to press on, regardless of their domestic economic problems? Were Britain and Denmark being wisely cautious or typically eurosceptic in their decisions to wait and see? Would the adoption of the euro prove to be a disruptive step too far, or one of the most far-sighted and creative decisions ever taken by Europe's leaders? What impact would it have, directly or indirectly, on economic development in Eastern Europe?

Whatever happens as the eurozone struggles to address the fallout from its recent crises, the single market has had widespread and irreversible implications for everyone living in the European Union, and for all the EU's trading partners. It has helped create new wealth and opportunity, has brought down many of the economic barriers that have for decades divided Europeans, and has paved the way for the creation of trans-European economic ties that have reduced national differences and promoted the idea of Europe as a powerful new actor on the world stage.

Chapter 8

Managing Resources

As we saw in the last chapter, the European Economic Community was mainly an exercise in economic integration, focused on helping make the European marketplace more open, efficient, competitive, and profitable. The Treaty of Rome made mention of the need to improve the living and working conditions of Europeans, but this was a general goal rather than the basis for specific policies. With the six founding states being roughly equivalent in terms of their levels of wealth, and their economic and social structures, there was little early focus on qualitative issues. But it soon became clear that wealth and opportunity would not be evenly distributed in the Community as long as there were differences in personal income, social services, education, and overall quality of life both within and among member states.

The Community soon found itself focused on efforts to ensure that Europeans had equal access to jobs and economic opportunity, and that the single market was not distorted by differences in regulatory standards, barriers to labour mobility, and access to funds for investment. Internal differences grew with the first enlargement in 1973, and problems worsened with the international economic turbulence of the 1970s, and new evidence during the 1980s that the Community was falling behind the United States and Japan on several fronts. With this in mind, there was a new focus on transferring resources and opportunities to those parts of the Community suffering the greatest handicaps. At the heart of these efforts were three key areas of policy revolving around the management and distribution of resources:

- *Agricultural policy* was factored in to the Treaty of Rome, the goal being to guarantee income for Community farmers. The Common Agricultural Policy (CAP) helped transform the rural economies of the EEC member states, but became both expensive and controversial, leading to efforts at reform that continue even today.
- *Cohesion policy* aims to even out regional economic differences within and among the member states by investing in economic development and focusing on issues relating to employment, including job creation, the free movement of labour, improved living and working conditions, and the rights and benefits of workers.
- *Environmental policy* first appeared on the political agenda in the late 1960s as the air and water pollution created by economic

growth prompted a reaction from increasingly affluent Europeans. With differences in standards and regulations posing a barrier to the single market, the environment by the 1990s had become a primary policy interest of the EU and is today widely recognized as an example of a policy area in which regional integration has clear benefits over independent national approaches.

Europeans today – particularly those in the western EU – are among the most affluent and privileged people on earth, living longer and healthier lives, and having better access to jobs, education, housing, nutrition and consumer goods than the citizens of almost every other part of the world. But they do not have to look far to find decaying industrial areas, underdeveloped rural areas, pockets of poverty and high unemployment, and social dysfunction. EU policies have helped address many of these problems, but the effective management of resources – and the creation of a more even playing field – remain critical priorities.

Levelling the playing field

All societies contain economic and social divisions. This was true of the early EEC; in spite of the relative economic and social similarity of the six founding states, it remained true in the 1970s and 1980s with enlargement to Ireland, Greece, Portugal, and Spain, and even more so with the 2004–07 enlargement, when 15 countries with a per capita gross domestic product (GDP) mainly in the range of $20,000–30,000 were joined by 12 countries with a per capita GDP mainly in the range of $2,000–5,000. The differences remain even today:

- Levels of economic productivity vary significantly. Expressing the average per capita GDP for the EU as 100, in 2009 levels ranged from a high in Luxembourg of 271 to lows in Lithuania, Latvia, Romania and Bulgaria of about half the EU average (see Figure 8.1).
- Unemployment rates in Eastern Europe have fallen in recent years, but variations remain and overall numbers were made worse by the fallout from the 2007–10 global economic downturn. In December 2010, rates varied from lows of 4–6 per cent in the Netherlands, Austria and Malta to highs of 11 per cent (Hungary and Portugal), 14 per cent (Ireland and Slovakia), and 21 per cent in Spain (see Figure 8.2). The average for the EU-27 was 9.6 per cent (the same as the United States).
- Economic structures are becoming more similar, but while in 2009 77–79 per cent of wealth was generated by services in Germany, France, Britain, and Denmark, they accounted for 63–66 per cent of

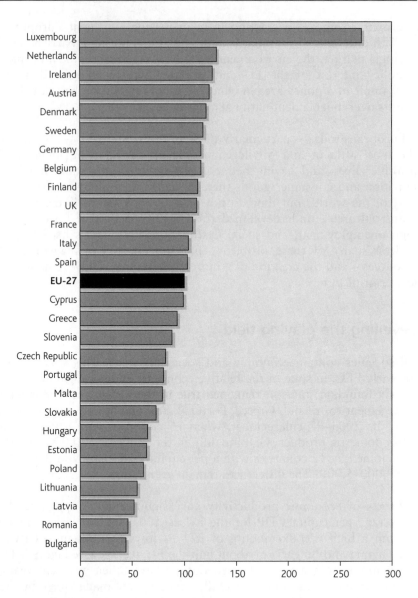

Data from Eurostat at http://epp.eurostat.ec.europa.eu (retrieved December 2010).
Figures are for 2009, and indicate per capita GDP adjusted for purchasing power relative to
the average for the EU-27, which is expressed as 100. For comparison, the figure for the
United States was 147.

Figure 8.1   *Per capita GDP in the European Union*

GDP in Bulgaria, Hungary, Poland, Lithuania and Slovakia (World Bank website, 2011).

Overall, the wealthiest parts of the EU are mainly in the north-central regions, particularly in the quadrilateral area between London, Paris, Milan and Hamburg. The poorest parts are mainly on the eastern, southern, and western margins: Eastern Europe, eastern Germany, Greece, southern Italy, Spain, Portugal, western Ireland, and western Scotland. The relative poverty of these regions has different causes: some are depressed agricultural areas with little industry and high unemployment, some are declining industrial areas with outdated factories and machinery, some (notably islands) are geographically iso-lated from the opportunities offered by bigger markets, and most suffer lower levels of education and health care and have underdeveloped infrastructure, especially roads and utilities.

The preamble to the Treaty of Rome included the sentiment that eco-nomic unity was tied to 'harmonious development by reducing the dif-ferences existing between the various regions and the backwardness of the less favoured regions'. As well as the obvious moral need to address poverty and economic handicaps wherever they existed, there was a clear strategic need as well: variations in the economic wealth of the member states would interfere with the functioning of the single market by creating barriers to trade and opportunity. As a result, jobs would move to the poorer parts where cheaper labour was available, inequality would interfere with the development of a skilled labour force, Europe would lack the well-educated and affluent consumers needed for a vibrant marketplace, and poorer regions would not attract the kind of investment and infrastructure needed to help the EU compete at the global level.

Recognizing these problems, the EU has given priority to reducing economic and social disparities in the interests of broader progress, working to help bring the poorer member states closer to the level of their wealthier partners. While free marketeers have always hoped that the single market would have a trickle-down effect by directing more investment towards the poorer parts of Europe, the EU has taken a more proactive approach by setting up several so-called structural funds:

- The European Social Fund (ESF), created under the Treaty of Rome and designed to promote job creation and worker mobility, to combat long-term unemployment and help workers adapt to techno-logical change; particular attention is paid to the needs of migrant workers, women, and the disabled.
- The European Regional Development Fund (ERDF), created in 1975 to support underdeveloped areas (particularly those affected by the

decline of traditional industries such as coal, steel, and textiles) and inner cities. Its goal is to encourage sustainable integrated economic development, particularly in the areas of transport, energy, health and social infrastructure, the environment, and tourism.

- The Cohesion Fund, created in 1992 to compensate poorer states (those with a per capita gross national income less than 90 per cent of the EU average) for the costs incurred by the tightening of environmental regulations, and to provide financial assistance for transport projects.

Additional structural funds have more focused goals: the Solidarity Fund (created in 2002 in response to serious floods in several countries) is designed to help the EU respond more quickly to natural disasters, the European Agricultural Fund for Rural Development was set up in 2006 to help modernize farming and forestry, and the Globalization Adjustment Fund was set up in 2007 to help workers who have lost their jobs as a result of trade liberalization. Among them, the funds in 2007–13 attracted a total of nearly €350 billion in spending, or about one-third of the EU budget, and were based on three key objectives:

- The Convergence Objective targets regions with a per capita GDP less than 75 per cent of the EU average, the goal being to encourage more investment, new jobs, and improved infrastructure. Spending comes out of all three structural funds, accounts for more than 80 per cent of all EU regional spending, and the biggest recipients are Poland, Spain, the Czech Republic, Hungary, and Italy.
- The Regional Competitiveness and Employment Objective covers parts of the EU not addressed by the Convergence Objective, the goal being to make these areas more competitive and more attractive for investment. Funds come from the ERDF and the ESF, and the biggest recipients in 2007–13 were France, Germany, the UK, and Italy.
- The Territorial Cooperation Objective focuses on encouraging cooperation between European regions, and the development of common solutions to the challenges of urban, rural, and coastal development. Financed out of the ERDF, it accounted for less than three per cent of structural fund spending in 2007–13.

Agricultural policy

Agriculture is not usually a headline issue in industrialized countries, because it accounts for only a small percentage of employment and economic activity. But in the meeting rooms of the EU institutions it has long been a bone of contention: it was for decades the most expensive,

Box 8.1   Living the European dream

Europeans are among the most privileged people in the world. They have access to an advanced system of education and health care, an extensive and generous welfare system, a vibrant consumer society, and a sophisticated transport and communications system. An African infant is 21 times more likely to die at birth than a European infant, and a European can expect to live 24 years longer than an African and 18 years longer than an Indian. Europeans enjoy almost universal literacy, employed Europeans enjoy more paid holiday leave and leisure time than anyone else, and the provision of shelter and nutrition is more than adequate. Eastern Europe is still catching up, but the opportunities offered by European integration are helping it with investments in education, health care, and infrastructure, and its citizens are seeing significant change. One American author (Rifkin, 2004) has argued that the quality of life of Europeans as a whole is eclipsing that of Americans, long thought of as living in the world's most socially privileged country. Another (Hill, 2010) has reached a similar conclusion, suggesting that 'most of the world is recognizing the advantages of the European way', with its steady-state economy and emphasis on sustainable development.

Much can be attributed to the philosophy adopted by most Western European governments after the Second World War that the state should provide a wide range of basic social services, creating a safety net through which even the poorest and the most underprivileged would not be allowed to slip. Hence every EU member state has some form of state education and national health care, and provisions for children and the aged have increased as the number of lone-parent families and retirees has grown. Most wealthier European states even do well in comparison with the United States, which has the most technologically advanced health care in the world but lacks a comprehensive national health service, and is one of the richest economies in the world yet still has 15 per cent of its people living in poverty.

Not all of Europe's welfare policies have succeeded, and it is one of the great ironies of life in modern industrialized democracies that considerable want continues to exist in the midst of plenty. Poverty has not gone away and in several places has worsened, creating considerable differences across Europe. This is particularly true of the number of children living in poverty, which stands at less than 10 per cent in Germany, the Netherlands, and Sweden, but is almost twice as high in Britain and Italy. On these and other indicators, the Eastern European states still lag behind, but the benefits of EU membership will likely help them in much the same way as it has helped Greece, Ireland, Portugal, and Spain, all of which (at least until the 2007–10 economic downturn) saw dramatic improvements in quality of life. But there have been many troubling questions asked of late about how long the EU can continue to sustain this way of life, given its declining and ageing population.

the most complex, and sometimes the most politically charged of the policy areas in which the Community – and then the EU – was involved. At least until recently, the EU had more powers over agriculture, spent more money on agriculture, passed more legislation on agriculture, and saw more political activity on agriculture than was true of almost any other policy area. Its approach to agricultural policy was also structurally different from other EU policy areas in at least one key respect: while barriers were being removed and markets opened up in almost every area of EU economic activity, agriculture long remained heavily interventionist, efforts being made to keep agricultural prices high even in the face of criticism from within the EU and from the EU's trading partners.

The prominence of agriculture on the EU policy agenda traces its roots back to the early days of integration. In the 1950s, farming was important to European economies, accounting for about 12 per cent of the GDP and 20 per cent of the workforce of the Six. The Second World War had also made Europeans conscious of how much they depended on imported food, and of how prone those imports were to disruption. The focus on agriculture was also a key element in the tradeoff between France and Germany on the terms of integration (Dinan, 2004:94–7), with France worried that the common market would benefit German industry while providing the French economy with relatively few benefits. In the mid-1950s France had a large and efficient agricultural sector, which contributed significantly to employment and economic activity.

In fact, no discussion of EU agricultural policy would be complete without reference to the special case of France. Its farming population fell between 1950 and 2000 from nearly 31 per cent to just 3.4 per cent, and the contribution of agriculture to its GDP fell over the same period from 15 per cent to just over 2 per cent. But French farmers have long had a strong domestic political role, enhanced by the number of people who live in the rural areas of France, and by the role that those areas play in the French national psyche. All attempts to reform EU agricultural policy inevitably brought out protesting French farmers in their thousands. Today, more than one-fifth of EU agricultural production comes from France, which also takes the biggest share of EU farm spending (about one-sixth in 2010). But this is now changing: many small farmers live in poverty, thousands leave the land every year to look for other work, and the role of the French farm lobby has been on the wane.

At the core of EU activities is the Common Agricultural Policy (CAP), which was long based on three underlying principles: the promotion of a single market in agricultural produce, Community preference (a system of protectionism aimed at giving advantages to EU produce over imported produce), and joint financing (that is, the costs of the CAP had to be shared equitably across all the member states).

What this meant in practical policy terms for its first quarter-century was that Community farmers were guaranteed the same minimum price for their produce, regardless of how much they produced, of world prices, or of levels of supply and demand. Meanwhile, the EU's internal market was protected from imports by tariffs, and the member states shared the financial burden for making this possible.

In many ways this policy was a success: productivity increased, markets stabilized, supplies were secured, Western European farmers were protected from fluctuations in world prices, and became wealthier, and their livelihoods became more predictable and stable. The EU today is by far the world's biggest agricultural exporter, accounting in 2008 for 42 per cent of the world total, or more than four times as much as the United States and 13 times as much as China (World Trade Organization website, 2010). Encouraged by guaranteed prices, European farmers have squeezed more and more from their land, so that production has gone up in virtually every area, and the EU is now self-sufficient in almost every product it can grow or produce in its climate (including wheat, barley, wine, meat, vegetables, and dairy products). The CAP alone cannot be credited with all the successes, because farmers have also been helped by intensification, mechanization, and the increased use of agrochemicals, but it has certainly been at the core of agricultural change in the EU.

Unfortunately, the CAP also created many problems along the way:

- EU-15 farmers produced more than the market could bear, creating stockpiles of surplus produce, including cereal, powdered milk, beef, olive oil, raisins, figs, and even manure.
- The CAP created economic dependency by sustaining farmers who would have gone out of business, pushed up the price of agricultural land, and failed to close the income gap between rich and poor farmers, which grew with eastern enlargement.
- The CAP caused environmental problems by encouraging the increased use of chemical fertilizers and herbicides, the removal of hedges and trees, and the 'reclamation' of wetlands, in the interests of making farms bigger and more efficient.
- The CAP made food more expensive for consumers, despite the surpluses.
- Because so much of the EU budget was for so long swallowed up by agriculture, there was less available for spending in other areas.
- The CAP distorted world agricultural prices, soured EU relations with its major trading partners, and perpetuated the idea of a protectionist EU.
- Differences between EU prices and world prices posed an irresistible temptation for less honest farmers to make fraudulent claims (Grant, 1997: 99–101).

With these problems in mind, the case for reform of the CAP was clear. Early efforts to encourage small farmers to leave the land, and to amalgamate farms into bigger and more efficient units, were vehemently opposed by small farmers in France and Germany. Pressures for reform grew in the 1980s with efforts to reorganize the Community budget, and then with criticism levelled at the Community during international trade negotiations. In the early 1990s, agreement was reached to replace guaranteed prices with a system of direct payments if prices fell below a certain level, to reduce subsidies on grain, beef, and butter, and to encourage farmers to take land out of production (the 'set-aside' system) (Lewis, 1993: 337). Further reforms agreed between 1998 and 2003 led to ending the link between subsidies and production, with farmers instead receiving a single payment. Guaranteed prices on milk powder, butter, and other products were all reduced, direct payments for bigger farms cut, and the share of the EU budget devoted to agriculture fell.

Eastward enlargement added a new dimension to the issue, because of the small size and relatively low productivity of most Eastern European farms. Investment in agriculture also has greater political, economic, and social significance in the east, given its relatively large farming populations (about a quarter of Romanians and 15 per cent of Poles work in agriculture, compared to 3–4 per cent of Danish, Swedish, and French workers, and less than two per cent of Britons) (Rieger, 2005:163). Opening the CAP immediately to the new member states would likely have bankrupted the EU, but special efforts were also needed to make sure that Eastern European farmers were not made to feel like second-class citizens. The compromise agreed was to allow them a small but growing proportion of agricultural payments, €22 billion was budgeted to be spent in 2000–06 under the Special Accession Programme for Agriculture and Rural Development (SAPARD), designed to help applicant countries prepare for CAP, and it was agreed that direct aid would be phased in over ten years, starting at 25 per cent in 2004 and moving up in annual increments of 5 per cent.

Today's CAP is almost unrecognizable from its early days. Direct payments to farmers have fallen, more funds have been available for rural development, and guaranteed prices are now seen mainly as a safety net to be used only when global prices sink too low. Where the CAP was once about ensuring regular food supplies, today it is more about helping European farmers to survive and to compete in global markets. There is more of a focus on quality rather than quantity, driven mainly by changing consumer demands and concerns about the state of the environment. CAP payments have conditions attached, linked to food safety, animal health and welfare, sustainable development, and the management of rural landscapes.

Box 8.2   The Common Fisheries Policy

The fishing industry employs barely 400,000 people in the EU, or a fraction of the workforce, but the state of the industry has important implications for coastal communities all around the EU; especially important given that 22 of the 27 member states have coasts, and there are heavy concentrations of population in coastal areas. Disputes over fishing grounds in European waters once led to bitter confrontations, such as the infamous 'cod wars' of the 1960s between Britain and Iceland over access to fisheries in the north Atlantic, and to political battles such as the opposition from many in Britain in the 1990s to the presence of Spanish trawlers in traditional British fishing waters.

Although it has attracted much less controversy (or spending) than the CAP, the EU's Common Fisheries Policy (CFP) has occasionally attracted sustained political attention (see Lequesne, 2004). Tracing it origins to the 1976 changes in international law by which access to marine resources was expanded from 19km (12 miles) to 322km (200 miles) from the coastline, it was adopted in 1983. Aimed at supporting a competitive and sustainable fishing industry, it has focused on imposing national quotas (Total Allowable Catches, or TACs), setting rules on fishing gear and mesh sizes for fishing nets, requiring accurate reporting of catches and landings, setting rules on the protection of marine wildlife and vulnerable species of fish, requiring licensing for all EU fishing boats, operating a management policy that limits the size of EU fishing fleets, managing the market in order to monitor prices, quality, and competition, and reaching agreements with third countries on access to their fishing grounds.

The results have been mixed. Overfishing is a global problem, with estimates that as much as one-fifth of the worldwide fish catch is unregulated and illegal, fears that overfishing has left major fish stocks depleted, and concerns that – combined with the effects of pollution – the sustainability and the future of marine ecosystems is threatened (see Clover, 2005). Fisheries are a classic example of a common-pool resource, or one that does not come under the jurisdiction of a single state or authority, and so is open to unregulated exploitation. Rational self-interest encourages all those who have access to the resource to extract as much of it as possible, maximizing their benefits at the cost of the whole. For this reason, the CFP cannot function in isolation, but must be part of a global regime to manage fisheries.

Cohesion policy

The EU's cohesion policy is aimed at reducing differences in levels of wealth, income, and opportunity in the interests of promoting balanced economic and social development. The free market unavoidably contains inequalities, many of which defy attempts to address them, but there is strong political and public support in the EU for public programmes aimed at redistributing wealth and providing social safety nets. The wealthier EU member states have long had their own domestic programmes of economic and social development, aimed at encouraging new investment in poorer areas, at offsetting the effects of rural decline, and at trying to revive old industrial areas and the centres of large cities. But while these programmes may help offset disparities within member states, there is a limit to how much they can deal with such disparities among member states. And as long as those differences exist, attempts to build a level economic and social playing field throughout the European single market will be undermined.

Armstrong (1993) suggests that there are several benefits to a joint EU approach: it ensures that spending is concentrated in the areas of greatest need, it ensures coordination of the spending of the different member states, and it encourages the member states to work together on one of the most critical barriers to integration. A common cohesion policy also means that the member states have a vested interest in the welfare of their EU partners, helps member states deal with some of the potentially damaging effects of integration (such as loss of jobs and greater economic competition), and introduces an important psychological element: citizens of poorer regions receiving EU assistance are made more aware of the benefits of EU membership, while citizens of the wealthier states that are net contributors have a vested interest in ensuring that such spending is effective.

There are two elements to cohesion policy:

- Regional policy focuses on the reduction of disparities in wealth and income through investments in decaying industrial areas and poorer rural areas, promoting employment and equal opportunities, and improving living and working conditions. Its goal is to strengthen the European marketplace by reducing economic differences, promoting balanced economic development, addressing the handicaps posed by geographic remoteness or underdeveloped links between urban and rural areas, and dealing with the causes of social deprivation and poor education.
- Social policy addresses problems relating to employment, including job creation, the free movement of labour, improved living and working conditions, and protecting the rights and benefits of workers. At its heart are the European Employment Strategy, aimed

at addressing the worryingly high and curiously persistent unemployment rates in parts of the EU (although they have improved of late in the eurozone), and the Social Agenda, aimed at providing jobs, fighting poverty, reforming pensions and health care, and addressing inequality and discrimination.

European regional policy dates back to the 1950s when provision was made by the ECSC for grants to depressed areas for industrial conversion and retraining. In 1969, the Commission proposed a common regional policy, including the creation of a regional development fund, but found little support among the governments of the member states. The climate changed after the first round of enlargement in the early 1970s, when a complex pattern of political and economic interests came together to make the idea of a regional policy more palatable. Most importantly, the 'rich man's club' of the 1950s (Italy excepted) had been joined by Britain and Ireland, whose regional problems not only widened the economic disparities within the EEC, but also strengthened Italy's demands for a regional policy. The Commission-sponsored Thomson report argued in 1973 that regional imbalances were acting as a barrier to one of the goals of the Treaty of Rome ('a continuous and balanced expansion' in economic activity), threatened to undermine plans for economic and monetary union, and could even pose a threat to the common market (European Commission, 1973). Agreement was reached to create a European Regional Development Fund (ERDF) in 1975.

The Single European Act brought new attention to regional policy, introducing a Title V on Economic and Social Cohesion, and arguing the need to 'clarify and rationalize' the use of the structural funds. Reforms agreed in 1988, based on Britain's insistence on reduced CAP spending and increased spending under the structural funds, helped improve the efficiency of regional policy by setting up Community Support Frameworks under which the Commission, the member states, and the regions would work more closely together on agreeing the means to achieve regional development planning goals. More changes to regional policy came with Maastricht, under which a Committee of the Regions (COR) was created to give regional authorities a greater say in European policy, and the Cohesion Fund was created. The latter grew out of concern that economic and monetary union might worsen regional disparities, particularly given that poorer countries were going to be handicapped by the requirement (as a prelude to the single currency) for member states to limit their budget deficits to 3 per cent of GDP.

The jury is still out on the effectiveness of EU regional policy. An independent report commissioned by the European Commission and published in 2004 concluded that there was little hard evidence that the structural funds had either made a significant difference to closing regional disparities, or that they had not (Sapir *et al.*, 2004), but the Commission itself disagreed. There is still a substantial gap in per capita GDP between the richest and poorest member states, but it has been closing, and the case of Ireland stands as an example of what is possible. Once one of the poorest parts of the EU, it saw double-digit economic growth during much of the 1990s and falling unemployment. EU structural support cannot be given sole credit, but in combination with sensible domestic economic policies – including cuts in corporate and capital gains tax – and a general upturn in the economic fortunes of most capitalist economies, it certainly helped. Unfortunately the Irish miracle went into reverse in 2007–10 (see Box 8.3).

Meanwhile, EU social policy aims to reduce social differences among Europeans. A truly open single market demands equal pay, equal working conditions, comparable standards on workers' rights and women's rights, and an expansion of the skilled workforce. Without these qualities, poorer European states will suffer the effects of competition from their wealthier partners in the EU, while those with less progressive employment laws will lose jobs to those that offer better working conditions. These concerns, combined with the long history of welfare promotion in individual Western European states, have helped make social policy an important part of the EU agenda.

Social policy deals mainly with questions related to employment, or the rights, opportunities, and benefits provided to potential, actual, or former workers. These activities have proved controversial, because social policy treads on sensitive ideological and cultural toes. Conservatives and liberals will never agree on the best way of building a level social playing field, and programmes that may be regarded as progressive by one member state may be seen as a threat to economic welfare or even cultural identity by another. Generally speaking, national labour unions have been in favour of EU social policy, as have the Commission and Parliament (where social democratic parties have long been prominent), while business interests and conservative political parties have been opposed, arguing that social policy could make European companies less competitive in the global market (Geyer and Springer, 1998:208).

Concern about the competitive implications of different levels of social security payments and labour costs encouraged little direct discussion about social questions during the negotiations leading up to the Treaty of Rome. While the treaty made it the Community's business to deal with such matters as the free movement of workers, equal pay for equal work, working conditions, and social security for migrant workers, it was based on the naive assumption that the benefits of the single market would improve life for all European workers. This proved true to the extent that it helped increase wages, but

Box 8.3   The (bad) luck of the Irish

In few places have the possibilities and limitations of cohesion policy (more specifically) or membership of the EU (more generally) been more clearly illustrated than in the case of Ireland. Long a member of the relatively poor and underdeveloped periphery of the European Community, it saw double-digit annual economic growth in the 1990s (peaking in 2000 at a remarkable 11.5 per cent), and its unemployment rate fell to a record low. Fuelled by cuts in corporate and capital gains tax, and by the attractions of Ireland as an English-speaking toehold in the EU – with plenty of skilled workers – foreign investment boomed, most of it going into the high technology and financial sectors. Ireland moved up the league of the EU's richest countries, and – after decades during which the Irish had left to seek jobs in Britain and the United States – many started to return to Ireland. By 2005 it had a per capita gross national income of just over $40,000, ranking it fourth in the EU behind Luxembourg, Denmark, and Sweden, and ahead of Britain, France, Germany, and Italy. Borrowing from the growth of Southeast Asian 'tiger' economies, Ireland became known as the Celtic tiger.

There was no simple explanation for this remarkable story, and partial credit had to be given to the general upturn in economic growth that came to most capitalist economies during the 1990s, and to the economic policies of the Irish government. At the same time, membership of the EU was a boon for Ireland, not only because of the substantial flow of investments under the various structural funds, but also because of the opportunities provided by the single market. The Irish economy would no doubt have grown without the EU, but not at the same rate.

But then it all changed. The economic boom had begun to tail off by 2003 and there were worries about growing inflation, an unsustainable increase in the value of property, and pressures on infrastructure. The housing bubble burst in 2008, Ireland became the first EU country to declare itself in a recession at the start of the global economic downturn, government revenues fell (Ireland by 2009 had the biggest government deficit as a proportion of GDP in the eurozone), unemployment levels rose, and bad debts brought problems for Irish banks, obliging the government – which had given the banks a blanket guarantee in 2008 – to accept an €85-billion rescue package. By 2010 Ireland was among a small group of countries – the others being Greece, Portugal, and Spain – whose economic woes were such that they raised questions about the future of the entire eurozone.

market forces failed to deal with gender and age discrimination, wage disparities, different levels of unemployment, and safety and health needs in the workplace. Social issues were pushed down the EEC agenda while governments concentrated on completing the single market and resolving battles over agricultural policy, and the movement of workers was meanwhile heavily restricted.

When restrictions were eased so that labour shortages in the larger northern economies could be overcome, there was an influx of immigrants from southern Europe, mostly from non-EC states such as Greece, Portugal, Spain, and Turkey, and what was then Yugoslavia. Enlargement in 1973 brought an increase in the disparities in levels of economic wealth within the Community, so social policy was pushed up the political agenda. The first in a series of four-year Social Action Programmes (SAPS) was launched in 1974, aimed at developing a plan to achieve full employment, improved living and working conditions, and gender equality. However, a combination of recession and ideological resistance from several European leaders ensured that many of the words failed to be translated into practical change on the ground.

Because a core goal of the Single European Act (SEA) was the freedom of Europeans to live and work wherever they liked in the EC, social policy came to the fore again as questions were raised about the mobility of workers and about 'social dumping': money, services, and businesses moving to those parts of the Community with the lowest wages and social security costs. The Commission tried to focus the attention of national governments on the 'social dimension' of the single market, but economic recession made sure that the SEA initially lacked such a dimension. This encouraged the then Commission president Jacques Delors to launch an attempt in 1988 to draw more attention to the social consequences of the single market.

The Belgian government had raised the idea of a charter of basic social rights during its presidency of the Council of Ministers in 1987, modelled on its own new national charter. The idea was taken up by Delors, and was given a helping hand by the determination of the socialist government of François Mitterrand to promote social policy during the French presidency of the EC. Other countries with socialist governments – such as Spain and Greece – were in favour, as was the moderately conservative government of Helmut Kohl in Germany. The only opposition came from the conservative government in Britain. Margaret Thatcher considered it 'quite inappropriate' for laws on working regulations and welfare benefits to be set at the Community level, and dismissed the charter as one 'devised by socialists in the Commission and favoured predominantly by socialist member states' (Thatcher, 1993:750).

When the Community Charter of Fundamental Social Rights of Workers (known generally as the Social Charter) was adopted at the

1989 Strasbourg summit, Britain refused to go along. Plans to incorporate the charter into Maastricht were blocked by the refusal of Thatcher's successor, John Major, to agree to its content, and it was only when Britain changed its position following the 1997 election of Tony Blair that the charter was incorporated by the Treaty of Amsterdam. Among other things, it notes the right to freedom of movement, to fair remuneration for employment, to social protection (including a minimum income for those unable to find employment), to freedom of association and collective bargaining, to equal treatment, to health, safety, and protection in the workplace, and to a retirement income that allows a reasonable standard of living.

Despite all the rhetoric about social issues, most attention since the 1990s has focused on just one problem: the failure of the EU to ease unemployment, the persistence of which was once famously described as equivalent to the persistence of poverty in the United States (Dahrendorf, 1988:149). The single market has not been able to generate enough jobs for Europeans, for reasons which are unclear; at least part of the problem has been the large number of unskilled workers in the EU and the relative ease with which workers can be laid off. Another problem was that while millions of new jobs were created before the economic downturn in 2007–10, nearly half were temporary or part-time jobs, many of them in the service sector, and because most were being filled by men and women new to the job market, they did little to help ease long-term unemployment. The EU has launched a host of retraining programmes, and is shifting resources to the poorer parts of the EU through various cohesion programmes, but with mixed results. Geyer and Springer (1998:210) argue that EU employment policy has had 'high visibility but little focus', and that the search for solutions is hampered by a lack of support in the member states, which have been responsible for employment policy. They also note that the EU has the problem of trying to create jobs through increased competitiveness while preserving the traditional rights of employees.

One of the changes that came with the Amsterdam treaty was the introduction of an employment chapter that called on member states to 'work towards developing a coordinated strategy for employment'. However, it only requires the Commission and the member states to report to each other, and most of the responsibility for employment policy still remains with the member states. Unemployment has been high on the agendas of several recent European Council summits, which have agreed common guidelines on employment policy, including a fresh start for the young and the long-term unemployed, and simplified rules for small and medium-sized enterprises. The structural problems that had remained unresolved came home to roost in many EU states during the economic downturn, worsening the unemployment picture (see Figure 8.2).

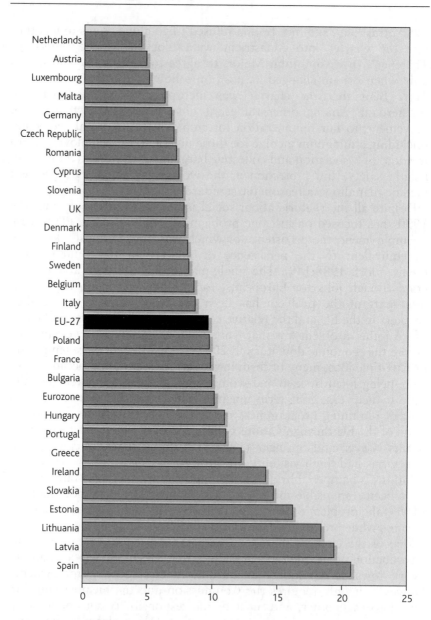

Data from Eurostat at http://epp.eurostat.ec.europa.eu (retrieved December 2010).
Figures are for October 2010. For comparison, the figure for the United States was 9.6.

Figure 8.2   *Unemployment in the European Union*

of encouraging an equitable distribution of the benefits of integration. The EU has tended to equate development with growth, but whether quantity and quality go hand in hand has long been debated. The free market can never entirely eliminate inequalities of opportunity, which is why regional policy has been based on a kind of grand welfare system that sees the redistribution of wealth as a means of encouraging equal opportunity.

Social policy has been aimed at reducing differences in income, opportunity, working conditions, and worker skills with a view to creating a level playing field in the labour market. The attempt to build a common approach has stepped on ideological toes, but has ultimately brought all the member states around to a standard set of objectives. The biggest failure has been the inability to reduce unemployment across the EU, a problem which only became worse with the global economic downturn, and which promises to compromise some of the achievements of the single market unless it can be turned around.

In the case of the environment, there is little question that international cooperation is desirable and even inevitable. Problems such as air and water pollution ignore national boundaries, and there are repeated examples from around the world of one state being a producer and downwind or downstream states being recipients. As the global economy expands, the barriers posed to trade by different environmental standards add a new dimension. There will always be ideological disagreement about the extent to which the state should manage natural resources and regulate industry, but there is a strong internal logic to international cooperation on environmental management. There is an emerging consensus that the EU has been a positive force in environmental protection, and that European environmental problems are better dealt with at the EU level than at the national or local level.

Chapter 9

The EU and the World

The EU presents a confusing image to the outside world. Should the member states still be thought of and dealt with separately, should the European Union be considered a single large bloc, or is the best approach something in between? The answer depends on the issue at stake. On foreign and security policy the EU has developed many common positions, but member states still have their own more limited interests, and the EU is still not regarded as a global actor in the same light as the United States, China, or Russia. But when trade issues are on the agenda, or third parties want access to the European marketplace, the EU can be thought of as a unit, and on monetary issues the states of the eurozone work and act collectively.

The long-time lack of focus, consistency, and policy leadership, and the resulting confusion felt by other countries, was neatly summed up in a (sadly, apocryphal) question credited to former US Secretary of State Henry Kissinger: 'When I want to speak to Europe, whom do I call?' More clarity was provided in 1999 when four external relations portfolios in the Commission were replaced with one, and the new position of High Representative was appointed to be the first point of contact on foreign and security policy matters. The office was confirmed under Lisbon, and given new powers, including a seat in both the European Commission and the Council of Ministers, and management of a new European diplomatic corps. But the EU is still represented in high-level meetings by the president of the Commission, and the waters were further muddied by the creation under Lisbon of a new president of the European Council.

Whatever efforts the EU institutions and the leaders of EU member states have made to redefine the global role of the EU, international events have probably had a more telling effect. European leaders were embarrassed in the 1990s by their divided response to the first Gulf war and the break-up of Yugoslavia, and again in 2003 by their disagreement over whether or not to support the US-led invasion of Iraq. The need for more and better coordination of policy was underlined by the teething troubles of the euro, the pressures of globalization, the effects of eastern enlargement, the emergence of new kinds of threats to international security (such as terrorism and climate change), the global economic crisis of 2007–10, and wider changes in the international system, including the revised global role of the United States and the rise of China and India.

While the steps taken by the EU to build a common foreign and security policy have been halting, there are few remaining doubts about its global economic status. It is the world's richest market-place, accounting for 28 per cent of global GDP, 17 per cent of merchandise trade, and 25 per cent of trade in commercial services. It is the dominating actor in global trade negotiations, the biggest market in the world for mergers and acquisitions, and the biggest source of (and target for) foreign direct investment. In spite of recent problems with the euro, its global economic profile continues to grow, and much more is now expected of the EU on the world stage, both by its own members and by other countries. The result has been new momentum on giving substance to the outlines of the EU as a global actor, and a reassertion of the European perspective in international affairs. The implications of this are not yet fully recognized or understood.

Towards a European foreign policy

In their attempts to build a common European foreign policy, EU leaders have found themselves being pulled in two directions. On the one hand it has been clear that the EU will punch below its weight unless its member states work as a group. On the other hand there has been the fear that coordination will interfere with state sovereignty and the freedom of member states to pursue matters of national interest. Complicating the picture, there are legal and constitutional issues regarding policy responsibility, and European leaders are divided over how far they should continue to follow the lead of the United States and how far they should (or could) build more policy independence for the EU (see later in this chapter). But while leaders are divided, many ordinary Europeans have made up their minds:

- In polls taken between 1999 and 2009, about 75 per cent supported a common EU defence and security policy, with only about 15 per cent opposed (Eurobarometer 70, June 2010:225).
- In the same period, about 65 per cent favoured a common EU foreign policy, with only about one-fifth opposed (Eurobarometer 70, June 2010:223).
- 75 per cent regard the EU as indispensable in meeting global challenges such as climate change and international terrorism (Eurobarometer 72, Spring 2010:193).
- 78 per cent support an EU foreign policy independent from that of the United States; even in Britain, the closest European ally of the

US, there is 72 per cent support (Eurobarometer 68, May 2008:128).
- 60 per cent feel that the EU can play a more positive role than the United States in promoting international peace, encouraging environmental protection, and pursuing the war on terrorism (Eurobarometer 66, September 2007:173).

The Treaties of Rome made no mention of foreign policy, and the EEC long focused on domestic economic policy. But the logic of spillover implied that the development of the single market would make it difficult to avoid the agreement of common external policies. Early moves in that direction included the failed European Defence and Political Communities, and Charles de Gaulle's plans for regular meetings among the leaders of the Six to coordinate foreign policy. It was only at their summit in The Hague in 1969 that leaders looked more closely at foreign policy, paving the way for the 1970 launch of European Political Cooperation (EPC), a process by which the foreign ministers met to discuss and coordinate policy positions. EPC remained a loose and voluntary arrangement outside the Community, but consultation became habit-forming, and led to the creation in 1974 of the European Council.

Regular meetings of senior officials from the foreign ministries provided continuity to EPC, and a small secretariat was set up in Brussels to help the country holding the presidency of the Council of Ministers, which provided most of the momentum. Larger or more active states such as Britain and France had few problems providing leadership, but policy coordination put a strain on smaller and/or neutral countries such as Ireland and Luxembourg. And while changes in the presidency of the Council of Ministers every six months gave each member state its turn at the helm, they complicated life for non-Community states, which had to switch their attention from one member state to another, and to establish contacts with ministers and bureaucrats in six, then nine, then 12 capital cities.

EPC was given formal recognition with the Single European Act, which confirmed that the member states would 'endeavour jointly to formulate and implement a European foreign policy'. But the Gulf War of 1990–91 – set off by the Iraqi invasion of Kuwait in August 1990 – found the Community both divided and unprepared. The United States orchestrated a multinational response, but while the Community was quick to ban Iraqi oil imports, suspend trade agreements, freeze Iraqi assets, and give emergency aid to frontline states (Ginsberg, 2001:193), in terms of hard military action, its member states were divided: Britain and France made major commitments of troops, warplanes, and naval vessels; Germany was limited by a postwar tradition of pacifism and constitutional limits on military deployments; Belgium, Portugal, and Spain made minimal military contributions; and Ireland remained neutral (van Eekelen, 1990; Anderson, 1992). The response, charged Luxembourg foreign minister Jacques Poos, underlined 'the political insignificance of Europe', while for Belgian foreign minister Mark Eyskens it showed that the EC was 'an economic giant, a political dwarf, and a military worm' (*New York Times*, 25 January 1991).

Under the terms of Maastricht, the EU adopted a Common Foreign and Security Policy (CFSP). Its goals were only loosely defined, with vague talk about the need to safeguard 'common values' and 'fundamental interests', 'to preserve peace and strengthen international security', and to 'promote international cooperation', but it encouraged a steady convergence of positions among the member states on key international issues. Their UN ambassadors met frequently to coordinate policy, the EU agreed several common strategies, such as those on Russia and Ukraine, joint actions such as transporting humanitarian aid to Bosnia and sending observers to elections in Russia and South Africa, and common positions on EU relations with other countries, including the Balkans, the Middle East, Burma, and Zimbabwe. The EU also coordinated western aid to Eastern Europe, Russia and the former Soviet republics during the 1990s, and became the major supplier of aid to developing countries (see later in this chapter).

But the examples of weakness and division remained, nowhere more so than in the Balkans in the 1990s (see Peterson, 2003). When the ethnic, religious, and nationalist tensions that had long been kept in check by the Tito regime (1944–80) broke into the open, and Croatia and Slovenia seceded from Yugoslavia in June 1991, the Yugoslav federal army responded with force. The EU organized a peace conference, but then lost its credibility when it recognized Croatia and Slovenia in January 1992, and it was left to the United States to broker the Dayton peace accords in 1995. Then there was the EU's feeble response to the 1998 crisis in the Yugoslav province of Kosovo: when ethnic Albanians in Kosovo began agitating for independence from Serb-dominated Yugoslavia, the government of Slobodan Milosevic responded with force, leading to a massive refugee problem and reports of massacres of both Kosovars and Muslims. When the military response eventually came, in March 1999, it was led not by the EU but by the United States under the auspices of NATO.

Some of the structural weaknesses in the CFSP were addressed by the Treaty of Amsterdam: as well as opening up the possibility of limited majority voting on foreign policy issues, the rotation of countries holding the presidency of the EU was changed so that large member states alternated with small ones, more effectively balancing leadership. A Policy Planning and Early Warning Unit was also created in Brussels to help the EU anticipate foreign crises, and the four different regional external affairs portfolios in the European Commission were replaced with a single foreign policy post and the appointment of a High Representative for the CFSP; the first office-holder was Javier Solana, former secretary-general of NATO. But these institutional changes were not enough to prevent the most open and famous of all recent foreign policy disputes: the split over the 2003 invasion of Iraq. While there was transatlantic political unity on the US-led invasion of Afghanistan in 2002, there was a dramatic parting of the ways over Iraq, with questions over the rationale behind the invasion: charges that Iraqi leader Saddam Hussein possessed weapons of mass destruction, aspired to build nuclear weapons, and posed a threat to neighbouring states.

EU governments fell into three camps: supporters of US policy included Britain, Denmark, Italy, the Netherlands, Spain, and many in Eastern Europe; opponents included Austria, Belgium, France, Germany, and Greece; those that took no position included Finland, Ireland, Portugal, and Sweden. But often overlooked, and yet far more significant, was the remarkable uniformity of public opposition to the war in the EU: 70–90 per cent were opposed in every EU member state, including those whose governments supported the invasion. Several of the latter found themselves in trouble with their electorates, and massive public demonstrations were held in most major European capitals, including Berlin, London, and Rome. A June 2003 opinion poll found reduced faith in American global leadership, and even in Germany – long a staunch US ally – 81 per cent felt that the EU was more important than the United States to their vital interests, up from 55 per cent in 2002 (Asmus *et al.*, 2003). Most remarkably, another survey found that 53 per cent of Europeans viewed the United States as a threat to world peace on a par with North Korea and Iran (Eurobarometer poll, October 2003).

The disagreement had three major effects. First, it shook the Atlantic Alliance to its core, raising new questions in the minds of Europeans about the extent to which the EU should continue to rely on US foreign and security policy leadership. Second, when the weapons of mass destruction were not found, and questions were asked about the extent to which the United States and Britain had manufactured the case for going to war, a major blow was dealt to the credibility of US policy leadership from which it has yet to recover. Finally, it reminded the EU once again just how poorly developed its foreign policy structures remained, decades after the first attempts had been made to build common European positions.

Lisbon brought the most recent round of institutional changes, not only confirming the revamped post of High Representative (HR), but making the office-holder a vice-president of the Commission, chair of the Foreign Affairs Council in the Council of Ministers, and director of a new diplomatic corps, the European External Action Service (EEAS) (see Box 9.1). Some consternation was created when the European Council opted to give the job to Baroness Catherine Ashton, a relatively unknown British politician then serving as commissioner for trade. Many saw the appointment as an opportunity to bring a well-known figure into the EU foreign policy structure and thus give it more international presence, and saw Ashton's appointment as an opportunity missed. But at least the EU had made a clear move towards providing the phone number that Henry Kissinger had asked for. The president of the Commission and the new president of the European Council are also part of the mix, but in the combination of the HR and the EEAS, the EU today has something very like a department of foreign affairs (or the State Department in the United States).

Towards a European defence policy

Dealing with the 'foreign' element of the CFSP – while not easy – has been less politically troubling than dealing with the 'security' element. Together the EU member states have formidable military power at their disposal, with nuclear weapons (in Britain and France), nearly 1.9 million active personnel, nearly 3,500 combat aircraft, and more non-nuclear submarines and surface naval combat vessels than the United States (aircraft carriers excepted) (see International Institute for Strategic Studies, 2007). Were it to agree a common defence policy and shared command structures, it could transform itself into a military superpower. But EU governments have independent opinions and priorities when it comes to committing their forces, there is still only limited coordination on policy, and progress on setting up a European defence force has been slow. There has also been an ongoing division of opinion within the EU about how to relate to NATO and the United States (see Box 9.2), and – as we saw in Chapter 2 – Europeans generally have a preference for using civilian rather than military means for the resolution of conflict. In short, the EU as a security actor is – in the opinion of Howorth (2007:3) – still in its 'early infancy'.

Maastricht stated that one of the goals of the EU should be 'to assert its identity on the international scene, in particular through the implementation of a common foreign and security policy including the eventual framing of a common defence policy'. But while the CFSP moved defence more squarely onto the EU agenda, Maastricht provided a loophole by committing member states to a common policy that would 'include all questions related to the security of the Union, including the *eventual* framing of a common defence policy, *which might in time* lead to a common defence' (emphasis added).

Box 9.1   The European External Action Service

The creation of a large new bureaucracy is not by itself the solution to a policy problem, and by creating new procedures and hierarchies it can also often create new problems. However, the EU has long lacked an institutional focus for its interests in external relations, and the creation of the EEAS may help address that problem. First proposed as one of the initiatives of the failed constitutional treaty, the EEAS reappeared in the Treaty of Lisbon, and was formally launched on 1 December 2010. It is a combination foreign ministry and diplomatic corps for the EU, charged with working with the diplomatic services of the member states to manage EU foreign and security policies, and supporting the work of the High Representative. It is unique in the EU institutional system, bringing together the external relations departments of the Commission and the Council of Ministers into an independent body with its own budget. It cannot make policy, but instead acts on decisions reached by the Council and Parliament, its job made easier by the fact that the HR has seats in both the Commission and the Council.

When Lisbon also created the new position of president of the European Council, there was speculation that this would cause confusion, and some debate about which of the two positions was potentially the more powerful. Many hoped that the presidency of the European Council would be given to a high-profile politician like Tony Blair, but it went instead to Belgian Prime Minister Herman van Rompuy, who had a track record as a conciliator and as someone whose ego would not outshine those of the heads of the member states. Meanwhile, the HR was given leadership of the EEAS, which seemed to suggest that it was actually the more powerful of the two positions.

There was a struggle for power in 2010 between the Commission (hoping to give up as few of its former responsibilities as possible) and Parliament (hoping to win as many oversight responsibilities as possible). With the final creation of the EEAS, departments and staff were transferred from the Council of Ministers (including those dealing with military matters, intelligence, and crisis management), and from the Commission, including the directorates-general for external relations and development. The overseas delegations that until then had been managed by the Commission were also transferred and renamed European Union delegations. It is too early to say what difference the EEAS will make, but as part of the ongoing pooling of responsibility for external relations, and efforts to give the EU a clearer presence on the world stage, its creation was a critical step forward.

In June 1992, EU foreign and defence ministers meeting at Petersberg, near Bonn, issued a declaration in which they agreed that military units from member states could be used to promote the Petersberg tasks: humanitarian, rescue, peacekeeping, and other crisis-management jobs (including peacemaking). Early indications of how this might work came when EU personnel worked with NATO in monitoring the UN embargo on Serbia and Montenegro, helped set up a unified Croat-Muslim police force to support the administration of the city of Mostar in Bosnia in 1994–96, and helped restructure and train the Albanian police force in 1997. The Treaty of Amsterdam incorporated the Petersberg tasks into the EU treaties, and at a meeting in St Malo in France in December 1998, British prime minister Tony Blair and French president Jacques Chirac declared that the EU should be in a position to play a full role in international affairs, 'must have the capacity for autonomous action, backed up by credible military forces, the means to decide to use them, and the readiness to do so', and suggested the creation of a European rapid reaction force. This was later endorsed by German chancellor Gerhard Schröder (for more details, see Collester, 2000).

The result was the launch in 1999 of the European Security and Defence Policy (ESDP) (see Howorth, 2003). An integral part of the CFSP, this was initially to consist of two key components: the Petersberg tasks, and a 60,000-member Rapid Reaction Force (RRF) that could be deployed at 60 days' notice and sustained for at least one year and could carry out these tasks. The Force was not intended to be a standing army, was designed to complement rather than compete with NATO, and could only act when NATO had decided not to be involved in a crisis. The plan was to have it ready by the end of 2003, but it proved more of a challenge than expected, and by 2004 the EU was talking of the more modest goal of creating 'battle groups' that could be deployed more quickly and for shorter periods than the RRF. The groups would consist of 1500 troops each that could be committed within 15 days, and could be sustainable for between 30 and 120 days. That same year, the European Defence Agency was created within which national defence ministers meet to promote planning and research in the interests of the ESDP.

The terrorist attacks on the World Trade Center in New York and on the Pentagon in Washington, DC in September 2001 brought new issues into the equation. The meaning of 'war' and 'defence' had already changed with the end of the cold war, but the attacks – and the response to them – forced a review of defence policy priorities on both sides of the Atlantic: terrorism (especially when it involved suicide attacks) could not be met with conventional military responses. Many European leaders hoped for a new era in transatlantic relations, with a new US emphasis on multilateralism and diplomacy, but these hopes

Box 9.2   A European or an Atlantic defence?

One of the core issues in the debate about European foreign policy is the question of how the EU should relate to the North Atlantic Treaty Organization (NATO) and the United States. Among governments, there are two main schools of thought:

- Atlanticists such as Britain, the Netherlands, Portugal, and several Eastern European states emphasize the importance of the security relationship with the United States, and are loath to do anything that could be interpreted as undermining or replacing the transatlantic security relationship.
- Europeanists such as France, Italy, Spain, and sometimes Germany look more towards European independence, and believe that the EU should reduce its reliance on the American policy lead.

During the cold war (1945–91), Atlanticists had the upper hand because the main defence issue was security against a Soviet attack, something that fell squarely under the remit of a US-dominated NATO. Furthermore, member states had different policy positions and different defence capacities: the British and the French had special interests in their colonies and former colonies, the Germans and the Dutch saw their armed forces as part of the broader NATO system, and several countries – notably Ireland – were neutral. Europeans became used to coordinating their defence policies within the NATO framework, guided by US leadership.

With the end of the cold war, Europeanists appeared to gain ground, in part thanks to changes in US policy. President Kennedy had spoken during his inauguration in 1960 of the willingness of the United States to 'bear any burden' and 'meet any hardship ... to assure the survival and success of liberty'. By the mid-1990s, though, American public opinion had turned against such an idea, and the term 'burden sharing' became more common in transatlantic discussions, with demands for the EU to take on greater responsibility for addressing its own security threats. Meanwhile, the ability of the EU to respond to security threats was clearly inadequate, a problem that became more critical during the 1990s as US defence spending fell (Barber, 1998). Then came the divisions over how to conduct the war on terrorism, and the transatlantic fallout over the 2003 US-led attack on Iraq, the latter in particular showing that European public opinion was taking an increasingly independent view.

were dashed in the fallout from the dispute over Iraq, which emphasized to many that the EU needed to more forcefully outline and pursue its distinctive position on security issues.

In 2003, the European Council adopted the European Security Strategy, the first ever declaration by EU member states of their strategic goals. It argued that the EU was 'inevitably a global player', and 'should be ready to share in the responsibility for global security', listing the key threats facing the EU as terrorism, weapons of mass destruction, regional conflicts, failing states, and organized crime. Against the background of a changing transatlantic relationship, the draft EU constitution included the stipulation that the EU should take a more active role in its own defence, talking of the 'progressive framing of a common Union defence policy' leading to a common defence 'when the European Council, acting unanimously, so decides'. But even if they are to be guided by the Petersberg tasks, the question still remains as to how European defence forces should be organized. Europeanists such as France continue to want to develop an independent EU capability. The United States is content to see the Europeans taking responsibility for those tasks from which NATO should best keep its distance, but insists that there should be no overlap or rivalry in the event of the creation of a separate European institution. Meanwhile, Atlanticists such as Britain continue to feel nervous about undermining the US commitment to Europe.

While there is no questioning the American superiority in the field of military power (the United States currently spends more on defence every year than the rest of the world combined), an issue often overlooked in the debate about the global role of the EU is the question of soft power. This is defined by Joseph Nye (2004:x), as 'the ability to get what you want through attraction rather than coercion', and is centred on culture, political ideals, and policies rather than on the threat of violence. Critics of US foreign policy argue that it relies too much on hard power rather than soft power, and that this has been one of the causes of the decline in the credibility of US foreign policy. By contrast, the EU – making a virtue of necessity, argue some, while pursuing a deliberate policy, argue others (see discussion in Chapter 2) – has become adept at using soft power in its dealings with other countries. In a world in which violence is increasingly rejected as a tool of statecraft (at least among wealthy liberal democracies), the use of diplomacy, political influence, and the pressures of economic competition may be giving the EU a strategic advantage that reduces the need to develop a significant common military capacity.

This is not to suggest that the EU is either unwilling or unable to use hard power. In spite of its internal political disagreements, the EU has achieved far more on security cooperation than most people think, driven by a desire to decrease its reliance on the US (Jones, 2007). It is also both willing and able to use hard power when needed (Giegerich and Wallace, 2004). In 2003, it deployed peacekeeping troops in Macedonia (Operation Concordia) and in the Democratic Republic of Congo (Operation Artemis), and in December 2004 launched its biggest peacekeeping mission when 7000 troops (many coming from outside the EU, it is true) took over from NATO in Bosnia. By 2006, the EU was contributing 50 per cent of the peacekeeping forces in Bosnia (where the office of High Representative in charge of implementation of the Dayton peace accords has always been held by an EU national), 60 per cent of the forces in Afghanistan, 70 per cent of the forces in Kosovo, and 72 per cent of the forces in Lebanon, while 12 EU states had 19,000 troops in Iraq. National military interventions have also continued, including Britain's operation in Sierra Leone in 2001 (establishing order after a UN force had failed) and France's operation in Côte d'Ivoire in 2002.

Europe's global economic presence

While there is little evidence to suggest that the EU could (or even wants to) become a military superpower, there are no doubts at all about its status as an economic superpower. The single market is all but complete, the euro has been adopted by 17 member states, the Commission has the authority to speak on behalf of the EU in global trade negotiations, and it is now well understood that the EU is the most powerful actor in those negotiations. The statistics paint a clear and incontestable picture:

- With just over 7 per cent of the world's population, the European Union accounts for 28 per cent of the world's GDP (more even than the United States) and for bigger shares of trade in merchandise and commercial services than either the United States or China (see Figure 9.1). Trade – argues Orbie (2008) – has become the EU's 'most powerful external policy domain'.
- With a population of nearly 500 million, the EU has 61 per cent more consumers than the United States. More importantly, the personal wealth of Europeans – combined with the largely open internal market that now exists in the EU – means that the EU is the wealthiest market in the world. China and India may have many more people but they are on average much poorer; German gross national income is nearly 12 times greater than that in China and nearly 36 times greater than that in India (see Appendix 1).
- Seventeen of the 27 member states (which among them account for 76 per cent of the GDP and 66 per cent of the population of the EU) have a shared currency that is the only substantial competitor with the US dollar in terms of credibility and influence – China and India have nothing that comes close to comparing. At least until its problems in 2010–11 the euro was earning new attention as a challenger to the status of the US dollar, with suggestions that it might eventually become the primary international reserve currency (Chinn and Frankel, 2005). The euro has been helped by declining faith in the

dollar, based in part on concerns about the snowballing US national debt, and in part on questions about American economic leadership in the world.

- As we saw in Chapter 7, the EU has become the biggest mergers and acquisitions market in the world, a trend that has helped create new European multinationals with a global presence comparable only to their US counterparts. The EU is now the source of two-thirds of all investment coming from OECD member states, and more than three times as much as the United States (OECD website, 2010).
- The EU has become the engine of economic growth for Eastern Europe and Russia, which have a combined population of more than 240 million, enormous productive potential, and a wealth of largely untapped natural resources.

The global economic presence of the EU has been built on the foundations of the single market and the Common Commercial Policy, to which end the EU has built a complex network of multilateral and bilateral trading networks and agreements, some based on proximity (agreements with Eastern Europe and Mediterranean states), some on former colonial ties (see the section on development cooperation below), and some on expediency (agreements with the United States and Japan). The growth of European trade power has also been helped by an institutional structure that promotes common positions among the member states. The Commission generates policy initiatives, is responsible for investigating and taking action against unfair trading practices, and makes suggestions to the Council of Ministers when it thinks that agreements need to be negotiated with other countries or international organizations. Most importantly, once the member states have agreed a position among themselves, the Commission is left to negotiate external trade agreements on behalf of the EU as a whole. So if Henry Kissinger was to ask to whom he should speak in Europe regarding trade matters, the answer would be clear.

The power of the EU is particularly clear in the role it has played in global trade negotiations. In 1948, the General Agreement on Tariffs and Trade (GATT) was founded to oversee a programme aimed at removing trade restrictions and liberalizing trade; it was replaced in 1995 by the World Trade Organization (WTO). The GATT/WTO negotiations have taken place in successive rounds in which the EU states negotiate as a group, and are typically represented by the European commissioner for trade. The round that began in 2001 in Doha, Qatar, was designed to open up world markets for agricultural and manufactured goods. By 2006 they had stalled because rich and poor countries could not agree over farm subsidies and import taxes. The poor countries accused the EU in particular of supporting and protecting its farmers through CAP export subsidies (which has made

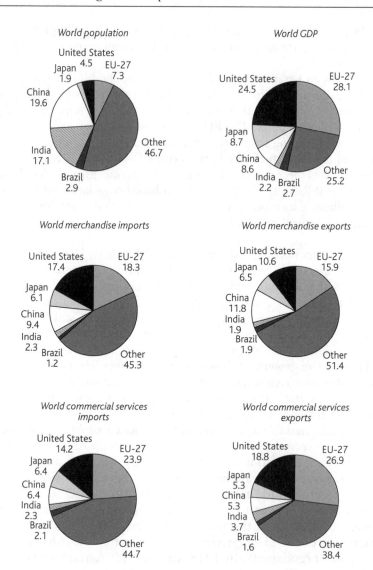

Figure 9.1   *The EU in the global economy*

Sources: Population data for 2010 from UN Population Division at http://www.un.org/esa/popula-tion, economic data for 2009 from World Development Indicators database at http://www.world-bank.com, and trade figures for 2008 (excluding data for intra-EU trade) from World Trade Organization at http://www.wto.org.

European farmers more competitive and productive), and of 'dumping' their produce cheaply in poor countries, undermining the efforts of local farmers. (The United States was also criticized for its subsidies, particularly to cotton farmers.)

But more telling as a measure of EU trading power has been the frequency with which it has been at odds with the United States, the other giant at the table. If a country adopts a trade policy measure or takes an action that is considered to be a breach of a WTO agreement, the dispute can be taken to the WTO, which investigates and issues a judgment that is binding upon member states. The EU and the United States have brought more cases before the WTO than anyone else, and in many instances the disputes have been between the EU and the US; they have tussled in recent years over hormone-treated beef, banana imports, trade with Cuba, tariffs on steel, subsidies to aircraft manufacturers, intellectual property rights, trade in services, and the tax regimes of third countries (Billiet, 2005).

Relations with the United States

The transatlantic relationship has blown hot and cold, which is only to be expected given that the EU and the United States are both major allies and major competitors (see McGuire and Smith, 2008: ch. 1). Relations were strong after the Second World War, the United States having played a critical role in ridding Europe of Nazism, then guaranteeing European reconstruction and integration with the investments it made under the Marshall Plan and the security umbrella it provided for Western Europe during the cold war. US administrations saw integration as a way of helping the region recover from the ravages of war and of improving European (and American) security in the face of the Soviet threat. Relations cooled in the early 1960s with Charles de Gaulle's concerns about American influence in Europe, and continued to cool as the US and its European allies fell out over Vietnam, and over West German diplomatic overtures to Eastern Europe.

The 1971 collapse of the Bretton Woods system – precipitated by the decision of the Nixon administration to cut the dollar's link with gold – not only marked the beginning of a steady withdrawal of the US responsibility for global leadership, but also emphasized to many Europeans the unwillingness of the United States always to take heed of European opinion on critical issues. The Community was by then rapidly catching up with the United States in economic wealth, it traded less with the United States and more with Eastern Europe, and disagreement over the Arab–Israeli issue in the 1970s was followed by the revival of the Western European anti-nuclear movement in the early 1980s, both placing a further strain on transatlantic relations.

Box 9.3   The overlooked superpower

Since the end of the cold war there has been a vigorous debate about the character and dynamics of the international system. During the cold war it was clearly bipolar, driven by the tensions between the United States and the Soviet Union. With the collapse of the Soviet Union in 1991, it became usual to hear discussion of a new unipolar arrangement with a dominating United States. But then new attention was drawn to the rise of the BRIC states: Brazil, Russia, India, and China (Wilson and Purushothaman, 2003). While less attention is now paid to Brazil and Russia, the preponderance of public and political opinion is that China and India are the new great powers (in spite of their poverty, and China's poor human rights record), and that the United States is in relative decline.

Missing from much of this debate about the changing international system has been the place of the European Union. Several studies have suggested that it is on the ascendant (see Reid, 2004; Haseler, 2004; Leonard, 2005; McCormick, 2007) but few consider it one of the great powers on a par with the United States or China, for four main reasons:

- Convention equates great power with military power, and the EU has neither a combined military nor a clear common defence policy.
- Convention associates power with states. Taken individually, even the larger EU states have only a modest international reach, while the EU itself, say the cynics, is not sufficiently coordinated to express its collective power at a global level.
- Power is more impressive when it is expressed visibly, and nothing is more visible than the sight of American 'shock and awe' bombardments of Iraq or Afghanistan, or American aircraft carriers being despatched for a show of force. The EU has little to match this kind of raw power, its influence being subtle and latent rather than obvious and assertive.
- The EU has regularly failed to provide leadership, reflected in its dithering in the Balkans in the 1990s, the often public disagreements among its leaders, or evidence that the United States is taken more seriously by North Korea, Iran, or Israel.

How we think about the global role of the EU depends in large part on how we define power. The EU expresses its influence differently, through civilian means, and through the subtle and sometimes unconscious offering of a different example of power, and of different approaches to the resolution of global problems. We are still in an early phase of our understanding of the effects.

The end of the Soviet hegemony in Eastern Europe in the late 1980s led to a new volatility in Europe that encouraged the first Bush administration to call for stronger transatlantic ties on political matters. The result was the signature in November 1990 of a Transatlantic Declaration committing the United States and the Community to regular high-level meetings. Contacts were taken a step further in 1995 with the adoption of a New Transatlantic Agenda and a Joint EU–US Action Plan under which both sides agreed to move from consultation to joint action aimed at promoting peace and democracy around the world, expanding world trade, and improving transatlantic ties. Biannual meetings have since taken place between the presidents of the United States, the Commission and the European Council, between the US Secretary of State and EU foreign ministers, and between the Commission and members of the US cabinet.

The EU and the United States are each other's major trade partners, and the largest sources and destinations of foreign direct investment. They hold common views on the merits of democracy and capitalism, but divisions of opinion have become more common and more substantial with time. This has been partly a result of the reassertion of European economic power since the end of the cold war, and partly a result of the relative decline of US influence in the wake of the Iraqi controversy and the global economic crisis of 2007–10. But it can also be explained by the fact that Americans and Europeans have many different values: Americans place more emphasis on military power than Europeans, unilateralism plays a greater role in their calculations than the multilateralist tendencies of the Europeans, the often unapologetic support given by the United States to Israel says much about the different worldviews of Americans and Europeans, and the two sides have quite different thoughts about the responsibilities of government (Europeans are more willing to tolerate state-run health-care and education systems, for example) and about a string of more focused issues, including capital punishment, climate change, the work of the United Nations, and the links between religion and politics (for more details, see McCormick, 2007: ch. 7).

The fallout over Iraq raised many new questions about the health of the transatlantic relationship that have not yet been answered (see, for example, Kopstein and Steinmo, 2008). At one level, the dispute could be dismissed as just another of the many that have coloured US–European relations since 1945, and perhaps as more reflective of the short-term goals and values of the Bush administration than of long-term US policy on Europe. But the depth of public opposition to US policy was remarkable, as was the division among the leaders of the EU's four major powers: Germany, Britain, France, and Italy. For some, the dispute represented the rapidly changing worldviews of the United States and the European Union, and an opportunity for the EU

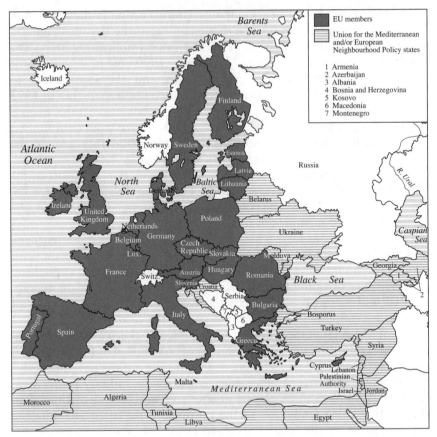

Map 9.1 *The EU and its neighbourhood*

to assert its often different analyses of – and prescriptions for – global problems (see Box 9.3). In this sense, the war on terrorism may ultimately be seen as emblematic of a fundamental change not just in the nature of the transatlantic relationship, but in the setting of priorities on international issues.

Relations with the neighbourhood

If there are many questions about the global influence of the European Union, there are far fewer about its impact on its immediate neighbourhood, where three distinct rings of influence can be identified: the states that have short-term potential to either become members of the EU (including Croatia, Iceland, Macedonia, and Montenegro) or have at least established strong economic links with the EU (notably

Norway and Switzerland), the states that have longer-term prospects of joining the EU (including Albania, Serbia, the Ukraine, and Turkey), and states that do not qualify for membership but cannot escape the gravitational pull of the EU (North Africa, Russia, and much of the Middle East) (see Map 9.1). In each of these rings the EU plays a critical role in reorganization of economic structures, while further afield its activities have critical implications for the spread of democracy and capitalism.

The Community was quick to take a leading role in responding to the fallout from the end of the cold war, coordinating western economic aid to the east and creating in 1990 the European Bank for Reconstruction and Development (EBRD), which has since channelled public money from the EU, the United States, and Japan into development of the private sector in the east. The EU subsequently signed trade and cooperation agreements with almost every Eastern European state, several billion dollars in loans were made available by the European Investment Bank, and several programmes were launched to help east European economic and social reform. More significantly, the end of the cold war generated several requests from Eastern Europe for associate or full membership of the EU. Europe Agreements were signed with several, arranging for the integration of Eastern European economies with those of the EU through the staged removal of barriers to trade in industrial and agricultural goods, and to the movement of workers. The Treaty of Amsterdam paved the way for eastward expansion, membership negotiations began in 1998 with the Czech Republic, Estonia, Hungary, Poland, and Slovenia, and the 2004–07 enlargements brought 12 new members into the EU, including three former republics of the Soviet Union: Estonia, Latvia, and Lithuania.

The significance (and the challenge) of eastern enlargement was considerable. It gave final confirmation to the end of the cold war, giving new meaning to the definition of Europe and reducing the distinctions between *Europe* and the *European Union*. But Eastern European governments and citizens struggled with the task of transforming their economies from central planning to the free market, and their political systems from one-party authoritarianism to multi-party democracy, and faced the daunting task of making sure that domestic laws were adapted to EU law. Eastern Europe was also relatively poor: while the 12 countries that joined in 2004–07 increased the population of the EU by 20 per cent, they increased its GDP by less than 5 per cent. In the west, meanwhile, an 'enlargement fatigue' set in, raising questions about how long it would be before more countries would join the EU.

Alongside enlargement, the EU has been pursuing agreements and cooperation with its neighbours that have different intentions. In 1995 the Barcelona Process (formally the Euro-Mediterranean Partnership) was launched with the goal of strengthening ties between the EU and

214 Understanding the European Union

all other states bordering the Mediterranean. It was handicapped by the lack of progress on the Middle East peace process, by concerns among some partner countries about the dominant role of the EU, and by the inclusion of the many EU states that do not border the Mediterranean. In 2008 the Barcelona Process evolved into the Union for the Mediterranean, a pet project of French President Nikolas Sarkozy that was intended originally to have focused only on Mediterranean states, but ultimately expanded to include the whole of the EU; it now has 43 members: the 27 EU states and 16 neighbouring states. Meanwhile the European Neighbourhood Policy was launched in 2004, encouraging a relationship that the EU describes as 'privileged', and with the goals of promoting democracy, human rights, the rule of law, good governance, and market economics. Both initiatives include a mix of states with prospects for joining the EU and those without.

Even if there are still many doubts about the substance and potential for success of the EU foreign and security policies as a whole, few now question the critical and dominating role that EU policy has had in ensuring the spread of democracy and free-market ideas to the former Soviet bloc (Leonard, 2005:56, 103–4). The EU's leading role in this area has not only helped define EU foreign policy, but has also made the EU a major regional political actor. In only three cases can major qualifications be added. First, while it has a far greater interest than the United States in seeing peace in the Middle East (given its proximity, its oil interests, and its concerns about illegal immigration and terrorism), it has played only a supporting role and has been unable to exert much influence on Israel (see Pardo and Peters, 2009). Second, the story of EU–Russian relations has not been a happy one (Antonenko and Pinnick, 2005). During the 1990s the Russians looking for the respectability and economic opportunities that would come from a good relationship with the EU, while the EU looked for Russian support for eastern enlargement, and needed some of the oil and natural gas that Russia has in abundance. But neither side fully trusts the other, and the EU has to balance staying on good terms with Russia against its criticism of the remnants of Russian authoritarianism. Finally, the EU has had little influence on bringing change to Belarus, the last remaining outpost of Soviet-style authoritarianism in Europe and a close ally of Russia.

Development cooperation

The long history of European colonialism has left the European Union with a heritage of close economic and political ties to the South: Latin America, South Asia, and Africa. Several of the founding members of the Community – notably France and Belgium – still had colonies when the Treaty of Rome was signed, and when Britain joined the EU in 1973 it brought several dozen more mainly former colonies into the equation. As a result, the South has been a significant factor in the external relations of the EU, the core of the relationship being a programme of aid and trade promotion involving several dozen former European colonies in Africa, the Caribbean, and the Pacific – the so-called ACP states (see Table 9.1).

EU development aid policies have been based partly on remedying quality of life issues such as poverty and hunger, but there are also less altruistic motives: Africa in particular is a key source of illegal immigrants to the EU, and the EU continues to rely on the South as a source of oil and of key raw materials such as rubber, copper, and uranium. The EU aid programme has several different aspects. As well as allowing all Southern states to export industrial products to the EU tariff- and duty-free (subject to some limitations on volume), the EU provides food and emergency aid, and sponsors development projects undertaken by NGOs. The EU has also negotiated a series of cooperative agreements with the ACP countries, mainly non-Asian former colonies of Britain and France. These began with the 1963 and 1969 Yaoundé Conventions (named for the capital of Cameroon, where they were signed), which gave 18 former colonies preferential access to Community markets. The 18 in turn allowed limited duty-free or quota-free access by the EC to their markets. The provision of trade concessions was expanded by the four Lomé Conventions (named after the capital of Togo), which were signed in 1975, 1979, 1984, and 1989.

Lomé IV, which covered the period 1990–2000 and was revised in 1995, had three main elements. First, it provided financial aid to 71 ACP states under the European Development Fund, in the form mainly of grants for development projects and low-interest loans. Second, it provided free access to the EU for products originating in ACP countries, with the exception of agricultural products covered by CAP. About 95 per cent of ACP exports entered the EU duty-free, compared to just 10 per cent of agricultural goods from other countries, and other goods were subject to tariffs in the range of 17–23 per cent. Finally, it offered an insurance fund for ACP exports called Stabex, designed to offset falls in the value of 50 specified ACP agricultural exports. If prices fell below a certain level, Stabex made up the deficit. If they went above that level, ACP countries invested the profits in the fund for future use.

Opinions were mixed about the effects of the Yaoundé and Lomé conventions. On the one hand, they helped build closer commercial ties between the EU and the ACP states, and there was an overall increase in the volume of ACP exports to Europe from the 1960s to the 1990s.

Table 9.1 *The ACP states*

AFRICA (48)	Mali	Dominica
Angola	Mauritania	Dominican Republic
Benin	Mauritius	Grenada
Botswana	Mozambique	Guyana
Burkina Faso	Namibia	Haiti
Burundi	Niger	Jamaica
Cameroon	Nigeria	St Kitts and Nevis
Cape Verde	Rwanda	St Lucia
Central African Republic	São Tomé and Principe	St Vincent and Grenadines
Chad	Senegal	Suriname
Comoros	Seychelles	Trinidad and Tobago
Congo (Brazzaville)	Sierra Leone	
Congo (Kinshasa)	Somalia	PACIFIC (15)
Djibouti	South Africa	Cook Islands
Equatorial Guinea	Sudan	Fiji
Eritrea	Swaziland	Kiribati
Ethiopia	Tanzania	Marshall Islands
Gabon	Togo	Micronesia
Gambia	Uganda	Nauru
Ghana	Zambia	Niue
Guinea	Zimbabwe	Palau
Guinea-Bissau		Papua New Guinea
Côte d'Ivoire	CARIBBEAN (16)	Samoa
Kenya	Antigua and Barbuda	Solomon Islands
Lesotho	Bahamas	Timor-Leste
Liberia	Barbados	Tonga
Madagascar	Belize	Tuvalu
Malawi	Cuba	Vanuatu

But the conventions were widely criticized for promoting economic dependence, and for perpetuating the flow of low-profit raw materials from the ACP to the EU, and the flow of high-profit manufactured goods from the EU to the ACP. Questions were also raised about the extent to which they helped the ACP states invest in their human capital, and helped them develop greater economic independence.

Other problems were structural. Stabex did not help countries that did not produce the specified commodities, payments from the European Development Fund were small by the time the fund had been divided among 71 countries, the ACP programme excluded the larger Southern states that had negotiated separate agreements with the EU (for example, India and China), too little attention was paid to the environmental implications of the focus on cash crops for export, and the programme neither helped deal with the ACP debt crisis nor really much changed the relationship between the EU and the ACP states.

The biggest problem was internal to the ACP states themselves. They mostly failed to diversify their exports, to invest in infrastructure, to build up a more skilled labour force, and to become more competitive in the world market. The EU provided them with a generous set of trade preferences, and yet imports from the ACP as a share of the EU total fell from 6.7 per cent in 1976 to just 3 per cent in 1998. Oil, diamonds, gold, and other industrially related products accounted for about two-thirds of ACP exports to the EU, the balance being made up by agricultural products (30 per cent) and fish (5 per cent). Four countries – Nigeria, Côte d'Ivoire, Cameroon, and Mauritius – between them accounted for more than 40 per cent of EU imports from the ACP countries. At the same time, economic growth in many sub-Saharan African states was sluggish, and there was very little trade taking place among African ACP states.

A new agreement was signed in Cotonou, Benin, in 2000, designed to run for 20 years with revisions every five years. It added seven more countries to the ACP group (including Cuba), places a stronger requirement on ACP states to improve domestic political, economic, and social conditions, and emphasizes the importance of human rights and democracy. Its objectives include the promotion of the interests of the private sector, gender equality, sustainable environmental management, and the replacement of trade preferences with a progressive and reciprocal removal of trade barriers. Whether this will be enough to address the structural problems of the ACP programme remains to be seen.

Meanwhile, the EU has become the biggest source of official development assistance in the world, collectively accounting for 56 per cent of the total of $120 billion given in 2009 by the 24 members of the Development Assistance Committee of the OECD (compared to 22 per cent from the United States and 8 per cent from Japan) (OECD website, 2010). Most EU aid (15 per cent of which is channelled through the EU) goes to sub-Saharan Africa, but an increasing proportion is going to Latin America. The EU also provides emergency humanitarian aid (nearly €500 million in 2001), much of which has gone in recent years to the victims of conflicts in Afghanistan, Armenia, Azerbaijan, and Tajikistan. It has also become the second largest provider of food aid in the world after the United States, supplying food worth about €500 million per year.

Conclusions

The process of European integration was born as a way to help Western Europe rebuild after the Second World War, and to remove the historical causes of conflict in the region. It began life with an introverted domestic agenda, leaving leadership on wider foreign and security policy issues to the United States. With the end of the cold war, the clear security threat posed by the Soviet Union was replaced by economic concerns, by regional security problems such as those in the Balkans and the Middle East, and by less easily defined threats such as nationalist pressures in Russia, the movement of political refugees, the spread of nuclear weapons, the implications of new technology, and environmental problems. Meanwhile globalization proceeded under the auspices of the World Trade Organization, and the wealth and competitiveness of China and India continued to grow, altering the balance of global economic power.

The EC/EU had no choice but to become more extroverted, and integration has since had implications not just for Europe but for Europe's relations with the rest of the world. While the EEC initially focused on bringing down the barriers to internal trade, it quickly became involved in external trade matters, and the EU by the 1990s had turned its attention squarely to common foreign and security policies. Problems were experienced along the way, and the EU become notorious for its often confused and bumbling responses to international problems, but cooperation acquired more consistency and substance, and the development of common foreign and security policies has become one of the core endeavours of European integration.

Events in 2001–04 were to prove a critical turning point: The September 2001 terrorist attacks in the United States were followed by the US-led invasion of Iraq in 2003, while the EU was coincidentally launching its new single currency, expanding its membership deep into Eastern Europe, and upgrading its common foreign, security, and defence policies. The new economic power of the EU combined with new levels of alarm at US foreign policy and growing criticism of US global leadership to make it clear that entirely new expectations were being directed at the EU. Where once Europeans followed the lead of the Americans, if not always willingly, it has become more clear of late that they are out of step with the United States not just on such immediate problems as international terrorism and peace in the Middle East, but also on a wide variety of longer-term issues relating to trade, security, the environment, and more.

The changes of the last few years have made it clear that the EU must work to give its international identity clearer definition, to assert itself on the global stage, and to build the kind of political influence that it needs as a superpower. Europe may never achieve the qualities of a military superpower that are so overtly on show in the United States, and increasingly in China, but it has few aspirations in that direction; it is more adept at using soft power, and at building on its political, economic, and diplomatic advantages as an alternative to the increasingly discredited policies of the United States. Even though the EU may still present a rather confused and confusing image to the outside world, the outline of that image is becoming sharper.

Appendix 1

Europe in Numbers

	Area (000 sq.km)	Population (million)	Gross domestic product (billion $)	Per capita gross national income ($)
European Union (27)				
Germany	357	82.0	3,330	42,450
France	549	62.6	2,649	42,620
UK	244	61.9	2,175	41,370
Italy	301	60.1	2,113	35,110
Spain	505	45.3	1,460	32,120
Netherlands	42	16.7	792	48,460
Belgium	31	10.7	471	45,270
Poland	313	38.0	430	12,260
Sweden	450	9.3	406	48,840
Austria	84	8.4	381	46,450
Greece	132	11.2	330	29,040
Denmark	43	5.5	310	59,060
Finland	338	5.3	238	45,940
Portugal	92	10.7	233	21,910
Ireland	70	4.6	227	44,280
Czech Republic	79	10.4	190	17,310
Romania	238	21.2	161	8,330
Hungary	93	10.0	129	12,980
Slovakia	49	5.4	88	16.130
Luxembourg	3	0.5	52	76,710
Slovenia	20	2.0	48	23,520
Bulgaria	111	7.5	49	6,060
Lithuania	65	3.3	37	11,410
Latvia	65	2.2	26	12,390
Cyprus	9	0.9	25	26,940
Estonia	45	1.4	19	14,060
Malta	0.3	0.4	8	16,690
Total	*4,329*	*497.5*	*16,377*	

Note: countries in bold are part of the eurozone.

	Area (000 sq.km)	Population (million)	Gross domestic product (billion $)	Per capita gross national income ($)
Non-EU Europe (17)				
Turkey	784	75.7	615	8,720
Switzerland	41	7.6	492	65,430
Norway	324	4.9	382	84,640
Ukraine	604	45.4	113	2,800
Croatia	57	4.4	63	13,720
Belarus	208	9.6	49	5,560
Serbia	88	9.9	43	6,000
Azerbaijan	87	8.9	43	4,840
Bosnia/Herzegovina	51	3.8	17	4,700
Iceland	103	0.3	12	43,430
Albania	29	3.2	12	4,000
Georgia	70	4.2	11	2,530
Macedonia	26	2.1*	9*	4,400
Armenia	30	3.1	9	3,100
Kosovo	11	1.8*	5	3,240
Moldova	34	3.6*	5	1,560
Montenegro	14	0.6	4	6,650
Total	*2,561*	*189.1*	*1,884*	

* Estimates

Other				
United States	9,364	308.7	14,256	46,360
Japan	378	127.0	5,069	38,080
China	9,600	1,331.5	4,985	3,650
Brazil	8,515	195.4	1,573	8,040
India	3,287	1,155.3	1,310	1,180
Russia	17,098	140.4	1,232	9,340
WORLD	134,593	6,775.2	58,228	

Source: Area figures from Food and Agriculture Organization of the UN at http://faostat.fao.org. Population figures for 2010 from UN Population Division at http://www.un.org/esa/population. Economic figures for 2009 from World Development Indicators database at http://www.world-bank.com. States are ranked by GDP. All figures retrieved December 2010.

Appendix 2

A Chronology of European Integration

1944	July	Bretton Woods conference
1945	May	Germany surrenders; European war ends
	October	Creation of United Nations
1947	June	Announcement of Marshall Plan
1948	January	Creation of Benelux customs union
	April	Organization for European Economic Cooperation founded
1949	April	North Atlantic Treaty signed
	May	Council of Europe founded
1950	May	Publication of Schuman Declaration
1951	April	Treaty of Paris signed, creating the European Coal and Steel Community
1952	March	Nordic Council founded
	May	Signature of draft treaty creating the European Defence Community (EDC)
	July	Treaty of Paris comes into force
1953	March	Plans announced for European Political Community (EPC)
1954	August	Plans for EDC and EPC collapse
	October	Creation of Western European Union
1956	June	Negotiations open on creation of European Economic Community (EEC) and Euratom
	October–December	Suez crisis
1957	March	Treaties of Rome signed, creating Euratom and the EEC
1958	January	Treaties of Rome come into force
	February	Benelux Economic Union founded
1960	May	European Free Trade Association (EFTA) begins operations
1961	February	First summit of EEC heads of government
	July–August	Britain, Ireland and Denmark apply to join EEC
1962	April	Norway applies for EEC membership

1963	January	De Gaulle vetoes British membership of the EEC; France and Germany sign Treaty of Friendship and Cooperation
1965	April	Merger treaty signed
	July	Start of empty-chair crisis (resolved January 1966)
1966	May	Britain, Ireland and Denmark apply for the second time to join EEC (Norway follows in July)
1967	November	De Gaulle again vetoes British membership of the Community
1968	July	Agreement of a common external tariff completes the creation of an EEC customs union
1970	June	Membership negotiations open with Britain, Denmark, Ireland and Norway; concluded in January 1972
1971	August	US leaves gold standard; end of the Bretton Woods system of fixed exchange rates
1972	September	Referendum in Norway rejects EEC membership
1973	January	Britain, Denmark and Ireland join the Community, bringing membership to nine
1975	March	First meeting of European Council in Dublin; creation of the European Regional Development Fund
	June	Greece applies to join Community
1977	March	Portugal applies to join Community
	July	Spain applies to join Community
1978	December	European Council establishes European Monetary System (EMS)
1979	March	EMS comes into operation; death of Jean Monnet
	June	First direct elections to the European Parliament
1981	January	Greece joins the Community, bringing membership to ten
1984	January	Free trade area established between EFTA and the EEC
1985	June	Schengen Agreement signed by France, Germany and Benelux states
	December	European Council agrees to drawing up of Single European Act (SEA)
1986	January	Portugal and Spain join Community, bringing membership to 12
	February	SEA signed in Luxembourg
1987	April	Turkey applies to join Community
	July	SEA comes into force
1989	April	Delors report on economic and monetary union
	July	Austria applies to join Community
	December	Adoption of Social Charter by 11 EC member states

1990	July	Cyprus and Malta apply to join Community
	August	Iraqi invasion of Kuwait
	October	German reunification brings former East Germany into the Community
1991	June	Outbreak of war in Yugoslavia
	July	Sweden applies to join Community
1992	February	Treaty on European Union (Maastricht treaty) signed
	March	Finland applies to join Community
	May	Switzerland applies to join Community
	June	Danish referendum rejects terms of Maastricht
	November	Norway applies again for Community membership
1993	May	Second Danish referendum accepts terms of Maastricht
	November	Treaty on European Union comes into force. European Community becomes a pillar of the new European Union
1994	January	Creation of the European Economic Area
	March	Hungary applies to join EU
	April	Poland applies to join EU
	May	Opening of Channel Tunnel, linking Britain and France
	June–November	Referendums in Austria, Finland and Sweden accept EU membership, but Norwegians again say no
1995	January	Austria, Finland and Sweden join the European Union, bringing membership to 15
	March	Schengen Agreement comes into force
	July	Europol Convention signed
	October–December	Bulgaria, Estonia, Latvia and Lithuania apply to join EU
	December	Dayton peace accords end war in Yugoslavia
1996	January	Czech Republic applies to join EU
	June	Slovenia applies to join EU
1997	October	Treaty of Amsterdam signed
1998	June	Establishment of European Central Bank
1999	January	Launch of the euro in 11 member states
	May	Treaty of Amsterdam comes into force
2000	September	Danish referendum rejects adoption of euro
2001	February	Treaty of Nice signed
	March	Swiss referendum rejects EU membership
	June	Irish referendum rejects terms of Nice
2002	January	Euro coins and notes begin circulating in 12 member states
	February	Opening of Convention on the Future of Europe
	October	Second Irish referendum accepts terms of Nice

2003	February	Treaty of Nice comes into force
	March	US-led invasion of Iraq sparks the most serious fallout in postwar transatlantic relations
	July	Publication of draft treaty establishing a constitution for Europe
	September	Swedish referendum rejects adoption of euro
2004	May	Cyprus, Czech Republic, Estonia, Hungary, Latvia, Lithuania, Malta, Poland, Slovenia, Slovakia join the EU, bringing membership to 25
	June	European Council accepts terms of draft constitutional treaty
	October	European leaders sign the treaty on the European constitution
	November	Lithuania becomes the first EU member to ratify the constitution
2005	May	French referendum rejects constitution
	June	Dutch referendum rejects constitution
2007	January	Bulgaria and Romania join the EU, bringing membership to 27; Slovenia becomes 13th country to adopt the euro
	December	Treaty of Lisbon signed
2008	January	Cyprus and Malta adopt the euro
	June	Irish referendum rejects terms of Lisbon
2009	January	Slovakia adopts the euro
	October	Second Irish referendum accepts terms of Lisbon
	November	Treaty of Lisbon comes into force
	November–December	Breaking of budget crisis in Greece
2010	December	Launch of European External Action Service
2011	January	Estonia adopts the euro

Sources of Further Information

Publishing on the European Union has grown exponentially in the last few years, with the number of new books, journal articles and websites increasing to match the pace of change in the EU itself, and of expanding interest in EU affairs. As a result, the following list of sources can offer no more than a flavour of what is currently available. For new titles, monitor acquisitions at your nearest library, watch the catalogues of the publishers with the best lists on the European Union (including Lynne Rienner, Oxford University Press, Palgrave Macmillan, Routledge, and Rowman & Littlefield), and search online book dealers such as Amazon.

Books

For general introductions to the history, institutions and policies of the EU, see Bache, George and Bulmer (2011), Hix and Hoyland (2011), McCormick (2011), Ginsberg (2010), Dinan (2010), Nugent (2010), Cini and Perez-Solorzano Borragan (2009), and Bomberg, Peterson and Stubb (2008). Edited collections on recent developments in the EU include Meunier and McNamara (2007), Jabko and Parsons (2005), and Cowles and Dinan (2004).

The best summaries of integration theory are offered by Wiener and Diez (2009) and by Rosamond (2000). An assessment of the key debates about the political identity of the EU is offered by Magnette (2005), and an illuminating set of discussions about the comparative character of European federalism can be found in Menon and Schain (2006) and Burgess (2000). Discussions about the meaning of Europe can be found in Dunkerley *et al.* (2002), Pagden (2002), Heffernan (2000), and Unwin (1998).

For histories of the EU, see Blair (2010), Eichengreen (2007), Dinan (2004), Gilbert (2003), Gillingham (2003), Henig (2002), and Stirk and Weigall (1999). For general histories of postwar Europe, see Judt (2005) and Hitchcock (2004), and for the best history of postwar transatlantic relations see Lundestad (2003).

For general surveys of EU institutions and decision making, see Peterson and Shackleton (2006) and Warleigh (2001). Regarding specific institutions:

- The Commission is covered by Cini (2007), Spence (2006), Smith (2004), and Nugent (2001).
- The Council of Ministers is assessed by Hayes-Renshaw and Wallace (2006) and Westlake and Galloway (2004). For the role of the presidency of the Council of Ministers, see Elgström (2003).
- Parliament is the subject of studies by Judge and Earnshaw (2008) and Corbett, Jacobs and Shackleton (2007), and EP committees are assessed by Whitaker (2010).
- Remarkably, Werts (2008) is the only up-to-date book-length study of the European Council currently available.
- For general surveys of the European Court of Justice, see Lasok *et al.* (2001) and Brown and Kennedy (2000). For more political analysis see Alter (2009), Sweet (2004), and Conant (2002). For an explanation of the EU legal system, see Hartley (2007).
- The work of the European Central Bank has been reviewed by Kaltenthaler (2006) and Howarth and Loedel (2005), and of Europol by Occhipinti (2003).

For edited collections dealing with EU policy in general, see Wallace *et al.* (2010) and Richardson (2006). Neal (2007), de Grauwe (2007), and McDonald and Dearden (2005) offer assessments of EU economic policy and the single market, while Marsh (2008), Chang (2008), and Hosli (2005) have written about the euro. Publication on specific areas of EU policy has been on the rise in recent years, with studies of agriculture (Ackrill, 2000; Grant, 1997), cohesion (Baun and Marek, 2008), competition (Cini and McGowan, 2009), development (Mold, 2007), energy (Matláry, 1997), the environment (Knill and Liefferink, 2007; Jordan, 2005), immigration (Geddes, 2008), justice and home affairs (Mitsilegas *et al*, 2003), social policy (Hantrais, 2007), and terrorism (von Hippel, 2005).

In spite of all the debates about the problems related to EU foreign and security policy, it has been the subject of a burgeoning literature. For example, see Keukeleire and MacNaughtan (2008), Orbie (2008), Smith (2008), Bretherton and Vogler (2006), Adamski *et al.* (2006), and Hill and Smith (2005). For security and defence policy, see Howorth (2007). For a discussion of the new international role of the EU, see McCormick (2007). One particular area of recent growth has been assessments of the transatlantic relationship: for example, see McGuire and Smith (2008) and Kopstein and Steino (2008), as well as Kagan (2003).

Periodicals and EU publications

The Economist

A weekly news magazine that has stories and statistics on world politics, including a section on Europe (and occasional special supplements on the EU). Selected headline stories can be found on *The Economist* website at http://www.economist.com.

The Economist also publishes two series of quarterly reports that are treasure-houses of information, but they are expensive, and not every library carries them: *Economist Intelligence Unit Country Reports* (these cover almost every country in the world, and include a series on the European Union), and *European Policy Analyst.* Both provide detailed political and economic news and information.

The Economist also publishes *European Voice,* a weekly newspaper published in Brussels that is packed with all the latest news and information on the EU. Selected headline stories can be found on its website at http://www.european-voice.com.

Academic journals

A wide range of these deal either wholly or partially with the European Union, including the following:

> *Common Market Law Review*
> *Comparative European Politics*
> *European Foreign Affairs Review*
> *European Journal of International Relations*
> *European Journal of Political Research*
> *European Union Politics*
> *International Organization*
> *Journal of European Social Policy*
> *Journal of Common Market Studies*
> *Journal of European Integration*
> *Journal of European Public Policy*
> *Parliamentary Affairs*
> *West European Politics*

Official sources

There are several of these, all of which are available through the Europa website at http://europa.eu.

Websites

The variety of useful websites changes often, as do their URLs, so instead of listing useful sites here, I have set up a short series of links on my home page at http://mypage.iu.edu/~jmccormi.

Palgrave Macmillan also has a website for books in the European Union series which provides information on key developments and links to other internet sources. The URL is http://www.palgrave.com/products/Series.aspx?s=EU.

Bibliography

Ackrill, Robert (2000) *The Common Agricultural Policy* (London: Continuum).

Adamski, Janet, Mary Troy Johnson and Christina M. Schweiss (eds) (2006) Old Europe, New Security: Evolution for a Complex World (Aldershot: Ashgate).

Albert, Michel (1993) *Capitalism v. Capitalism: How America's Obsession with Individual Achievement and Short-Term Profit Has Led to the Brink of Collapse* (New York: Four Walls Eight Windows).

Allen, David (1996) 'Competition Policy: Policing the Single Market', in Helen Wallace and William Wallace (eds), *Policy-Making in the European Union*, 3rd edn (Oxford: Oxford University Press).

Alter, Karen J. (2009) *The European Court's Political Power: Selected Essays* (Oxford University Press).

Andersen, Svein and Kjell A. Eliassen (eds) (1995) *The European Union: How Democratic Is It?* (London: Sage).

Anderson, Scott (1992) 'Western Europe and the Gulf War', in Reinhardt Rummel (ed.), *Toward Political Union: Planning a Common Foreign and Security Policy in the European Community* (Boulder, CO: Westview).

Antonenko, Oksana and Kathryn Pinnick (eds) (2005) *Russia and the European Union* (London: Routledge).

Archer, Clive (2000) *The European Union: Structure and Process*, 3rd edn (New York: Continuum).

Armstrong, Harvey (1993) 'Community Regional Policy', in Juliet Lodge (ed.), *The European Community and the Challenge of the Future* (London: Continuum and New York: Palgrave Macmillan).

Armstrong, Kenneth and Simon Bulmer (1998) *The Governance of the Single European Market* (Manchester: Manchester University Press).

Asmus, Ronald, Philip P. Everts and Pierangelo Isernia (2003) 'Power, War and Public Opinion: Thoughts on the Nature and Structure of the Trans-Atlantic Divide' (Washington, DC: German Marshall Fund, September).

Aspinwall, Mark and Justin Greenwood (1998) 'Conceptualising Collective Action in the European Union: An Introduction', in Mark Aspinwall and Justin Greenwood (eds), *Collective Action in the European Union: Interests and the New Politics of Associability* (London: Routledge).

Bache, Ian and Matthew Flinders (2004) *Multi-Level Governance* (Oxford: Oxford University Press).

Bache, Ian and Stephen George (2006) *Politics in the European Union*, 2nd edn (Oxford: Oxford University Press).

Bache, Ian, Stephen George and Simon Bulmer (eds) (2011) *Politics in the European Union*, 3rd edn (Oxford: Oxford University Press).

Balme, Richard and Didier Chabanet (2008) *European Governance and Democracy: Power and Protest in the EU* (Lanham, MD: Rowman and Littlefield).

Barber, Lionel (1998) 'Sharing Common Risks: The EU View', *Europe*, 374: 8–9.

Bardi, Luciano (2002) 'Transnational Trends: The Evolution of the European Party System', in Bernard Steunenberg and Jacques Thomassen (eds), *The European Parliament: Moving Toward Democracy in the EU* (Lanham, MD: Rowman and Littlefield).

Barnes, Ian and Pamela M. Barnes (1995) *The Enlarged European Union* (London: Longman).

Baun, Michael and Dan Marek (eds) (2008) *EU Cohesion Policy after Enlargement* (Basingstoke: Palgrave Macmillan).

Beck, Ulrich and Edgar Grande (2007) *Cosmopolitan Europe* (Cambridge: Polity Press).

Billiet, Stijn (2005) 'The EC and WTO Dispute Settlement: The Initiation of Trade Disputes by the EC', in *European Foreign Affairs Review*, 10(2): 197–214.

Blair, Alasdair (2010) *The European Union Since 1945*, 2nd edn (Harlow: Longman).

Bomberg, Elizabeth, John Peterson and Alexander Stubb (eds) (2008) *The European Union: How Does it Work?* 2nd edn (Oxford: Oxford University Press).

Booker, Christopher and Richard North (2005) *The Great Deception: Can the European Union Survive?* Rev. edn (London: Continuum).

Bretherton, Charlotte and John Vogler (2006) *The European Union as a Global Actor*, 2nd edn (London: Routledge).

Brown, L. Neville and Tom Kennedy (2000) *The Court of Justice of the European Communities*, 5th edn (London: Sweet & Maxwell).

Bugge, Peter (1995) 'The Nation Supreme: The Idea of Europe 1914–1945', in Kevin Wilson and Jan van der Dussen (eds), *The History of the Idea of Europe* (London: Routledge).

Burgess, Michael (2000) *Federalism and European Union: The Building of Europe, 1950–2000* (London: Routledge).

Burgess, Michael (2006) *Comparative Federalism: Theory and Practice* (London: Routledge).

Carr, William (1987) *A History of Germany, 1815–1985*, 3rd edn (London: Edward Arnold).

Chang, Michelle (2008) *Monetary Integration in the European Union* (Basingstoke: Palgrave Macmillan).

Chinn, Menzie and Jeffery Frankel (2005) 'Will the Euro Eventually Surpass the Dollar as the Leading International Reserve Currency?', Washington DC, National Bureau of Economic Research Working Paper 11510, July.

Chryssochoou, Dimitris I. (2000) *Democracy in the European Union* (London: I.B. Tauris).

Cini, Michelle (2007) *From Integration to Integrity: Administrative Ethics and Reform in the European Commission* (Manchester: Manchester University Press).

Cini, Michelle and Lee McGowan (2009) *Competition Policy in the European Union*, 2nd edn (London: Palgrave Macmillan).

Cini, Michelle and Nieves Perez-Solorzano Borragan (eds) (2009) *European Union Politics*, 3rd edn (Oxford: Oxford University Press).

Clover, Charles (2005) *The End of the Line: How Overfishing is Changing the World and What We Eat* (London: Ebury Press).

Collester, J. Bryan (2000) 'How Defense "Spilled Over" into the CFSP: Western European Union (WEU) and the European Security and Defense Identity (ESDI)', in Maria Green Cowles and Michael Smith (eds), *The State of the European Union: Risks, Reform, Resistance and Revival* (Oxford: Oxford University Press).

Conant, Lisa (2002) *Justice Contained: Law and Politics in the European Union* (Ithaca, NY: Cornell University Press).

Corbett, Richard (2001) 'The European Parliament's Progress, 1994–99', in Juliet Lodge (ed.), *The 1999 Elections to the European Parliament* (Basingstoke and New York: Palgrave Macmillan).

Corbett, Richard, Francis Jacobs and Michael Shackleton (2005) *The European Parliament*, 6th edn (London: John Harper).

Corbett, Richard, Francis Jacobs and Michael Shackleton (2007) *The European Parliament*, 7th edn (London: John Harper).

Cornell, Tim and John Matthews (1982) *Atlas of the Roman World* (Oxford: Phaidon).

Cowles, Maria Green and Desmond Dinan (eds) (2004) *Developments in the European Union 2* (Basingstoke and New York: Palgrave Macmillan).

Criddle, Byron (1993) 'The French Referendum on the Maastricht Treaty, September 1992', *Parliamentary Affairs* 46(2): 228–39.

Dahrendorf, Ralf (1988) *The Modern Social Conflict* (London: Weidenfeld & Nicolson).

de Grauwe, Paul (2007) *The Economics of Monetary Union* (Oxford: Oxford University Press).

Delanty, Gerard (1995) *Inventing Europe: Idea, Identity, Reality* (Basingstoke and New York: Palgrave Macmillan).

den Boer, Pim (1995) 'Europe to 1914: The Making of an Idea', in Kevin Wilson and Jan van der Dussen (eds), *The History of the Idea of Europe* (London: Routledge).

de Rougemont, Denis (1966) *The Idea of Europe* (London: Macmillan).

Dinan, Desmond (2004) *Europe Recast: A History of European Union* (Boulder, CO: Lynne Rienner, and Basingstoke: Palgrave Macmillan).

Dinan, Desmond (2010) *Ever Closer Union: An Introduction to European Integration*, 4th edn (Boulder, CO: Lynne Rienner, and Basingstoke: Palgrave Macmillan).

Dunkerley, David, Lesley Hodgson, Stanislaw Konopacki, Tony Spybey and Andrew Thompson (2002) *Changing Europe: Identities, Nations and Citizens* (London: Routledge).

Dye, Thomas (2002) *Understanding Public Policy*, 10th edn (Upper Saddle River, NJ: Prentice Hall).

Dye, Thomas and Harmon Zeigler (2000) *The Irony of Democracy* (Fort Worth, TX: Harcourt Brace).

Edwards, Geoffrey and David Spence (eds) (2006) *The European Commission*, 3rd edn (London: John Harper).

Eichengreen, Barry (2007) *The European Economy Since 1945: Coordinated Capitalism and Beyond* (Princeton: Princeton University Press).

Elgström, Ole (ed.) (2003) *European Council Presidencies: A Comparative Perspective* (London: Routledge).

Eriksen, Erik Oddvar, John Erik Fossum and Agustín José Menéndez (eds) (2004), in their introduction to *Developing a Constitution for Europe* (London: Routledge).

Etzioni, Amitai (ed) (1998) *The Essential Communitarian Reader* (Lanham, MD: Rowman & Littlefield).

Eurobarometer polls can be found on the Europa website at http://europa. eu.int/comm/public_opinion/index_en.htm

European Commission (1973) *Report on the Regional Problems of the Enlarged Community* (The Thomson Report), COM(73)550 (Brussels: European Commission).

European Commission (1985) *Completing the Internal Market* (The Cockfield Report), COM(85)310 (Brussels: European Commission).

European Commission (2001a) *European Governance: A White Paper*, COM428 (Brussels: European Commission).

European Commission (2001b) 'Interim Report from the Commission to the Stockholm European Council: Improving and Simplifying the Regulatory Environment', COM130 Final (Brussels: European Commission).

European Commission (2008) *European Agencies: The Way Forward* (Luxembourg: CEC).

European Commission (various years), *Annual Report on Monitoring the Application of Community Law*.

Eurostat (2007) *Europe in Figures: Eurostat Yearbook 2006–07* (Brussels: European Commission).

Fligstein, Neil (2008) *Euroclash: The EU, European Identity, and the Future of Europe* (Oxford: Oxford University Press).

Forsyth, Murray (1981) *Unions of States: The Theory and Practice of Confederation* (Leicester: Leicester University Press).

Franklin, Mark (1996) 'European Elections and the European Voter', in Jeremy Richardson (ed.), *European Union: Power and Policy-Making* (London: Routledge).

Geddes, Anthony (2008) *Immigration and European Integration: Towards Fortress Europe?* 2nd edn (Manchester: Manchester University Press).

George, Stephen (1996) *Politics and Policy in the European Community*, 3rd edn (Oxford: Oxford University Press).

Geyer, Robert and Beverly Springer (1998) 'EU Social Policy After Maastricht: The Works Council Directive and the British Opt-Out', in Pierre-Henri Laurent and Marc Maresceau (eds), *The State of the European Union*, vol. 4 (Boulder, CO: Lynne Rienner).

Giegerich, Bastian and William Wallace (2004) 'Not Such a Soft Power: The External Deployment of European Forces', *Survival* 46(2):163–82.

Giersch, Herbert (1985) *Eurosclerosis* (Kiel: Institut für Weltwirtschaft).

Gilbert, Mark (2003) *Surpassing Realism: The Politics of European Integration since 1945* (Lanham, MD: Rowman & Littlefield).

Gill, Graeme (2003) *The Nature and Development of the Modern State* (Basingstoke: Palgrave Macmillan).

Gillingham, John (1991; reissued 2002) *Coal, Steel, and the Rebirth of Europe, 1945–1955* (Cambridge: Cambridge University Press).

Gillingham, John (2003) *European Integration, 1950–2003: Superstate or New Market Economy?* (Cambridge and New York: Cambridge University Press).

Ginsberg, Roy H. (2001) *The European Union in International Politics: Baptism by Fire* (Lanham, MD: Rowman & Littlefield).

Ginsberg, Roy H. (2010) *Demystifying the European Union: The Enduring Logic of Regional Integration*, 2nd edn (Lanham, MD: Rowman & Littlefield).

Grabbe, Heather (2004) 'What the New Member States Bring into the European Union', in Neill Nugent (ed.), *European Union Enlargement* (Basingstoke and New York: Palgrave Macmillan).

Grant, Wyn (1997) *The Common Agricultural Policy* (Basingstoke and New York: Palgrave Macmillan).

Graziano, Paolo and Maarten P. Vink (eds) (2007) *Europeanization: New Research Agendas* (Basingstoke: Palgrave Macmillan).

Greenwood, Justin (2003) *Interest Representation in the European Union* (Basingstoke and New York: Palgrave Macmillan).

Haas, Ernst B. (1958) *The Uniting of Europe: Political, Social, and Economic Forces, 1950–57* (Stanford, CA: Stanford University Press).

Habermas, Jürgen and Jacques Derrida (2003 [2005]) 'February 15, or What Binds Europe Together: Plea for a Common Foreign Policy, Beginning in Core Europe', *Frankfurter Allgemeine Zeitung*, 31 May. Reproduced in Daniel Levy, Max Pensky and John Torpey (eds), *Old Europe, New Europe, Core Europe* (London: Verso, 2005).

Hantrais, Linda (2007) *Social Policy in the European Union*, 3rd edn (Basingstoke: Palgrave Macmillan).

Hartley, T.C. (2007) *The Foundations of European Community Law*, 6th edn (Oxford: Oxford University Press).

Haseler, Stephen (2004) *Super-State: The New Europe and its Challenge to America* (London: I.B. Tauris).

Hay, David (1957) *Europe: The Emergence of an Idea* (Edinburgh: Edinburgh University Press).

Hayes-Renshaw, Fiona and Helen Wallace (2006) *The Council of Ministers*, 2nd edn (Basingstoke: Palgrave Macmillan).

Heater, Derek (1992) *The Idea of European Unity* (London: Continuum and New York: Palgrave Macmillan).

Heater, Derek (2004) *Citizenship: The Civic Ideal in World History, Politics and Education*, 3rd edn (Manchester: Manchester University Press).

Heath, Anthony, Iain McLean, Bridget Taylor and John Curticel (1999) 'Between First and Second Order: A Comparison of Voting Behaviour in European and Local Elections in Britain', *European Journal of Political Research*, 35(3): 389–414.

Heffernan, Michael (2000) *The Meaning of Europe: Geography and Geopolitics* (London: Edward Arnold).

Heidenreich, Martin and Gabriele Bischoff (2008) 'The Open Method of Co-ordination: A Way to the Europeanization of Social and Employment Policies?', *Journal of Common Market Studies*, 46(3): 497–532.

Heisler, Martin O., with Robert B. Kvavik (1973) 'Patterns of European Politics: The European Polity Model', in Martin O. Heisler (ed.), *Politics in*

Europe: Structures and Processes in Some Postindustrial Democracies (New York: David McKay).

Henig, Stanley (2002) *The Uniting of Europe: From Consolidation to Enlargement* (London: Routledge).

Hill, Christopher and Michael Smith (eds) (2005) *International Relations and the European Union* (Oxford: Oxford University Press).

Hill, Steven (2010) *Europe's Promise: Why the European Way is the Best Hope in an Insecure Age* (Berkeley: University of California Press).

Hitchcock, William I. (2004) *The Struggle for Europe: The Turbulent History of a Divided Continent* (New York: Anchor Books).

Hix, Simon (2005) *The Political System of the European Union*, 2nd edn (Basingstoke and New York: Palgrave Macmillan).

Hix, Simon and Bjørn Hoyland (2011) *The Political System of the European Union*, 3rd edn (Basingstoke: Palgrave Macmillan).

Hix, Simon and Christopher Lord (1997) *Political Parties in the European Union* (Basingstoke and New York: Palgrave Macmillan).

Hobsbawm, Eric (1991) *The Age of Empire 1848–1875* (London: Cardinal).

Hoffman, Stanley (1964) 'The European Process at Atlantic Crosspurposes', *Journal of Common Market Studies*, 3: 85–101.

Hogan, Michael J. (1987) *The Marshall Plan: America, Britain, and the Reconstruction of Western Europe, 1947–52* (New York: Cambridge University Press).

Hosli, Madeleine O. (2005) *The Euro: A Concise Introduction to European Monetary Integration* (Boulder, CO: Lynne Rienner).

Hourani, Albert (1989) 'Conclusions', in William Roger Louis and Roger Owen (eds), *Suez 1956: The Crisis and Its Consequences* (Oxford: Clarendon Press).

Howarth, David and Peter Loedel (2005) *The European Central Bank: The New European Leviathan?* 2nd edn (Basingstoke: Palgrave Macmillan).

Howorth, Jolyon (2003) 'Foreign and Defence Policy Cooperation', in John Peterson and Mark A. Pollack (eds), *Europe, America, Bush: Transatlantic Relations in the Twenty-First Century* (London: Routledge).

Howorth, Jolyon (2007) *Security and Defence Policy in the European Union* (Basingstoke: Palgrave Macmillan).

Hutton, Will (2003) *The World We're In* (London: Abacus).

International Institute for Strategic Studies (2007) *The Military Balance 2007* (London: Routledge).

Jabko, Nicolas and Craig Parsons (eds) (2005) *The State of the European Union, Vol. 7: With US or Against US? European Trends in American Perspective* (Oxford and New York: Oxford University Press).

Jones, Seth G. (2007) *The Rise of European Security Cooperation* (Cambridge: Cambridge University Press).

Jordan, Andrew (2005) *Environmental Policy in the European Union: Actors, Institutions and Processes* (London: Earthscan).

Jordan, Andrew, Dave Huitma, Harro van Asselt and Frans Berkhout (eds) (2010) *Climate Change Policy in the European Union: Confronting the Dilemmas of Mitigation and Adaptation?* (Cambridge: Cambridge University Press).

Judge, David and David Earnshaw (2008) *The European Parliament*, 2nd edn (Basingstoke: Palgrave Macmillan).

Judt, Tony (2005) *Postwar: A History of Europe since 1945* (New York: Penguin).

Kagan, Robert (2003) *Of Paradise and Power: America and Europe in the New World Order* (New York: Alfred A. Knopf).

Kaltenthaler, Karl (2006) *Policy-making in the European Central Bank: The Masters of Europe's Money* (Lanham, MD: Rowman & Littlefield).

Keating, Michael and Liesbet Hooghe (1996) 'By-passing the Nation State? Regions and the EU Policy Process', in Jeremy Richardson (ed.), *European Union: Power and Policy-Making* (London: Routledge).

Keohane, Robert O. and Stanley Hoffmann (eds) (1991) *The New European Community: Decisionmaking and Institutional Change* (Boulder, CO: Westview Press).

Keukeleire, Stephan and Jennifer MacNaughtan (2008) *The Foreign Policy of the European Union* (Basingstoke: Palgrave Macmillan).

Knill, Christoph and Duncan Liefferink (2007) *Environmental Politics in the European Union: Policy-making, Implementation and Patterns of Multi-level Governance* (Manchester: Manchester University Press).

Kopstein, Jeffrey and Sven Steinmo (eds) (2008) *Growing Apart? America and Europe in the Twenty-First Century* (New York: Cambridge University Press).

Laffan, Brigid and Johannes Lindner (2010) 'The Budget: Who Gets What, When and How?' in Helen Wallace, Mark A. Pollack and Alasdair R. Young (eds), *Policy-Making in the European Union*, 6th edn (Oxford: Oxford University Press).

Lasok, Dominik *et al.* (2001) *Law and Institutions of the European Communities*, 7th edn (London: LexisNexisUK).

Lasok, K.P.E. (2007) *European Court Practice and Procedure*, 3rd ed. (Haywards Heath: Tottel).

Lavenex, Sandra (2010) 'Justice and Home Affairs: Communitarization with Hesitation', in Helen Wallace, Mark A. Pollack and Alasdair R. Young (eds), *Policy-Making in the European Union*, 6th edn (Oxford: Oxford University Press).

Layton, Lyndsey (2008) 'Chemical Law Has Global Impact', in *Washington Post*, 12 June.

Leonard, Mark (2005) *Why Europe will Run the 21st Century* (London: Fourth Estate).

Lequesne, Christian (2004) *The Politics of Fisheries in the European Union* (Manchester: Manchester University Press).

Lewis, David P. (1993) *The Road to Europe: History, Institutions and Prospects of European Integration 1945–1993* (New York: Peter Lang).

Lijphart, Arend (1971) 'Comparative Politics and the Comparative Method', *American Political Science Review*, 65(3):682–93.

Lindberg, Leon N. (1963) *The Political Dynamics of European Economic Integration* (Stanford: Stanford University Press).

Lindberg, Leon N. and Stuart A. Scheingold (1970) *Europe's Would-Be Polity: Patternsof Change in the European Community* (Englewood Cliffs, NJ: Prentice Hall).

Lindberg, Leon N. and Stuart A. Scheingold (1971) *Regional Integration: Theory and Research* (Cambridge, MA: Harvard University Press).

Lindblom, Charles (1959) 'The Science of "Muddling Through"', *Public Administration Review*, 19(2): 79–88.

Lister, Frederick K. (1996) *The European Union, the United Nations, and the Revival of Confederal Governance* (Westport, CT: Greenwood).

Lundestad, Geir (2003) *The United States and Western Europe Since 1945: From 'Empire' by Invitation to Transatlantic Drift* (Oxford: Oxford University Press).

Magnette, Paul (2005) *What is the European Union? Nature and Prospects* (Basingstoke: Palgrave Macmillan).

Mair, Peter (2001) 'The Limited Impact of Europe on National Party Systems', in Simon Hix and Klaus H. Goetz (eds), *Europeanised Politics? European Integration and National Political Systems* (London: Frank Cass).

Majone, Giandomenico (2006) 'Federation, Confederation, and Mixed Government: An EU–US Comparison', in Anand Menon and Martin Schain (eds), *Comparative Federalism: The European Union and the United States in Comparative Perspective* (Oxford: Oxford University Press).

Marks, Gary (1993) 'Structural Policy and Multi-level Governance in the EC', in Alan Cafruny and Glenda Rosenthal (eds), *The State of the European Community*, vol. 2 (Boulder, CO: Lynne Rienner).

Marsh, David (2008) *The Euro: The Politics of the New Global Currency* (New Haven, CT: Yale University Press).

Matláry, Janne Haaland (1997) *Energy Policy in the European Union* (Basingstoke and New York: Palgrave Macmillan).

Mazey, Sonia and Jeremy Richardson (1996) 'The Logic of Organisation: Interest Groups', in Jeremy Richardson (ed.), *European Union: Power and Policy-Making* (London: Routledge).

Mazey, Sonia and Jeremy Richardson (1997) 'The Commission and the Lobby', in Geoffrey Edwards and David Spence (eds), *The European Commission*, 2nd edn (London: Cartermill).

McCormick, John (1995) *The Global Environmental Movement*, 2nd edn (London: John Wiley).

McCormick, John (2007) *The European Superpower* (Basingstoke: Palgrave Macmillan).

McCormick, John (2010) *Europeanism* (Oxford: Oxford University Press).

McCormick, John (2011) *European Union Politics* (Basingstoke: Palgrave Macmillan).

McDonald, Frank and Stephen Dearden (eds) (2005) *European Economic Integration*, 4th edn (New York and Harlow: Prentice Hall Financial Times).

McGuire, Steven and Michael Smith (2008) *The European Union and the United States* (Basingstoke: Palgrave Macmillan).

Menon, Anand, Kalypso Nicolaidis and Jennifer Welsh (2004) 'In Defence of Europe – A Response to Kagan', *Journal of European Affairs*, 2(3): 5–14.

Menon, Anand and Martin Schain (eds) (2006) *Comparative Federalism: The European Union and the United States in Comparative Perspective* (Oxford: Oxford University Press).

Meunier, Sophie and Kathleen R. McNamara (eds) (2007) *Making History: European Integration and Institutional Change at Fifty* (Oxford: Oxford University Press).

Milward, Alan S. (1984) *The Reconstruction of Western Europe, 1945–51* (Berkeley: University of California Press).

Mitrany, David (1966) *A Working Peace System* (Chicago, IL: Quadrangle).

Mitsilegas, Valsamis, Jörg Monar and Wyn Rees (2003) *The European Union and Internal Security: Guardian of the People?* (Basingstoke: Palgrave Macmillan).

Mold, Andrew (ed) (2007) *EU Development Policy in a Changing World: Challenges for the 21st Century* (Amsterdam: Amsterdam University Press).

Monar, Jörg (2001) 'The Dynamics of Justice and Home Affairs: Laboratories, Driving Factors and Costs', in *Journal of Common Market Studies*, 39(4): 747–64.

Monnet, Jean (1978) *Memoirs* (Garden City, NY: Doubleday).

Moravcsik, Andrew (1998) *The Choice for Europe* (Ithaca, NY: Cornell University Press).

Moravcsik, Andrew (2002) 'In Defence of the 'Democratic Deficit': Reassessing Legitimacy in the European Union', *Journal of Common Market Studies*, 40(:4): 603–24.

Moravcsik, Andrew (2007) 'The European Constitutional Settlement', in Sophie Meunier and Kathleen R. McNamara (eds), *Making History: European Integration and Institutional Change at Fifty* (Oxford: Oxford University Press).

Morris, Chris (2005) *The New Turkey: The Quiet Revolution on the Edge of Europe* (London: Granta).

Müller, Jan-Werner (2007) *Constitutional Patriotism* (Princeton: Princeton University Press).

Neal, Larry (2007) *The Economics of Europe and the European Union* (Cambridge and New York: Cambridge University Press).

Nugent, Neill (2001) *The European Commission* (Basingstoke and New York: Palgrave Macmillan).

Nugent, Neill (2006) *The Government and Politics of the European Union*, 6th edn (Basingstoke: Palgrave Macmillan).

Nugent, Neill (2010) *The Government and Politics of the European Union*, 7th edn (Basingstoke: Palgrave Macmillan).

Nye, Joseph S. (1971a) *Peace in Parts: Integration and Conflict in Regional Organization* (Boston, MA: Little, Brown).

Nye, Joseph S. (1971b) 'Comparing Common Markets: A Revised Neofunctionalist Model', in Leon N. Lindberg and Stuart A. Scheingold (eds), *Regional Integration: Theory and Research* (Cambridge, MA: Harvard University Press).

Nye, Joseph (2004) *Soft Power: The Means to Success in World Politics* (New York: Public Affairs).

Occhipinti, John D. (2003) *The Politics of EU Police Cooperation: Toward a European FBI?* (Boulder, CO: Lynne Rienner).

OECD website (2010) http://www.oecd.org

Orbie, Jan (2008) 'The European Union's Role in World Trade: Harnessing

Globalisation?', in Jan Orbie (ed), *Europe's Global Role: External Policies of the European Union* (Aldershot: Ashgate).

Pagden, Anthony (ed.) (2002) *The Idea of Europe: From Antiquity to the European Union* (Cambridge: Cambridge University Press).

Page, Edward C. (2003) 'Europeanization and the Persistence of Administrative Systems', in Jack Hayward and Anand Menon (eds), *Governing Europe* (Oxford: Oxford University Press).

Palmer, Michael (1968) *European Unity: A Survey of European Organizations* (London: George Allen & Unwin).

Pardo, Sharon and Joel Peters (2009) *Uneasy Neighbors: Israel and the European Union* (Lanham, MD: Lexington Books).

Peters, B. Guy (1992) 'Bureaucratic Politics and the Institutions of the European Community', in Alberta Sbragia (ed.), *Euro-Politics: Institutions and Policy-making in the 'New' European Community* (Washington, DC: Brookings Institution).

Peters, B. Guy (2001) 'Agenda-Setting in the European Union', in Jeremy Richardson (ed.), *European Union: Power and Policy-Making*, 2nd edn (New York: Routledge).

Peterson, John (2003) 'The US and Europe in the Balkans', in John Peterson and Mark A. Pollack (eds), *Europe, America, Bush: Transatlantic Relations in the Twenty-First Century* (London: Routledge).

Peterson, John and Michael Shackleton (eds) (2006) *The Institutions of the European Union*, 2nd edn (Oxford: Oxford University Press).

Prestowitz, Clyde (2003) *Rogue Nation: American Unilateralism and the Failure of Good Intentions* (New York: Basic Books).

Puchala, Donald J. (1975) 'Domestic Politics and Regional Harmonization in the European Communities', *World Politics*, 27(4): 496–520.

Pye, Lucien (1966) *Aspects of Political Development* (Boston, MA: Little, Brown).

Reid, T.R. (2004) *The United States of Europe: The New Superpower and the End of American Supremacy* (New York: Penguin).

Reiff, K. and H. Schmitt (1980) 'Nine Second-Order National Elections: A Conceptual Framework for the Analysis of European Election Results', *European Journal of Political Research*, 8(1): 3–44.

Richardson, Jeremy (ed.) (2006) *European Union: Power and Policy-Making*, 3rd edn (London and New York: Routledge).

Rieger, Elmar (2005) 'Agricultural Policy: Constrained Reforms', in Helen Wallace, William Wallace and Mark A. Pollack (eds), *Policy-Making in the European Union*, 5th edn (Oxford: Oxford University Press).

Rifkin, Jeremy (2004) *The European Dream: How Europe's Vision of the Future is Quietly Eclipsing the American Dream* (New York: Tarcher/Penguin).

Rittberger, Berthold (2005) *Building Europe's Parliament: Democratic Representation Beyond the Nation-State* (Oxford: Oxford University Press).

Rosamond, Ben (2000) *Theories of European Integration* (Basingstoke and New York: Palgrave Macmillan).

Ross, George (1995) *Jacques Delors and European Integration* (New York: Oxford University Press).

Rumford, Chris (ed.) (2007) *Cosmopolitanism and Europe* (Liverpool: Liverpool University Press).

Salmon, Trevor and Sir William Nicoll (eds) (1997) *Building European Union: A Documentary History and Analysis* (Manchester: Manchester University Press).

Sapir, André, *et al.* (2004) *An Agenda for a Growing Europe: Making the EU Economic System Deliver* (Oxford: Oxford University Press).

Sbragia, Alberta (1992) 'Thinking about the European Future: The Uses of Comparison', in Alberta Sbragia (ed.), *Euro-Politics: Institutions and Policymaking in the 'New' European Community* (Washington DC: Brookings Institution).

Schlesinger, Philip and Francois Foret (2006) 'Political Roof and Sacred Canopy?', *European Journal of Social Theory*, 9(1): 59–81.

Schmitter, Philippe C. (1971) 'A Revised Theory of Regional Integration', in Leon N. Lindberg and Stuart A. Scheingold, *Regional Integration: Theory and Research* (Cambridge, MA: Harvard University Press).

Scruton, Roger (1996) *A Dictionary of Political Thought*, 2nd edn (London: Macmillan).

Smith, Andy (ed.) (2004) *Politics and the European Commission: Actors, Interdependence, Legitimacy* (London: Routledge).

Smith, Graham (1999) *The Post-Soviet States: Mapping the Politics of Transition* (London: Edward Arnold).

Smith, Karen E. (2008) *European Union Foreign Policy in a Changing World*, 2nd edn (Cambridge: Polity).

Smith, Michael (2006) 'The Commission and External Relations', in David Spence (ed.), *The European Commission*, 3rd edn (London: John Harper).

Snyder, Francis (2003) 'The Unfinished Constitution of the European Union: Principles, Processes and Culture', in J.H.H. Weiler and Marlene Wind (eds), *European Constitutionalism Beyond the State* (Cambridge: Cambridge University Press).

Spence, David (ed.) (2006) *The European Commission*, 3rd edn (London: John Harper).

Spinelli, Altiero (1972) 'The Growth of the European Movement Since the Second World War', in Michael Hodges (ed.), *Europe Integration: Selected Readings* (Harmondsworth: Penguin).

Springer, Beverly (1992) *The Social Dimension of 1992: Europe Faces a New EC* (Westport, CT: Praeger).

Stirk, Peter M.R. and David Weigall (eds) (1999) *The Origins and Development of European Integration: A Reader and Commentary* (London and New York: Pinter).

Strange, Susan (1996) *The Retreat of the State: The Diffusion of Power in the World Economy* (Cambridge: Cambridge University Press).

Sweet, Alec Stone (2004) *The Judicial Construction of Europe* (New York: Oxford University Press).

Taggart, Paul and Aleks Szczerbiak (2004) 'Supporting the Union? Euroscepticism and the Politics of European Integration', in Maria Green Cowles and Desmond Dinan (eds), *Developments in the European Union 2* (Basingstoke: Palgrave Macmillan).

Thatcher, Margaret (1993) *The Downing Street Years* (New York: HarperCollins).

Tsoukalis, Loukas (1997) *The New European Economy Revisited: The*

Politics and Economics of Integration, 3rd edn (Oxford: Oxford University Press).

UN Framework Convention on Climate Change website (2007) http://unfccc.int

Unwin, Tim (1998) 'Ideas of Europe', in Tim Unwin (ed.), *A European Geography* (Harlow: Longman).

Urwin, Derek (1995) *The Community of Europe*, 2nd edn (London: Longman).

van Creveld, Martin (1999) *The Rise and Decline of the State* (Cambridge: Cambridge University Press).

van Eekelen, Willem (1990) 'WEU and the Gulf Crisis', *Survival*, 32(6): 519–32.

Vincent, Andrew (1987) *Theories of the State* (Oxford: Blackwell).

von Hippel, Karin (ed) (2005) *Europe Confronts Terrorism* (Basingstoke: Palgrave Macmillan).

Walkenhorst, Heiko (2008) 'Explaining Change in EU Education Policy', *Journal of European Public Policy*, 15(4): 567–87.

Wallace, Anthony (2004) 'Completing the Single Market: The Lisbon Strategy', in Maria Green Cowles and Desmond Dinan (eds), *Developments in the European Union* 2 (Basingstoke: Palgrave Macmillan).

Wallace, Helen, Mark A. Pollack and Alasdair R. Young (eds) (2010) *Policy-Making in the European Union*, 6th edn (Oxford: Oxford University Press).

Wallace, William (1990) *The Transformation of Western Europe* (London: Royal Institute of International Affairs).

Waltz, Kenneth N. (2008) *Realism and International Politics* (Abingdon: Routledge).

Warleigh, Alex (2001) *Understanding European Union Institutions* (London: Routledge).

Watts, Ronald J. (2008) *Comparing Federal Systems*, 3rd edn (Montreal: Institute of Intergovernmental Relations).

Weigall, David and Peter Stirk (eds) (1992) *The Origins and Development of the European Community* (London: Pinter).

Werts, Jan (2008) *The European Council* (London: John Harper).

Westlake, Martin and David Galloway (2004) *The Council of the European Union*, 3rd edn (London: John Harper).

Wexler, Immanuel (1983) *The Marshall Plan Revisited: The European Recovery Program in Economic Perspective* (Westport, CT: Greenwood).

Whitaker, Richard (2010) *The European Parliament's Committees* (London: Routledge).

Wiener, Antje and Thomas Diez (eds) (2009) *European Integration Theory*, 2nd edn (Oxford: Oxford University Press).

Williams, Shirley (1991) 'Sovereignty and Accountability in the European Community', in Robert O. Keohane and Stanley Hoffmann (eds), *The New European Community: Decisionmaking and Institutional Change* (Boulder, CO: Westview Press).

Wilson, Dominic and Roopa Purushothaman (2003) 'Dreaming With BRICs: The Path to 2050', Global Economics Paper No. 99, Goldman Sachs, 1 October.

World Bank website (2011) http://www.worldbank.org/data

World Tourism Organization website (2010) http://www.world-tourism.org

World Trade Organization website (2010) http://www.wto.org

World Travel and Tourism Council website (2010) http://www.wttc.org

Wurzel, Rüdiger and James Connelly (eds) (2010) *The European Union as a Leader in International Climate Change Politics* (Abingdon: Routledge).

Young, Alasdair R. (2010) 'The European Policy Process in Comparative Perspective', in Helen Wallace, Mark A. Pollack and Alasdair R. Young (eds), *Policy-Making in the European Union*, 6th edn (Oxford: Oxford University Press).

Zurcher, Arnold J. (1958) *The Struggle to Unite Europe, 1940–58* (New York: New York University Press).

Index

ACP programme   215–17
acquis communautaire   65
Adonnino report   107–8
aerospace industry in Europe   157
agricultural policy   172, 176, 178–80
    see also Common Agricultural Policy
air transport in Europe   155–6
Airbus 157
Amsterdam, Treaty of   66, 140, 199
Armenia   34
Ashton, Catherine   201
asylum   153
Atlantic Alliance   55, 70, 200
Azerbaijan   34

Balkans   35–6, 199
Barcelona Process   213–4
Barroso, José Manuel   82, 189
Belarus   34
Berlin airlift   50
Blair, Tony   79, 187, 202, 203
Bologna process   109
Bretton Woods   49, 59, 209
Briand, Aristide   31
BRIC states   210
Britain   57
budget see European Union, budget
buildup   11

Charlemagne   27
Charter of Fundamental Rights of the
    European Union   66–7
Charter of Fundamental Social Rights
    of Workers see Social Charter
chemicals policy   192–3
Chirac, Jacques   203
Churchill, Winston   50, 52
citizens initiative   120–1
citizenship see European Union
    'citizenship'
climate change policy   193–4
Cockfield report   150
Cohesion Fund   176
cohesion policy   62, 172, 182–90
cold war   61, 211, 213
comitology   82

Committee of the Regions   64, 95,
    117, 183
Common Agricultural Policy   56, 138,
    172, 178–80
Common Commercial Policy   207
Common Fisheries Policy   181
Common Foreign and Security Policy
    63–4, 199, 201
  High Representative for   66, 200
common market see single market
Common Security and Defence Policy
    95
communitarianism   41–2
Community method   139
comparative politics   2, 14–15, 142
competence   126
competition policy   159–61
confederalism   19–22
conferral   126
Constitution for Europe, Treaty
    Establishing a   49, 70
constitutional patriotism   41
constitutional treaty see Constitution
    for Europe, Treaty Establishing a
constitutions
  European Union   75–8
  United States   75–6
Convention on the Future of Europe
    69–70
convergence criteria see euro
Copenhagen conditions   64–5
cosmopolitanism   41
Cotonou agreement   217
Coudenhove-Kalergi, Count Richard
    30
Council of Europe   48, 52, 67
Council of Ministers   84–8, 10
  Coreper   86
  powers and role   87
  presidency   86
  voting options   87–8
Council of the European Union see
    Council of Ministers
Court of First Instance see European
    Court of Justice, General Court
cultural policy   44

defence policy   201, 203–6
de Gaulle, Charles   57, 144, 209
Delors, Jacques   60, 82, 150, 163,
   186
democratic deficit   104–7, 120
Denmark   116
derogation   140
Derrida, Jacques   40
development cooperation   214–17
direct action   92, 94

EADS   157
economic and monetary union   59–60
economic crisis, global   72, 169–70
economic disparities in EU   173–5
education policy   109
elections *see* European Parliament,
   elections
employment policy   187
empty chair crisis   144
enhanced cooperation   139
enlargement of the EEC/EU *see*
   European Union, enlargement
Environmental Action Programmes
   190
environmental policy   172–3, 190–4
euro   67, 72, 138, 162–4, 166–70
   convergence criteria   67, 164, 168
   costs and benefits   167–9
   eurozone crisis   169–70
   global impact   206–7
   launch of   48, 162–4, 166–7
   stability and growth pact   168–9
Eurojust   153
Europe
   boundaries of   32–9
   identity of   25–32
   languages in   33, 109
   migration within   108–9, 152
   origin of term   26, 27
   postwar situation   49–50
Europe 2020 Strategy   68, 162
Europe Day   108
European Aeronautic Defence and
   Space company *see* EADS
European anthem   108
European arrest warrant   153
European Atomic Energy Community
   (Euratom)   54, 55
European Bank for Reconstruction and
   Development (EBRD)   213
European Central Bank   95, 164, 165,
   169

European Coal and Steel Community
   10, 31–2, 48, 53–4, 127
European Commission   80–4, 105
   College of Commissioners   81
   directorates-general   82
   powers and role   82–4
   president   81–2, 105
European Convention on Human
   Rights   67
European Council   63, 78–80, 105
   powers and role   78–9
   president   79
   summits   80
European Court of Human Rights   67
European Court of Justice   92–5, 105
   advocates-general   93–4
   General Court   94
   judges   93
   powers and role   92–3
   president   93
European Credit Transfer and
   Accumulation System   109
European currency unit (ecu)   59–60
European Defence Community   50,
   198
European dream   177
European Economic and Social
   Committee   117
European Economic Area   65–6
European Economic Community   32,
   48, 54–9
European Employment Strategy
   182–3
European Environment Agency   192
European evidence warrant   153
European External Action Service
   201, 202
European Free Trade Association
   (EFTA)   55, 57
European identity   25–32
European Investment Bank   55
European Monetary System   59, 79,
   163
European Neighbourhood Policy   214
European Ombudsman *see*
   Ombudsman, European
European Parliament   88–92, 105
   committees   91
   elections   111–15
   Members of the European Parliament
   89–90
   political groups in   112–13
   powers and role   91–2

European parliament – *continued*
  president   90
  site   90
European Police Office *see* Europol
European Political Community   50,
  63, 198
European Political Cooperation   63,
  198
European Regional Development Fund
  62, 175–6
European Security and Defence Policy
  203
European Security Strategy   204–5
European Social Fund   55, 62, 175
European Union
  and member states   124–7
  and Russia   214
  and United States 52, 55, 70, 71–2,
    200, 203–4, 209, 211–12
  as international organization   13–14
  as superpower   210
  budget   142–6
  'citizenship'   64, 110–1
  confederal features   21–2
  constitution *see* constitutions,
    European Union
  economic disparities in   173–5
  enlargement   48, 48–9, 55–9, 64–6,
    68–9, 161–2, 194, 213
  federal features   17–18
  flag   108
  interest groups in   116–20
  law   85
  languages, official   33
  membership requirements *see*
    Copenhagen conditions
  passport   108
  policies
    agricultural   172, 176, 178–80
      see also Common Agricultural
        Policy
    chemicals   192–3
    climate change   193–4
    cohesion   62, 172, 182–90
    competition   159–61
    cultural   44
    defence   201, 203–6
    development cooperation
      214–17
    education   109
    employment   187
    environmental   172–3, 190–4
    fisheries   181

foreign   127, 197–201
  see also Common Foreign and
    Security Policy
immigration   186
justice and home affairs   153
monetary *see* euro
neighbourhood   212–14
regional   182, 183–4
single market   60–1, 149–62
social   62, 182–3, 184–90
trade   206, 207
  see also Common Commercial
    Policy
public opinion in/on   99–104
referendums *see* referendums on
  Europe
treaties *see* treaties, European
  women's issues in   189–90
European Union Civil Service Tribunal
  94
European Union, Treaty on   63–4,
  105
Europeanism   24, 39–46
Europeanization   118, 141
Europol   64, 153
Euroscepticism   64, 84, 102, 144
Eurosclerosis   67
Exchange Rate Mechanism   59–60,
  163–4
Exchange Rate Mechanism II   165
external relations *see* foreign policy

federalism   7, 16–18
financial services market in Europe
  161
fisheries policy   181
foreign direct investment   158–9
foreign policy   127, 197–201
  see also Common Foreign and
    Security Policy
freedom of movement   151–2
functionalism   9

Galileo GNSS   155
General Agreement on Tariffs and
  Trade (GATT)   56
General Court *see* European Court of
  Justice
Georgia   34
globalization   3
governance   15
government   15
Greece   57

Haas, Ernst 9
Habermas, Jürgen 40
hard power 43, 205
Herriot, Edouard 31
High Representative for foreign and
    security affairs 78, 196, 200–1
Hitler, Adolf 31

Iceland 66
immigration policy 186
integrative potential 11–13
interest groups 116–20
intergovernmental conferences (IGCs)
    77
intergovernmentalism 5, 13
internal market *see* single market
international organizations 4–5
international relations 2, 14, 142
Iraq, invasion of 70, 200, 211–12
Ireland 57, 66, 71
    economic fortunes 185

joint ventures 158
justice and home affairs 153

Kagan, Robert 45
Kissinger, Henry 196
knowledge deficit 103

languages in Europe 33, 109
law *see* European Union, law
Lisbon Strategy 67–8, 162
Lisbon, Treaty of 49, 70–1
Lomé conventions 215–16

Maastricht treaty *see* European Union,
    Treaty on
Marshall Plan 50, 51, 209
Martel, Charles 27
Merger treaty 56
mergers and acquisitions 156–9,
    207
Microsoft 161
Mitrany, David 8
Mitterrand, François 63, 64, 186
Moldova 34
monetary policy *see* euro
Monnet, Jean 8, 10, 52–3, 54, 77
multiculturalism 41
multilateralism 45
multi-level governance 15–16
multi-speed integration 139–40
mutual recognition 108, 151

nation 3
neighbourhood policy 212–14
neofunctionalism 9, 10, 11
Nice, Treaty of 66
North Atlantic Treaty Organization
    (NATO) 50, 204
Norway 57, 66

official development assistance 217
Ombudsman, European 120, 136
open method of coordination 135
Organization for European Economic
    Cooperation (OEEC) 51

Paris, Treaty of 54
patriotism 41
people's Europe 107–11
permissive consensus 64
Petersberg tasks 203, 205
policies
    adoption 135
    agenda-setting 132–4
    compromise and bargaining 138
    Europeanization of 141
    evaluation 136, 138
    formulation 134–5
    implementation 135–6
    incrementalism 140
    influences on 129–32
    multi-speed integration 139–40
    policy cycle 132–8
    policy environment 127–32
    political games 139
    see also specific policies by
        subject area *or* European Union,
        policies
Portugal 57–8
preliminary ruling 92, 94
Prodi, Romano 82, 169
proportional representation 111–12
public opinion in Europe 99–104,
    131, 197–8
public policy 127–9
    changing balance of authority
        124–7, 128

qualified majority voting 87–8

rail transport in Europe 154
REACH regulation 193
realism/realist theory 7, 9
referendums on Europe 63, 64, 66,
    70, 71, 101, 105, 115–16, 117

regional integration 5–13
  around the world 12
  costs and benefits 6
regional integration association 4–5
regional policy 182, 183–4
religion in Europe 43
retrenchment 11
Rome, Treaty of 54, 55
Russia 34, 154, 214

Santer, Jacques 82
Schengen Agreement 61, 66, 140,
  150
Schuman, Robert 8, 10, 48, 52–3
Schuman Declaration 53
security policy *see* defence policy
Single European Act 48, 56, 60–1,
  150
  content and effects 60–1
single market 60–1, 149–51
  effects of 151–62
Social Action Programmes 186–7
Social Charter 62, 186
social policy 62, 182–3, 184–90
soft power 43, 205
sovereignty 2, 15, 127, 168
Spain 57–8
specialized agencies of the EU 95–6
spillaround 11
spillback 11
spillover 9–11, 125, 127, 130,
  141–2
Stabex 215–16
state, the 1–2
state system 2–3, 124–5
structural funds 62, 175–6
subsidiarity 125, 126
Suez crisis 50, 52
supranationalism 5
sustainable development 190

Switzerland 66

terrorism 153, 203
Thatcher, Margaret 145, 186, 190
Thomson report 183
Tindemanns report 107
tourism 154
trade policy 206, 207
  see also Common Commercial
    Policy
treaties, European 75–8
  Amsterdam 66, 140, 199
  Constitution for Europe, Treaty
    Establishing a 49, 70
  European Union, Treaty on 63–4,
    105
  Lisbon 49, 70–1
  Merger 56
  Nice 66
  Single European Act 48, 56, 60–1,
    150
trans-European networks 152, 154–5
Turkey 36, 27

Ukraine 34
unemployment 187–8
Union for the Mediterranean 214
Ural Mountains 34

value-added tax 150
van Rompuy, Herman 79, 202

Warsaw Pact 50, 52
Werner Committee 163
Western European Union 50
women's issues in the EU 189–90
World Trade Organization (WTO)
  207, 209

Yaoundé conventions 215–16